In the Tradition Nhat Hanh: Mindfulness and Engaged Buddhism

Dr. Lauri Bower

Copyright © 2016 Lauri Bower

ISBN: 978-1-326-75593-5

All rights reserved, including the right to reproduce this book, or portions thereof in any form. No part of this text may be reproduced, transmitted, downloaded, decompiled, reverse engineered, or stored, in any form or introduced into any information storage and retrieval system, in any form or by any means, whether electronic or mechanical without the express written permission of the author.

Acknowledgements

This thesis has benefited from the inspiration, challenge and detailed attention provided by my supervisors, Professor Pauline Kollontai and Professor Sebastian Kim. I am grateful to those who agreed to participate by being interviewed. I am also indebted to the many family and friends who have supported and encouraged this endeavour. In particular, Greg, who inspired me to take this path in the first place; my fellow Ph.D. students in the G-lab, who critiqued my writing and boosted my spirits by remaining positive and confident throughout the process; the York Sangha, who have provided much spiritual refreshment and laughter; and the SoS retreatants who, with their pertinent and penetrating questions, stimulated and nourished the work. Finally, my husband Tim and children Grace and Gabriel, who have kept me reassured, sane, well-fed and entertained on this journey.

Front cover photo: image taken at Upper Hamlet in Plum Village, January 2015.

Table of Contents

1. Introduction 7
   1:1 Thich Nhat Hanh 7
   1:2 Addressing the key issues 10
   1:3 Key terms of Buddhism and Interbeing in Thich Nhat Hanh's Teaching 14
   1:4 Thich Nhat Hanh's body of work 19
   1:5 Methodology 21
   1:6 Transplantation 28
   1:7 Chapter contents 29
   1:8 Conclusion 33

2. Mindfulness in early Buddhism and its relevance for Thich Nhat Hanh 35
   Introduction 35
   2:1 Deconstructing *Sati* 36
     2:1:1 Memory 37
     2:1:2 Non-judgement 39
     2:1:3 Bare attention 41
     2:1:4 Four characteristics of *Sati* 42
     2:1:5 A summation of Thich Nhat Hanh's elucidation of Mindfulness 45
   2:2 The Satipatthana Sutta 47
   2:3 Conclusion 49

3. Learning Mindfulness in Vietnam: the Formulation of Thich Nhat Hanh's Teachings 51

Introduction 51
3:1 The historical context of Vietnam 53
3:2 Thich Nhat Hanh's experience of Vietnam in the 1940s – 1960s 56
    3:2:1 Buddhism in the 1940s – 1960s 59
    3:2:2 The Buddhist response to occupation and war 63
3:3 Thich Nhat Hanh's inspirations and influences 71
    3:3:1 Prosperous and flourishing Vietnam 71
    3:3:2 A nonviolent approach 73
    3:3:3 Meditation in action 76
    3:3:4 Being peace 77
3:4 Theory into practice through engagement and Mindfulness 79
    3:4:1 *Phuong Boi*, Fragrant Palm Leaves 79
    3:4:2 The School of Youth for Social Services (SYSS) 81
    3:4:3 *Tiep Hien*, the Order of Interbeing 83
3:5 Reflections on Thich Nhat Hanh's Engaged Buddhist methodology 85
3:6 Conclusion 90

4. 'Entering into Life': The Development of Engaged Buddhism 94

Introduction 94
4:1 Thich Nhat Hanh's definition of Engaged Buddhism .. 96

4:2 Defining Engaged Buddhism 99
    4:2:1 A new *yana*? 102
    4:2:2 Applied Buddhism 106
    4:2:3 The social dimension of Engaged Buddhism 107
4:3 The interviewee's understanding of Engaged Buddhism 109
4:4 Critiques of Community of Interbeing practice of Engaged Buddhism 116
4:5 Reflections on the definition of Engaged Buddhism 121
    4:5:1 The balance of being and doing 122
    4:5:2 Participation in the world 123
    4:5:3 The interbeing aspect of Engaged Buddhism 124
    4:5:4 A summation of Engaged Buddhism 125
4:6 Conclusion 126

5. A Manifestation of Mindfulness: the Plum Village Meditation Practice Centre 129
    Introduction 129
    5:1 The instigation of Plum Village 130
    5:2 Plum Village practice centre 133
    5:2 The mindful practices 137
        5:2:1 Sitting meditation 138
        5:2:2 Silence 143
        5:2:3 Walking meditation 148
        5:2:4 Eating meditation 151
        5:2:5 Singing 153

5:3 Emotional connections 155
    5:3:1 The bell 156
    5:3:2 Thich Nhat Hanh 158
5:4 A familial atmosphere 164
    5:4:1 Family *Dharma* sharing group 165
    5:4:2 Beginning Anew ceremony 169
5:5 Plum Village as a metaphor 172
5:6 *Meditation in action:* the Plum Village model 174
5:7 Reflections on the retreat experience 176
    5:7:1 A critique of Thich Nhat Hanh 176
    5:7:2 Issues arising from a retreat 178
5:8 Conclusion 181

6. 'The Miracle of Mindfulness': Transforming Suffering into Happiness 185

Introduction 185
6:1 The Mindfulness trainings 186
    6:1:1 An assessment of the 5 Mindfulness trainings 190
    6:1:2 Comparison of the original and revised versions of the 14 Mindfulness trainings 200
6:2 Please call me by my true names 202
6:3 Thich Nhat Hanh's teaching on suffering and happiness 206
6:4 The expansion of Mindfulness from Thich Nhat Hanh's teaching 211
6:5 Conclusion 212

7. The Transplantation of Thich Nhat Hanh's Teachings into the West 216
Introduction 216
7:1 Home traditions 219
7:2 Relocating into a Christian country 223
    7:2:1 Host traditions 224
    7:2:2 Host response 225
7:3 Identity of the individual 230
    7:3:1 How does the individual self-describe? 231
    7:3:2 What is the individual's role within the *Sangha*? 232
7:4 Leadership 236
7:5 The impact of Western religious ideas 242
7:6 The retransplantation process 245
    7:6:1 The Community of Interbeing units 246
    7:6:2 Challenges of the Community of Interbeing units 251
    7:6:3 Moving the Plum Village model forward 253
    7:6:4 Are the growing numbers of monasteries sustainable? 254
    7:6:5 Is a satellite monastery possible for the UK? 256
7:7 Conclusion 258

8. Conclusion 262

Postscript 2016 272

Bibliography 275
Website addresses 288
Semi-structured Interviews (SI) 290

Informal Conversations (IC) 292
Public Talks 292
DVD 292
Unpublished Theses 293
List of Abbreviations 294

Appendices 295
Appendix 1: Field research 295
Appendix 2: Interview questions 296
Appendix 3: The 14 Mindfulness trainings (14MTs) 298
Appendix 4: Plum Village satellite monasteries 306
Appendix 5: A unit meeting 309
Appendix 6: Details of the 4 units researched 311
Appendix 7: What the geese know 313

About the author 314

List of Figures
    Figure 1   46
    Figure 2   126
    Figure 3   174

1. Introduction

My path is the path of stopping, the path of enjoying the present moment. It is a path where every step brings me back to my true home. ... That is my life; that is my practice (Nhat Hanh 2003c: 13).

1:1 Thich Nhat Hanh

Thich Nhat Hanh[1] is a Vietnamese Zen Buddhist monk, teacher, poet, peace-maker and, as author of over one hundred books, promotes Mindfulness as a key to transforming suffering into happiness, resolving conflicts, and living simply and happily by awakening to the present moment, in which we 'penetrate the nature of our world and understand the cause of suffering ... [as] Each moment we are mindful, the mind is pure, free of clinging, hating and delusion' (Kornfield 1996: 13). Through his teaching and his way of living Nhat Hanh demonstrates that it is possible to live a peaceful and happy life, without negating the suffering that is inherent to life.

Whilst he is generally recognised as 'the father of Engaged Buddhism' (Toms 1998: 29; Tricycle 1995: 37) this book will demonstrate he is more than this as he is now acknowledged as a Mindfulness teacher through his books and retreats. He has an important message to offer society about the accessibility of the

---

[1] Thich Nhat Hanh is the *Dharma* name he was given on being ordained a *Dharmacharya* (teacher) in 1966. Nhat Hanh means 'one action' and Thich indicates he is of the *Sakya* (Sakyamuni *Buddha*) clan. He is often referred to as Thay by his students, the Vietnamese word meaning teacher. In the quotations from my interviews I retain the term Thay as the speaker has used it.

present moment due to the prominence he gives to Mindfulness. His teachings elucidate one definition Jon Kabat-Zinn gives to Mindfulness, '… as a real and commonsensical choice … as balm and medicine for our anguished hearts and agitated minds' (2005: 578). Nhat Hanh indicates Mindfulness offering 'balm and medicine' to an agitated mind by demonstrating it has the ability to settle, in the same way a glass of juice settles allowing the pulp to sink to the bottom and the juice become clear (Nhat Hanh 1992e: 4). This simple yet evocative analogy establishes the ability of the mind to settle in the present moment when the mind is no longer caught up with agitated or circular thinking. It is the epitome of his teachings, enabling both academics and practitioners access to his vast understanding of Buddhism. Whilst his pedagogy developed in the particular context of war its relevance now extends to any and every aspect of daily life.

Within Buddhist circles Nhat Hanh is the second most famous Buddhist teacher and practitioner after the Dalai Lama, with both following a similar vision for world peace (Henry 2008: 233) yet he is not as well-known generally. This could be because he entered France as an individual rather than with an entourage of fellow countrymen as the Dalai Lama had in India. Furthermore, he spent several years after the end of the Vietnam/American War[2] quietly meditating and writing, apparently in retreat (Coleman 2001: 89; Chapman 2007: 304) before deciding what his next step would be. Nonetheless, I propose his teachings are worthy of academic research because, whilst research into Mindfulness in a clinical and mental health setting has been growing exponentially since the late 1990s (Williams & Kabat-Zinn 2011: 2), research of Mindfulness as a fundamental Buddhist teaching is comparably scarce. Nhat Hanh's simple yet penetrating approach has much to offer many people in the twenty-first century who find the pace of life and stresses inherent in a modern lifestyle incompatible with the way they wish to

---

[2] It must be acknowledged here that the Vietnam War is how it is recognised in the West, in Vietnam it was known as the American War. For this reason I will refer to it from now on as the Vietnam/American War.

live. He accentuates the present moment is the only place where change can happen; 'we are very good at preparing to live, but not very good at living ... we have difficulty remembering that we are alive in the present moment, the only moment there is for us to be alive' (Nhat Hanh 1995: 5). Whilst his prolific library often repeats this key theme there are few monographs or journal articles that thoroughly critique his teachings with the breadth and depth that I employ throughout this book.

Recent academic studies of Nhat Hanh's work have concentrated on comparing his teachings with others in particular contexts. These include a comparison with Aloysius Pieris in order to present a '... constructive contribution to a Christian spirituality informed by Buddhist-Christian encounters' (Alden 2006), a study of socially engaged Buddhism in the UK, in which the Community of Interbeing (CoI) (laypeople following the Plum Village tradition) is one of five communities examined (Henry 2008), and an appraisal of the methods of healing justice applied in three comparative communities, Plum Village, Hollow Water in Canada and the Iona Community in Scotland (Sawatsky 2009). Whilst Nhat Hanh's work represents a portion of these studies, I intend to concentrate solely on his teachings and the ways in which the context of transplantation has shaped their development. Whilst his own writing is prolific (see section 1:4) academic study on Nhat Hanh is '... almost totally absent' (Alden 2006: 32) and again comprises chapters in extended studies such as Queen (2000; 2003) and King (2005; 2009). Furthermore, these articles tend to focus on the social activism side of his work as Engaged Buddhism in Vietnam. I will demonstrate there is more to Nhat Hanh's teachings than Engaged Buddhism. My thesis makes an original contribution to the body of knowledge on Nhat Hanh by presenting him and his teachings as the sole case study and thereby focusing in-depth on his progression from Engaged Buddhist to Mindfulness teacher.

1:2 Addressing the key issues

The research questions considered in this book are; 1) how and why has Nhat Hanh's pedagogy of Engaged Buddhism and Mindfulness developed and what is the relationship between the two? 2) How is the evolution of his teaching of Mindfulness, due to transplantation, demonstrated in Plum Village? 3) How have his teachings been re-transplanted through other monasteries, institutes and lay Sanghas (Units[3])? Here I highlight some of the literature relating to these key issues.

The scholarly debates concerning Engaged Buddhism relate to whether it is a new movement (Queen 1996: 10; 2000: ix) led by Nhat Hanh as an interaction with Westernisation or an integral aspect of Buddhism. Nhat Hanh advocates Buddhism has always been engaged (Hunt-Perry & Fine 2000: 36). This is a discussion conducted between modernists and traditionalists (Yarnall 2003: 286-287); modernists such as 'Gary Snyder, Joseph Kitagawa, Richard Gombrich, Cynthia Eller, Kenneth Kraft' and traditionalists such as 'the Dalai Lama, Thich Nhat Hanh, Sulak Sivaraksa, Joanna Macy, and Bernard Glassman, ... Robert Thurman ... and Yarnall himself' (Queen 2003: 18-19).

Engaged Buddhism is seen as addressing social concerns that traditionally have been paid little attention by Buddhists who emphasised otherworldliness (Loy 2004), by 'applying Buddhist teachings in a more activist way than had hitherto been the case' (Keown 2003: 86) and is 'radical in Buddhist terms' because of this social dimension (Henry 2008: 5). Yet, other scholars question this (Bell 2000: 400; Jones 2003:178-179) because of the implication that 'Buddhism is normally disengaged from society' (Harris 2001: 99). Engaged Buddhism is deeply connected to Nhat Hanh as the person

---

[3] To distinguish between the monastic and lay Sanghas I am using the term Unit to denote the regular meetings of the lay community, as opposed to the permanent establishments for monastics (see Chapter 7).

to coin the term (Toms 1998: 29; Jones 2003: 178-179; Yarnall 2003: 286) yet I question whether he should be considered the 'father of Engaged Buddhism' as his struggle movement against war and conflict in Vietnam (King 2005: 172; Fasching & Dechant 2001: 154) coincided with a rise in Engaged Buddhism throughout several countries in Southeast and East Asia. Therefore, due to its diversity in application (Puri 2006: 147; Powers 2000: 75) can it be considered one movement as Queen (1996: 10; 2000: ix) argues?

Mindfulness which is at the heart of Nhat Hanh's teaching on Engaged Buddhism, on the other hand, is described as 'an alert state of mind that should be cultivated constantly as the foundation for understanding and insight' (Keown 2003: 270). Currently prevalent as a means of dealing with stress (Kabat-Zinn 1996: 34) it is a full awareness of the present reality (Kraft 1995: 156; Fasching & Dechant, 2001: 159) which restores the mind 'to its original undistracted state' (Laumakis 2008: 247). From this standpoint one can make decisions without the mind being prejudiced by 'one's own ever-changing physical, emotional, and mental states' (Clough 2005: 119).

The significance that Nhat Hanh accords to Mindfulness goes beyond other Buddhist practices where Mindfulness is restricted to sitting meditation practice (Gunaratana 2002; Shaw 2009: 263). Whilst Mindfulness can be seen as a personal practice of bringing the mind back to its natural state of living in the present moment, Nhat Hanh suggests one practices Mindfulness in order to bring peace and happiness to many people (1999d: 33; 2007c: 45) and reduce violence in society (2003a: 1) by 'developing peace both in oneself and in the world' (Laumakis 2008: 257). Mindfulness and meditation, which are synonymous according to Nhat Hanh (2003a: 5), are not seen as purely spiritual practices but are observed for their practical effects as well (King 2009: 48). In the practice of Mindfulness one develops inner peace and outer peace thereby nurturing the individual whilst simultaneously having a beneficial effect on wider society (Nhat Hanh 2007c: 96). King assents to this, calling the work for world peace as a basis of inner peace 'the signature contribution of Engaged Buddhism to spiritual social activism' (2009: 48). This statement indicates a relationship between Engaged Buddhism and Mindfulness which I will investigate throughout the book. It is too simplistic to postulate, as I had originally presumed, that Engaged Buddhism is only social activism concerned with helping a specific group of people or society in general whereas Mindfulness is the inner nurturing of one's individual personal practice. I will demonstrate how they interrelate with and nurture one another as complementary practices which Nhat Hanh has implemented and developed over the past seventy years. Once in France, his teaching centred on Mindfulness as a contextual response to the transplantation process that had been imposed upon him by exile from Vietnam. This alteration due to context has led some scholars to question whether his pedagogy has changed from collective social action to an emphasis on the individual (Brazier 2001: 72-74; Minh Pham 2001: 66-67; Henry 2008: 201-205), who accuse him of quietism in their critiques. The issue of transplantation, which these scholars are addressing, is the theoretical framework for parts of the book and Chapter 7 in particular.

Plum Village, as a manifestation of *Sangha*, has three goals; 'to model a community based on the practices of compassion and lovingkindness; to be a support and advocate base for the plight of people in Vietnam; to be a teaching and practice centre for those who want to learn about Engaged Buddhism' (Sawatsky 2009: 178). By implementing these goals Nhat Hanh 'makes a significant departure from much past Buddhist tradition ... in his conviction that one need not – and, in fact, should not – practice meditative cultivation in isolation from the world. Active care for others must be involved' (Clough 2005: 119). It is this combination of 'active care' and a rejection of meditation in isolation that has created Nhat Hanh's pedagogy relating to *Sangha*, which is demonstrated at the other worldwide monasteries as well as within a growing lay community, practising under the title the Community of Interbeing (CoI) in the UK and the Community of Mindful Living in America and elsewhere.

The scholarly debate concerning *Sangha* focuses on whether it includes laity or just 'those noble persons ... who have attained the supermundane path' (Keown 2003: 20). Many traditions restrict *Sangha* to monastics who have made progress along the path (Cantwell & Kawanami 2002: 46) and are therefore distinct from laypeople who practice the Five Precepts (Gowans 2003: 168). Whilst the *Buddha* 'envisaged the need for a "fourfold sangha" ... of fully ordained men and women ... as well as laymen and laywomen' (Tomalin 2009: 83) *Sangha* is often understood to be the 'community that renounces the world and its concerns entirely and has as its ultimate goal the transcendence of the world and of the personal individuality in the attainment of nirvana' (Ward 2000: 53-54) and is considered to be the Buddhist elite (Conze 2001: 38). Nhat Hanh, however, adopts the *Buddha's* vision for *Sangha* as fourfold incorporating laity as well as monastics (2007c: 89). Some traditions give less importance to the *Sangha* as the supportive community which in Nhat Hanh's teachings is an essential element and he suggests one needs a *Sangha* to support one's own practice (2007c: 75).

In addressing the research questions I plot Nhat Hanh's journey from a novice monk in Vietnam to a Mindfulness teacher in France with a worldwide following of monastic and lay people, examining key points along the way that have determined his path and guided his philosophy. Buddhist terms are italicised and their meaning either identified in the text or in a footnote. Following the example of Alden and Nhat Hanh himself I will not use diacritics as those familiar with Buddhist terms have no need of them and '... for those who are not familiar, they are most probably of little help' (Alden 2006: 32).

1:3 Key terms of Buddhism and Interbeing in Thich Nhat Hanh's Teaching

In order to understand Nhat Hanh's teachings one has to have a grasp of his particular practice of Buddhism because one cannot write of Buddhism as if it were one 'monolithic phenomenon about which one can make generalized statements applicable to the entire tradition' (Habito 2007: 132). I also propose interbeing is a fundamental concept in his pedagogy and this will also be discussed in this section.

Buddhism[4] denotes following the teachings of the *Buddha* (Keown 2003: 45) called the Three Jewels (*Triratna*) of *Buddha, Dharma*, and *Sangha*; i.e. following the teachings of a particular individual who took on the name of *Buddha* to indicate his awakened or enlightened nature, which represent the law or *Dharma* through a *Sangha* or community. As with the term Christianity this is a general name to encompass many different practices; all of which relate in some way to the Three Jewels. It differs from coexisting Indian practices (now referred to as *Hinduism*) in the concept of *anatman*, no self, closely related to dependent origination (*pratitya-samutpada*[5]) as well as rejecting the caste system prevalent in Indian society. Furthermore, Buddhism is defined by its focus on the realisation of enlightenment (Mitchell 2002: 1) or *nirvana*.

There are two kinds of *nirvana*, *nirvana* with remainder attainable during present existence and final *nirvana* (*parinirvana*) when there is no rebirth due to the extinction of *karma* [the consequences of actions] (Keown 2003: 195; Mitchell 2002: 62). In *Mahayana* Buddhism 'the Bodhisattva ideal diminishes the importance of nirvana as a religious goal' as the *bodhisattva* vows to take all living

---

[4] A western term referring to the teachings of the *Buddha*. 'There is no direct equivalent for this term in Sanskrit or Pali' (Keown 2003: 45).
[5] '... all phenomena arise in dependence on causes and conditions and lack intrinsic being' (Keown 2003: 221). See also Nhat Hanh 1999d: 221-249.

beings with him or her; furthermore, Zen Buddhism emphasises 'for those who are awakened and perceive with insight, nirvana saturates every aspect of samsara'[6] (Keown 2003: 195). It is this aspect of *nirvana* accessible in the present moment and not as a future goal that Nhat Hanh accentuates. He refutes the idea that *nirvana* is 'annihilation, the extinction of everything, and that Buddhists aspire to nonbeing' (2008b: 71) and instead recommends it is 'the extinction of all concepts ... birth, death, being, non-being, coming and going' (1992e: 121). He recommends that the recognition of one's true nature as unconditioned removes all fear and makes *nirvana* attainable 'right here and now. You don't have to die in order to reach nirvana' (2008g: 33).

The particular Buddhism that Nhat Hanh observes and teaches comes from a *Thien* (*Zen*[7]) tradition practised in Vietnam for centuries introduced by Indian monks (Nguyen 2008: 13-15), but heavily influenced by the Chinese, incorporating both Confucianism and Taoism (Topmiller 2002: 10). Vietnam is unusual for its region in offering a form of Buddhism that combines *Theravada*[8] and *Mahayana*[9] traditions with *Mahayana* prevalent in the north and *Theravada* in the south (Nhat Hanh 1967: 13). *Theravada* is generally considered to be a more conservative, older path (Gethin 1998: 1) recognised by the Pali canon whereas *Mahayana* emerged around the beginning of the Christian era (Gethin 1998: 1) as a movement away from the conservatism of *Theravada* and has added

---

[6] The cycle of birth and death.
[7] A Japanese pronunciation of the Chinese Ch'an meaning meditation and an umbrella term for various schools in Japan (Keown 2003: 346). Zen emphasises the practice of meditation over theory and scholasticism (Gethin 1998: 38).
[8] The way of the elders.
[9] The great vehicle.

sutras[10] in Sanskrit or Chinese. The *Theravada* teachings concentrate on *arhatship* (gaining enlightenment having been a disciple) whereas the *Mahayana* emphasised the concept of a *bodhisattva*, a Buddha-to-be '... who practiced and taught for the benefit of everyone' (Nhat Hanh 1999d: 16). Thus *Mahayana* came to indicate the *Buddha's* full or perfect awakening compared to his disciples (Gethin 1998: 224). Bhikkhu Bodhi refutes the stereotypes that have thus arisen suggesting *Theravadin* monastics are only concerned with individual enlightenment whereas *Mahayana* ones concentrate more on social service and do not practise meditation, as many *Theravadin* monastics teach the *Dharma*, and diligent training in meditation supports the *bodhisattva* ideal (2010).

The *bodhisattva* ideal came from the Jataka Tales demonstrating the *Buddha's* previous existences. They form part of the *Khuddaka Nikaya* in the *Sutta Pitaka*[11] of the Pali canon (Behm 1971: 30) and are recognised by both traditions. However, Mahayana traditions have accentuated and further developed the notion of the *bodhisattva* by creating a host of millions of *Buddhas* and *bodhisattvas*, such as those who reputedly paid respect to the *Buddha* in the womb (Nhat Hanh 1992e: 38).

Nhat Hanh has incorporated *Theravada sutras* into his *Mahayana* teachings demonstrating that *Mahayana* teachings originate within *Theravada* ones (Nhat Hanh 1992b: 576). These include the *Satipatthana Sutta*[12] (MN10) (the four establishments of Mindfulness) and the *Anapanasati*[13] *Sutta* (MN118) (the full

---

[10] A *sutra* is a text, *sutta* in Pali. *Sutta* refers to the discourses of the *Buddha* in the Pali Canon, in the Mahayana tradition other *sutras* were added.
[11] One of the three baskets that make up the *Theravadin* Pali canon.
[12] For the full text and commentary see *Transformation and Healing* (Nhat Hanh 2006c).
[13] For the full text and commentary see *Breathe! You Are Alive* (Nhat Hanh 1992a).

awareness of breathing), both of which inform many of the practices that Nhat Hanh teaches. In writing about Buddhism as it relates to Nhat Hanh therefore, I refer to a *Mahayana* Zen practice which incorporates *Theravada* teachings (King 1996: 322) and emphasises interbeing.

Interbeing is a neologism that Nhat Hanh invented (2000a: 6) in order to put forward interconnectedness as a worldview in which each being (including animals, plants and minerals) is dependent on each other for life. Whilst this is recognised in a scientific way through the reciprocal relationship of the carbon dioxide-oxygen cycle, Nhat Hanh's meaning of interbeing expresses the opposite of an anthropocentric view and the apparent separation from the rest of the universe that this can cause. It 'is a challenge to practitioners to look beyond the world of dualistic opposites and concepts' (Henry 2008: 195) as taught in the *Heart Sutra* (*Prajnaparamita*) (Nhat Hanh 2006b: 19) and *Avatamsaka Sutra* (Nhat Hanh 1992d: 78), both important *Mahayana sutras*. Interbeing, or non-duality, can be described as a bio-centric approach in which human life is a 'microorganism that is interlinked with other organisms' (Truong 2006: 285).

The concept of interbeing comes from a collective rather than an individual worldview and as a Westerner growing up in a society where considerations for the individual are foremost interbeing can be a difficult concept to grasp. Truong suggests this is due to an 'unwholesome mind [that] ... tends to cling to an unchanging notion of self and its craving' (2006: 286). The term unwholesome here is used in a Buddhist sense that describes mind as wholesome, unwholesome or neutral depending on whether it clings to concepts or is capable of discerning errors of perception (Truong 2006: 286) and is not intended to be a derogatory term. Furthermore, 'a worldview can be described as an individual's psychological framework through which reality is perceived, sense made of life and the world around us' (Kollontai 2007: 65). The Vietnamese worldview with which Nhat Hanh grew up based on Buddhist teachings is one of integration, whereas the European worldview based on a mainly Christian heritage is one of differentiation. David Krus & Harold Blackman's table denoting East-West styles of thought (1980: 951) indicates differences in worldviews that would be apposite to Nhat Hanh as a Vietnamese settling in exile in France (Europe). Whilst I do not agree with all classifications here in relation to Nhat Hanh's teachings, in particular the categories of dogmatic, anti-science and irrational, I find the overall tenure of the argument sympathetic with what I experienced as a Westerner in Plum Village, particularly the taxonomies of synthesis, totality and integration. It demonstrates a Vietnamese cultural system with an emphasis, as in other Asian traditions, on 'collective duty and responsibility instead of individual rights' (Tomalin 2006: 99). These differing worldviews between Vietnam and Europe in which interbeing is common to the Vietnamese perspective but more alien to the European one can further be explained by considering a circle in which the centre point represents the individual and the circumference humanity.

Broadly speaking, the European perspective is from the individual looking out and trying to find his or her place within the circle, whereas the Vietnamese perspective is from the circumference where although there is an apparent individual in reality this does not exist. The individual in this respect is only manifest for the play of creation and does not have any ultimate reality; 'in Buddhism there is no such thing as an individual' (Nhat Hanh 2007a: 45). According to Nhat Hanh individualism is a Western concept in opposition to the teachings of interbeing (1992e: 89) as 'one of the deepest causes of our suffering is our insistence on seeing reality in a dualistic way' (2014: 13). Highlighting these disparate approaches enables one to be aware of the problems Nhat Hanh would have faced in developing a retreat centre based on Vietnamese traditions and culture in a European setting. He indicates the difficulties encountered in living in a society so different from one he grew up in; '... living in an apartment house where there are many kinds of families, but people are not interested in each other. It's quite different from being in a village where everybody knows everybody' (Nhat Hanh & Berrigan 2001: 41-42). As discussed in Chapter 4 the village is the ideal retained in developing Plum Village as the most effective means of living and working as a community. Before proceeding further it is necessary to consider the extensive body of work Nhat Hanh has compiled and written since becoming a noviciate.

1:4 Thich Nhat Hanh's body of work

Nhat Hanh has written prolifically over sixty years, producing over one hundred books translated into many different languages. I have undertaken a thorough examination of his books covering several genres, including commentaries on Buddhist *sutras*, meditations, poetry, children's books and guides for implementing Mindfulness into one's day-to-day life.

He began with articles written in 1954 proposing the idea of Engaged Buddhism (Nhat Hanh 2008c: 5). His early books were letters (*The Miracle of Mindfulness* 2008e) or diaries (*Fragrant Palm Leaves* 1999b). *The Miracle of Mindfulness* indicates his growing awareness that Mindfulness is 'the essential discipline ... [and one to be adopted] right now in one's daily life, not only during meditation sessions' (Nhat Hanh 2008e: 6-12). This consistent message is the content of all the books published since then, initially by himself and now through Parallax Press, a non-profit publishing company set up almost exclusively for Nhat Hanh's books and others with a Buddhist theme. His books fall into two categories, firstly translations and commentaries on Buddhist *sutras* and teachings and secondly those delivering the message of Mindfulness to a mainly lay audience. Those in the second category are written in an approachable language, easily accessible for the lay practitioner and those new to his teachings and may not be considered academic. Nonetheless they closely reflect the deep Buddhist teachings of the first category that he has spent his life studying and realising. The first category are a direct analysis of the *Buddha*'s teachings accompanied by commentaries on how they are applicable to daily life, whereas the others focus on the applied aspect, with occasional reference to the *sutras* they are drawn from.

As mentioned previously two Buddhist *sutras* (the *Satipatthana Sutta* and the *Anapanasati Sutta*) are the basis of all of Nhat Hanh's teachings, in specific books (*Transformation and Healing* 2006c and *Breathe! You Are Alive* 1992a) as well as comprising the content of many others. The aspects of 'practicing breathing and contemplating our body, feelings, mind, and objects of mind, we practice peace in the present moment' (Nhat Hanh 1995: 108) as taught in the *Satipatthana Sutta* are also apparent in other books. To give just a couple of examples, in the detail of *Being Peace*; 'this capacity of waking up, of being aware of what is going on in your feelings, in your body, in your perceptions, in the world, is called Buddha nature, the capacity of understanding and loving' (Nhat Hanh 2007a: 9) as well as in the chapter content of *The Blooming of a Lotus* (2009b). Furthermore, the recommendation to focus on the breathing is the basis of many books as well as guided meditations; 'breathing in and out mindfully, I become fully present and fully alive, and now I see myself as a miracle' (Nhat Hanh 2002a: 11).

Many of the recently published books are transcripts of *Dharma* talks edited by a group of monastics who make the decision about publishing a new book, not Nhat Hanh himself; he merely checks they are his own words before approving publication (SI, Sr Chan Khong 2011). Some of the early book titles reflect his focus on calling for peace in Vietnam such as *Being Peace; Touching Peace; Peace is Every Step* whereas his more recent books aim at bringing Mindfulness into specific areas such as *Work; Fear; Anger*. As suggested previously, these books are aimed at a lay audience who may be Nhat Hanh's students or who have an interest in his teachings and in this respect are not considered to be academic, however, given the experience and years of practice he has, neither are they merely for the populist market. Furthermore the commentaries on Buddhist *sutras* reflect a deep academic understanding, and this same material is evident in the more accessible ones almost without the reader realising. It is only on thorough examination that one comes to comprehend the depth of Nhat Hanh's books and how closely they reflect the *Buddha's* teachings. He has adopted the concept of awareness of breathing from the *Satipatthana Sutta* to become the basis of many guided meditations and teachings, termed '... conscious breathing' (Nhat Hanh 1995: 54). I propose that whilst his books cannot be considered as purely academic there is a depth to them that puts them in a category of their own, somewhere between academic and populist.

1:5 Methodology

Before proceeding I will present my ontological and epistemological perspectives that shape the position I take as a researcher. This is a subjective, postmodernist stance in which there are multiple versions of reality (Johnson & Duberley 2000: 180&183) as opposed to 'universal agreement, or certainty, and ... a grand narrative account of being created human' (Anderson 2005: 45). This is consistent with Nhat Hanh's teachings of Buddhism and particularly the Fourteen Mindfulness Trainings (14MTs, see Chapter 6) which express being free from doctrines, theories and ideologies in order to examine one's life and actions openly with the insight of interbeing (1st MT). My ontological beliefs are founded, like many of those interviewed, in a Christian tradition, chiefly maintained through my maternal grandfather and quickly dissolved after his death. From the age of nineteen I joined a Practical Philosophy group whose teachings are based in the *Advaita*[14] tradition offering a more inclusive, universal worldview together with meditation. I practised with this group for twenty-five years and whilst I found the teachings, based on the *Vedas* and the *Upanishads*[15], accessible I eventually found the organisation prescriptive and domineering. Thus, when I discovered Nhat Hanh's teachings through his book *Touching Peace* I left the organisation to pursue his path which was comparatively simple and open. The simplicity combined with the depth of Nhat Hanh's teachings is one reason I chose to research them.

---

[14] Not two (Skt).
[15] Ancient Indian texts and teachings.

In researching Nhat Hanh and his key teachings I adopted an ethnographic methodology by gathering data from a number of sources to throw light on the emerging issues (Hammersley & Atkinson 2007: 3). This qualitative method involved immersing myself in the community (Bryman 2008: 402) who have chosen to associate themselves with Nhat Hanh and Plum Village to a greater or lesser degree by means of their adherence to his teachings. In order to achieve this I participated in several retreats (see Appendix 1) as well as becoming a member of the Community of Interbeing (CoI) in the UK. Whilst this increased my understanding of how the CoI operates than could have been achieved as a researcher this was not purely pragmatic. I took a personal decision to become an insider as my affiliation with the teachings increased. However, I do not consider this compromised the efficacy of the research.

There is some research on the insider/outsider debate including Russell T McCutcheon's book, a collection of writings exploring the problem from several perspectives, beginning with the premise highlighted in Harper Lee's *To Kill a Mockingbird* that to understand another's perspective one needs to stand in their skin and walk around in it (McCutcheon 1999: 1). One assessment is that of the etic (outsider) and emic (insider) standpoints coined by Kenneth L Pike; he indicates emic descriptions represent '... the views of one familiar with the system and who knows how to function within it' (Pike 1999: 29). From my own perspective I hesitate to take on the label of emic as my research began as an outsider and even though I have since joined the CoI I am still learning what this means. Each retreat I attended allowed me to deepen my understanding of 'the system and how it functions', offering a balance between '... familiarity and strangeness' (Hammersley & Atkinson 2007: 89) that one needs to be aware of as a researcher. Does familiarity lead to complacency or an acceptance of modes of behaviour that a stranger would question? One must be sensitive to issues such as these in conducting research.

The essays in McCutcheon's book indicate the debate is not a simple either/or perspective but a question of degree (1999: 21). Noble Ross Reat pursues a similar line of argument, examining four roles which he identifies as traditionalist (insider-to-insider), anthropological (insider-to-outsider), comparative (outsider-to-outsider) and dialogical (outsider-to-insider) (1983: 459-461). These concern not only the researcher's role but the relationship between the researcher and interviewee. For the purposes of this discussion, however, I focus on Kim Knott's continuum highlighting these four roles from the researcher's point of view, not only the insider/outside debate but also further nuances on the spectrum.

OUTSIDER   INSIDER

Complete   Observer-as-   Participant-   Complete
observer ---------- participant -------- as-observer ---------- participant
(Knott 2005a: 246).

In my particular situation it is the two middle categories that are relevant as I moved from Observer-as-participant to Participant-as-observer. My aim in adopting this second role was to retain the researcher's critical stance whilst endeavouring to gain from an insider's knowledge, keeping in mind that my role as researcher is one of '... critical inquiry rather than advocacy' (McCutcheon 1999: 369) as I indicate above.

The key point for any of the roles is to be aware of its limitations as well as its benefits. Ann Bonner & Gerda Tolhurst highlight the advantages and disadvantages of the insider/outsider roles relating to their experiences of participant observation (2002: 16). It is not that one is more right or wrong than another but whichever stance one takes one needs to be aware of the parameters. A further dimension is provided by Joseph Styles describing what he terms myths (1979: 148) centring on whether an insider can provide objectivity or an outsider can realise a true understanding of the group. Furthermore, there are the possibilities of '... methodological dangers' by *going native* and developing over-rapport (Hammersley & Atkinson 2007: 87). This infers the observational analysis is lost in participation. These are all warning signals I took with me in approaching my research, aiming for objectivity and distance.

Knott indicates the '... overlapping and interactive [nature of these roles making] ... the distinction between insider and outsider largely redundant [and dissolving] the boundaries' (2005a: 269). This is pertinent to Plum Village where Nhat Hanh states one does not need to become Buddhist to follow his teachings and instead invites retreatants to reconsider their own traditions in the light of these teachings (Nhat Hanh 2009a: 86-88). Furthermore, the practice of Mindfulness requires a non-judgemental open awareness of one's thoughts, feelings and emotions that maintains a critical distance between what one is experiencing and observing, and is apposite to the researcher's role. In seeking to maintain an objective view I used triangulation to provide a broad basis from which to study Nhat Hanh's teachings and practices.

I have employed triangulation because this offers validation (Hammersley & Atkinson 2007: 183) by, in this case, comparing Nhat Hanh's teachings and writings with data collected from qualitative interviews, participant observation and field notes and thereby assessing whether the theory and practice of his teachings are congruent. I have used the triangulation methodology to explore 'the richness and complexity of human behaviour by studying it from more than one standpoint' (Cohen, Manion & Morrison 2011: 195) as it offers 'complementary measures of concepts' and a more rounded set of results (Payne & Payne 2006: 230). In this respect my literature research combines with field research including participant observation and semi-structured interviews (SI) in order to provide a broad foundation of data from which to base my findings. Much information was gained from interviews and participant observation that could not be obtained from Nhat Hanh's books, in particular the praxis of his teachings.

In undertaking social research one has to be aware of the interpretivist view that human beings change their behaviour when they know they are being observed (Denscombe 2003: 19) therefore participant observation offers a solution 'by establishing relationships with those individuals who are being studied' (Saliba

2003: 137) through partaking (in a retreat or a Unit) in the same way as the interviewees. Participant observation requires detachment and evenness of thinking in order to critique what takes place without sentimental involvement, here termed bracketing; bracketing out one's own 'presuppositions, feelings and attitudes ... as far as possible' in order to present the beliefs, symbols and activities of the other from their own perspective (Smart 1987: 3-4). It is this same detached viewpoint that is recommended when practising Mindfulness in order to be aware of the mental world one is living in and is consistent with the participant observation method.

The ethnographer is a 'learner among the more knowledgeable' by trying to see through the eyes of the participants (Payne & Payne 2006: 73) and therefore I undertook SIs in order to focus on particular aspects of Plum Village practice and Nhat Hanh's teachings that required further investigation beyond my field notes. The SI utilises the same set of questions for each interview but offers freedom in terms of sequence or probing for more information (Fielding & Thomas 2005: 124). Having recorded and transcribed each interview thematic analysis was conducted using *NVivo* software to code the transcripts. In this way it was possible to draw out and collate, compare and contrast themes that arose from the interviews.

I conducted thirty-six SIs over a two-year period, twenty-four female and twelve male,[16] and apart from one student in their early twenties I suggest everyone was aged thirty or above with the majority in the age category of forty to sixty. I began with members of the Family group (see Chapter 5) with whom I resided at Plum Village on my first visit. These eight interviewees were likewise mainly first-time

---

[16] Of the thirty-six interviewees, five are Vietnamese with a Buddhist upbringing; two are Irish; one is French, all raised as Catholic; six are American, one with a Vietnamese (Buddhist) and one with an Indian (Hindu Brahmin) ethnicity, one Catholic, one Jewish and two unknown; twenty-two are British; two with an Indian ethnicity; seven brought up as Christian, two Quakers, one Christian and Hindu and ten unknown religiosity.

visitors to Plum Village with little experience of a local Unit. Only one person had been to Plum Village previously. These interviews were determined by those who agreed to be interviewed in the time available on the week's retreat. In the UK I further interviewed twenty-four Unit members and one Mindfulness teacher, all of whom had some experience of being on retreat with Nhat Hanh either at Plum Village, other monasteries, or in the UK. Here the degree of attendance on retreat varied from one UK retreat to many years of experience both at Plum Village and within the UK. There was also a wide variance in practice of which two are *Dharmacharya* (*Dharma* teachers ordained by Nhat Hanh), seven are Order[17] members and one an aspirant to the Order as well as those newer to the practice.

The twenty-four Unit members are linked to thirteen different Units within the UK;[18] it is quite normal for people to join one Unit and then start another closer to their home. In the cases of two interviewees one also practices with the Wake Up group (for young adults) and another with the Deep Listening Sangha a teleconference

---

[17] Within the CoI UK there is a distinction between the Community and the Order. When people join a Unit they may wish to also join the CoI – although there is no requirement to do so – which allows them access to a quarterly magazine, *Here and Now*, giving details of the Community's countrywide activities, involving retreats with members from other Units. Many will have formally received the 5MTs in a transmission ceremony, but again, this is not a stipulation. For those that wish to be involved in a more official capacity, there is a further opportunity to join the Order, which acknowledges the worldwide community, and includes monastics as well as laity. To do this (in the UK) one has to become an aspirant, and have two mentors with which to work for at least a year, whilst consolidating one's practice and deepening one's commitment to the 14MTs. Such people are usually involved in running and/or facilitating their local Unit as well as having some commitment to the UK Sangha. These aspects of the CoI will be further developed in Chapter 6.

[18] Bentham, Cambridge, Deep Listening, Hexham, Keighley, White Lotus (Leeds), Rolling Tide (Lancashire), Nottingham, Settle, Sheffield, Suffolk, Wake Up and York Units.

Unit for those who cannot access a Unit within their locality[19]. The interviews with Unit members were organised for me by a member of the Leeds Unit who had national contacts; I arranged the interviews with those who responded to her initial email. I either interviewed people in their houses or in a mutually agreed meeting place, some over Skype and two by email. All interviews were undertaken on an individual basis with the exception of one husband and wife who were interviewed together and their responses recorded separately. Ten follow-up interviews were undertaken by phone and Skype. The SIs were based on a qualitative interview[20] format with a consent form to be signed beforehand ensuring the interviewee understood what the information gathered would be used for and offering anonymity if desired. Aside from these informal conversations (IC) on retreats provided much useful data.

The demographics of the interviewee set are comparable with those Henry interviewed, being mainly '... ethnically white, Western converts, middle aged and largely middle class' (2008: 233). They represent the demographics of retreatants at Plum Village by being '... modernity's successful, the well-educated and financially strong Euro-American group of people' (Alden 2006: 29) who can afford Plum Village retreats and purchase many of the books. It is to these people that Nhat Hanh now addresses much of his teaching, those who represent the wealth of the West yet realise it '... is incapable of creating a good and meaningful life' (Alden 2006: 29).

My findings are mainly reliant on this lay community. Amongst the total of thirty-six interviews three were undertaken with monastics; I interviewed Sister (Sr) Chan Khong[21] twice and two monks at Blue

---

[19] for details of the Units see Appendix 6.
[20] See Appendix 2 for a list of the questions.
[21] Sr Chan Khong is the person who has lived and worked most closely with Nhat Hanh for more than fifty years.

Cliff Monastery NY state.[22] At the Plum Village Summer Retreat 2009 and both Nottingham retreats[23] I had the opportunity to ask Nhat Hanh one question in a public Question and Answer session (Q&A). He does not offer personal interviews (Alden 2006: 32) and for academics he insists people attend a retreat and practise with the community. I suggest this is not because he has anything to hide but because he wishes to emphasise the practical nature of the teachings. However, it was not as easy as I had supposed in obtaining interviews with monastics. On occasions my requests were turned down due to the busyness of the retreat; Sr Chan Khong and the two monks at Blue Cliff were the only monastics who agreed to my request. Having detailed the demographics of the interviewee set and the interview process I now turn to the theoretical framework, which is transplantation.

1:6 Transplantation

Transplantation is the relocation of a '... religious group and its tradition [into] ... a new geographical and social location' (Knott 1986: 10). The works of Kim Knott (1986: 10-13; 1991: 86-111) and David Kay (2004: 12-19) shed some useful insights into understanding the transplantation of Nhat Hanh's teachings. Knott identifies the 'home traditions' (1986: 10) as one of the several aspects contributing to the success, or otherwise, of transplantation. These are the religious and cultural traditions that individuals or communities bring with them in the diaspora process, i.e. they are not arriving empty handed. This is particularly relevant to Plum Village which began with a cohort of mainly Vietnamese diaspora before emerging into a Western teaching centre. Whilst 'Plum Village is not a Vietnamese temple set on European land' (Nhat

---

[22] One monk is the acting abbot at Blue Cliff and the second a visitor from Kim Son monastery in California, run by a Vietnamese abbot, who combines Pure Land practices with Nhat Hanh's teachings.

[23] In 2010 and 2012 I attended a six-day retreat on campus at the University of Nottingham led by Nhat Hanh.

Hanh 2003c: 21) but an integrated practice, there is a tension between maintaining a continuous link to its mother country and integrating into a new culture with a different worldview. This transcultural process (Kay 2004: 12-16) into countries with a mainly Christian heritage involves working with inherent values as well as responding to the current needs of people in a way that Christianity may be found wanting (Knott 2005b: 55). It is for this reason Nhat Hanh insists 'Buddhism is not one. The teaching of Buddhism is many. When Buddhism enters one country, that country always acquires a new form of Buddhism' (2007a: 84).

Transplantation is addressed in depth in Chapter 7 by considering the '...complex relationship between tradition and interpretation' (Pye 1969: 236). This is particularly pertinent to Nhat Hanh who encourages the use of interpretation based on a deep study of traditional teachings in order to keep Buddhism updated and relevant to current society. Transplantation in this circumstance is not only one removal from East to West, i.e. Vietnam to France, but also taken a stage further by questioning what happens to this new form of Buddhism in other locations, as it is re-transplanted in monastic centres in America and Germany and the lay community in the UK.

1:7 Chapter contents

Through the three research questions I will establish that Nhat Hanh did not leave Vietnam with a deliberate intention of creating a model of Engaged Buddhism and Mindfulness to be replicated in various settings. Conversely, this book shows that he has responded to each situation as it has arisen and did not have a vision to instigate in the West with Plum Village developing incrementally over time. Indeed, it was not even certain that Nhat Hanh would develop a teaching centre in the West when he left Vietnam, or even when he settled in France, as he did not expect to be out of Vietnam for long (Nhat Hanh 2003c: 25). Nonetheless, he already had the experience and desire for setting up communities of mindful living which he sees as the crucial means of establishing the practice (2007c: 75). Chapter 3 indicates *Phuong Boi* (Fragrant Palm Leaves) is the original practice centre out of which all others, including Plum Village, have developed. Thus, Plum Village was not a concept plucked out of the air but has been slowly forming over many years and has become a standard which is now being recreated in other settings. Chapter 7 explores this model in the monastic and lay setting through Knott's framework of transplantation (1986: 10-13 & 1991: 100-106), demonstrating the archetype is a fluid one that adapts to each new situation and not a static one that is merely cloned.

Likewise, as will be discussed in Chapter 3, although Nhat Hanh was one key component in the development of Engaged Buddhism he did not have the intention of starting a new movement merely of providing the Vietnamese people with a spiritual direction to alleviate their confusion (Nhat Hanh 2008c: 5). This aspect of combining meditation and social work is nonetheless transferable to different situations and is not only a remedy for the Vietnam/American War. It is a means of applying Buddhism to any and every aspect of one's daily life and is thus pertinent to any situation. The term Engaged Buddhism and its implications are examined in Chapter 4. A further development in this respect is the recent change from *Engaged* to *Applied* Buddhism also discussed in Chapter 4. I will adopt a mainly chronological rather than thematic approach in order to specify the development of his teachings responding to context.

The book begins with an examination of the *Satipatthana Sutta* a key text from the Pali canon that Nhat Hanh has adopted as crucial to his pedagogy. This chapter examines scholars' interpretations of *sati* (Mindfulness) and the various connotations it holds, before reflecting on Nhat Hanh's own interpretation which brings in a practical element of engaging with the world. Thus I introduce an important facet of Nhat Hanh's teachings, which is, that the 'teaching, no matter how lovely, if it cannot be applied to daily life it has no value at all' (*Dharma* talk 2010). This is a feature that identifies Nhat Hanh's teachings and is the foundation of all that has emanated from him in over sixty years of teaching.

Chapter 3 addresses the question as to how Nhat Hanh developed his pedagogy of Engaged Buddhism by investigating his early life as a novice monk who closely questioned what took place at both the monastery and the Buddhist Institute in which he was taught. This chapter highlights his inspirations which fed his aspirations to bring out the social dimensions of Buddhism. It clarifies the war-like context in which he grew up which formulated his aspiration as a peace-maker and questions how Nhat Hanh vocalised his opposition to war. It further denotes the two key statements that formed the path he took, *meditation in action* and *being peace*. In what ways have these statements informed and guided what he has undertaken?

Chapter 4 examines Nhat Hanh's clarification of Engaged Buddhism alongside other scholars' interpretations. The continuum, which Ken Jones uses to identify Engaged Buddhism (2003: 175), will be employed to place Nhat Hanh's work in comparison to others. This chapter also reflects on the social dimension of Engaged Buddhism and considers in what ways it is different to Buddhism which may emphasise an otherworldliness rather than this-worldly path. After considering the interviewees' understanding of Engaged Buddhism the chapter reflects on the key aspects of the balance of being and doing, participation in the world and the role interbeing plays, culminating in a diagram indicating my summation of Engaged Buddhism.

Chapter 5 demonstrates the establishment and growth of both Nhat Hanh as a teacher in a new situation and the community that formed around him, based in tradition but forward-looking. This chapter outlines the evolution and formation of Plum Village as a meditation practice centre and considers the balance between maintaining the Vietnamese culture and meeting the needs of Westerners. It examines the daily programme in order to establish how this encourages Mindfulness as a practice in everyday situations as well as addressing a need for conflict resolution within society. The Plum Village Model is represented in diagrammatic form here in order to incorporate the various aspects that come together to create a model that can be transplanted into different settings.

Chapter 6 investigates Nhat Hanh's interpretation of Mindfulness through an in-depth examination of the 5 and 14MTs. These ethical guidelines are offered to Plum Village and the wider community, but are also intended for anyone endeavouring to practice a mindful way of living. The chapter demonstrates both the close connections to the *Buddha*'s teachings and the ways in which they are updated to be relevant to current society. This chapter further explores the aspiration of the Plum Village Model, which is, transforming suffering into happiness. This is explored through some key pedagogical phrases Nhat Hanh uses to help his students deepen their understanding.

Chapter 7 utilises Knott's framework of transplantation to explore how the teachings are disseminating out beyond the hub of Plum Village to the satellite monasteries and the lay community. It investigates some of the relevant points on transplantation that are applicable to Nhat Hanh's situation, particularly home traditions, leadership, the identity of the individual and the group, and the effects of relocating into a country with a different culture and worldview and how Western religious ideas have impacted upon a Buddhist teaching. This chapter demonstrates how Nhat Hanh has embraced secularisation which allows the teachings to move out of the monastic setting into schools, prisons and different social settings. It further examines the emphasis Nhat Hanh places on *Sangha* as the means of supporting and sustaining the individual's practice.

Nhat Hanh's teachings are not unique in that they directly derive 'from the Zen School of Lin Chi, and [Nhat Hanh] is the 42nd generation of this school' (Nhat Hanh 2007a: 85) and rely on centuries of Buddhist teachings. He is, however, innovative in his emphasis of Mindfulness, a key theme that will be thoroughly examined throughout the book. I also propose that his gentle approach, which some interpret as having to only *breathe and smile* (see subsection 5:2:1), offers an accessible teaching through a 'powerful aura of tranquillity and compassion he seems to radiate' (Coleman 2001: 88). Given that he has been observing Buddhist meditation and nonviolent practices for over seventy years this is not surprising. Yet his way of being is inspiring to others by palpably demonstrating what he is teaching and encouraging that any situation can be approached nonviolently. 'Living for the sake of compassion, understanding, and nonviolence is very beautiful. I tread this path and I will never renounce it' (Nhat Hanh 2004a: 118-9). Throughout this book I tread the path with Nhat Hanh, examining his nonviolent method and the evolution of his teachings.

1:8 Conclusion

I will be arguing that Nhat Hanh's message has not changed in essence over the sixty years that he has been teaching, it is the context that has altered. The process of transplantation has necessitated an adjustment due to the way suffering in the West manifests differently from Vietnam, and the Western demographic he is now mainly teaching. As Buddhism permeated new countries it changed due to factors of adaptation with the local culture (Pye 1969: 237-238; Tomalin 2009: 91) and one cannot expect to find a replication of the Vietnamese practices in Europe. The factors of a diverse geographical context and a different worldview contribute to an inevitable alteration in pedagogy. However, Nhat Hanh's teachings in Vietnam enabled people to respond to the suffering of others from the insight gained in meditation and thereby being mindful, and this is no different to what he states in his *Dharma* talks every week. His aim is 'to bring peace to the heart of each person' (SI, Sr Chan Khong 2011) and the means of doing this is to recognise that 'your happiness and suffering depend on the happiness and suffering of others' (Nhat Hanh 2007d: 68). In order to facilitate this he recommends forming or joining a *Sangha* to access collective energy and to strengthen one's own practice (Chapter 7). Again, this is no different from the creation of *Tiep Hien* (the Order of Interbeing) in 1964. It is the transmission of the essence of his pedagogy that is relevant here rather than necessitating an exact replica. Similar to the *Kalama Sutta*[24] imparted by the *Buddha* Nhat Hanh only requires his students to consider for themselves what is useful to practise for their own situation. 'When you yourselves know' is what I propose he is offering his students. He emphasises trying out these practices and seeing for oneself if they work, so that one adapts the teachings to one's individual situation. This is demonstrated in Chapter 2 which examines the way Nhat Hanh has adopted the teachings from the *Satipatthana Sutta* and made them his own.

---

[24] A, Tika Nipata, Mahavagga, Sutta No. 65

2. Mindfulness in early Buddhism and its relevance for Thich Nhat Hanh

Mindfulness is like a light, enabling concentration to really be there, and that also makes it possible for us to look deeply into the heart of things (Nhat Hanh 2004b: 51).

Introduction

In Chapter 1 I established the importance of Mindfulness in Thich Nhat Hanh's teachings. Before investigating how this manifests practically in his work this chapter explicates the origins of Mindfulness in early Buddhism, which will enable me to locate Nhat Hanh's approach to Mindfulness. Secondly I examine his usage of the *Satipatthana Sutta* in order to ascertain how this influences his pedagogy. He has also adopted the *Anapanasati Sutta* from the *Theravadin* tradition yet, for the purposes of this discussion, I focus mainly on his usage of the *Satipatthana Sutta*, (2006c & 2012a). It appears that whilst Mindfulness was a key aspect of early Buddhist teaching, from which the *Theravada* stream evolved, it became less important in the *Mahayana* stream (Wallace 2008). Tse-fu Kuan indicates, 'many contemporary Buddhist teachers, especially those following the Theravada tradition, are advocates of mindfulness' (2008: 1) and yet includes Nhat Hanh within his list, indicating how

Nhat Hanh has embraced this *sutta*[25]. The key argument for this chapter is that Nhat Hanh's pedagogy is embedded in early Buddhist teachings on Mindfulness and in particular the *Satipatthana Sutta*.

It is necessary before discussing the *Satipatthana Sutta* to examine firstly how Mindfulness is understood in early Buddhist traditions. Following the example of scholars studied (Gethin 1998, 2001, 2008; Shaw 2006; Kuan 2008) I discuss Mindfulness using the Pali term *sati* rather than the Sanskrit *smrti*. The Pali teachings are recognised as being earlier and containing many of the ideas formulated in the Mahayana texts (Nhat Hanh 1992: 576). Initially passed on orally, the Pali canon is thought to have been written down in the first century BCE (Gethin 1998: 42; Nhat Hanh 2012a: 1). *Sati* is given prominence by being one of the steps of the noble eightfold path (Bodhi 2011: 20) as Right Mindfulness, as well as the *Satipatthana Sutta* being the '... only sutta of the Pali canon to occur in both the Digha-nikaya and Majjhima- nikaya' (Gethin 2008: 141). I begin by examining some definitions of *sati*.

2:1 Deconstructing *Sati*

Firstly it must be indicated that there is no one definitive interpretation of *sati* as there is a lack of agreement as to its definition (Grossman & Van Dam 2011: 219; Baer 2011: 245) reflected by the understanding that Buddhism is a not a single, monolithic tradition but a teaching of distinct manifestations that has evolved over centuries and includes diverse views about Mindfulness (Dreyfus 2011: 42; Dunne 2011: 71-72). More accurately, Mindfulness is a complex collection of '... phenomena that are collectively referred to as *mindfulness*' (Goss 2012: 108) and it is these that will be elucidated below, uncovering how the following definitions relate to Nhat Hanh's teachings.

---

[25] Nhat Hanh uses the term *sutra* in accordance with the *Mahayana* body of work written in Sanskrit rather than Pali.

Several scholars and Buddhist monastics have executed hermeneutical examinations of *sati* (Soma 1975; Nyanaponika 1996; Gethin 2001 and 2008; Analayo 2006; Shaw 2006: 76-85; Kuan 2008; Kabat-Zinn 2009 and 2011; Bodhi 2011: 19-39) and their findings inform this evaluation, beginning with the range of definitions. *Sati* is understood to be, '...reckoning just what is present' (Soma 1975: 2); 'bare attention' (Nyanaponika 1996: 30); 'remembering properly' (Gethin 2001: 42); 'presence of mind' (Gethin 2008: 141); 'clearly knowing' (Analayo 2006: 41-42); '... that quality that characterises the mind that is alert, awake and free from befuddlement' (Shaw 2006: 76); 'it enables one to overcome both cognitive and emotional problems' (Kuan 2008: 34); 'lucid awareness' (Bodhi 2011: 19); and one definition that is well-known in MBSR (Mindfulness based stress reduction) teachings, 'paying attention in a particular way: on purpose, in the present moment, and non-judgementally' (Kabat-Zinn 2009: 4). Here again the complexity of the term is discernible. As well as present moment awareness and clarity or insight several questions emerge from this list; one is the aspect of memory and what role Mindfulness plays here, secondly is whether non-judgement is a full enough description of Mindfulness and thirdly, whether non-judgement and bare attention are synonymous. These aspects will be examined in more detail and discussed in relation to Nhat Hanh's teachings and practices.

2:1:1 Memory

Sati derives from the root word for memory, however, several scholars deem this is not an adequate definition of Mindfulness as '... this does not quite accommodate all its shades of meaning, which is more an 'attentiveness directed towards the present'' (Shaw 2006: 76). It '... was given new connotations in early Buddhism ... such as "conscience", "attention", "meditation", "concentration" and "insight"' (Kuan 2008: 1) and 'lucid awareness'' (Bodhi 2011: 19) suggesting that translating *sati* as memory is insufficient. Furthermore, Analayo elucidates,

> *sati* is not really defined as memory, but as that which facilitates and enables memory ... if *sati* is present, memory

will be able to function well ... it is not concerned with recalling past events, but functions as awareness of the present moment ... it is due to the presence of *sati* that one is able to remember what is otherwise only too easily forgotten: the present moment (2006: 46-48).

Here s*ati* is not cognitive rumination or '... worrying about the past or predicting the future' (Nhat Hanh 2008a: 6) but remembering (Gethin 2001: 37) in the sense of '... remembering to come back to the present moment' (Nhat Hanh 1999d: 64). Re-membering simply means being mindful of again. Mindfulness is a moment-by-moment experience, one may be mindful one moment and forgetful the next, so one practises remembering to be mindful by coming back to the point of Mindfulness again and again. Sangharakshita (2003: 9-12) demonstrates the necessity of memory to Mindfulness with the illustration of a Dickens novel that suggests without memory one has no sense of who one is, and one's responsibilities to and relationships with others, concurring with Nhat Hanh's teaching that Mindfulness is '... not forgetting where we are, what we are doing, and who we are with' (Nhat Hanh 1999d: 215).

Furthermore, Dreyfus denotes Mindfulness, by which he means remembering or keeping in mind, as the cognitive and evaluative function that is missed out in interpreting *sati* as non-judgemental (2011: 45&47). Whilst this will be further discussed in the next subsection, this ability of the mind to remember experiences in the future (Dreyfus 2011: 48) concurs with what interviewees describe. Practices such as the walking meditation taught by Nhat Hanh can evoke a powerful reminder of the depth of Mindfulness one experienced on retreat. 'When doing walking meditation back at home I often visualise myself walking with them [Nhat Hanh and the monastics]' (SI, Tom 2011);

> I think mindful walking is one of the things that has stayed with me since that retreat. Whenever I think of walking in a mindful way ... an image of him [Nhat Hanh] comes into my head and it just reminds me of how you can just allow. I mean he's a very very busy person he's got so much to do, but he can just let that all drop away and when he's walking

he just allows himself to walk in a mindful way (SI, Person 24 2010).
In this respect it is not only present moment awareness but involves past actions of Mindfulness as well.

Nhat Hanh differentiates between the wholesome and unwholesome in order to choose the wholesome; 'every mental formation that manifests needs to be recognized. If it is wholesome, mindfulness will cultivate it. If it is unwholesome, mindfulness will encourage it to return to our store consciousness and remain there, dormant' (1999d: 74-75). This suggests Mindfulness is making judgements about what it is recognising and, furthermore, 'knowing this, we will be very careful in what we choose to be the object of our mindfulness and to what we give our attention' (Nhat Hanh 2003b: 32). This understanding is likewise taken by Soma, '… mindfulness distinguishes the worthy from the unworthy things, avoids the unworthy and obtains the worthy … Integrating mindfulness sees all lacks and deficiencies, brings in the needed qualities and suitably applies them' (Soma 1975: 4-5) which seems to contradict the understanding put forward by Jon Kabat-Zinn of Mindfulness as non-judgemental.

2:1:2 Non-judgement

Is there a difficulty in using the term non-judgemental? This suggests that one accepts everything and hints at acquiescence. In defining Mindfulness as non-judgemental 'the mind is simply aware of an object without evaluating the object' (Kuan 2008: 42), therefore it recognises experiences just as experiences, without defining them as pleasant or unpleasant (Teasdale 2004: 277). Is there a difference between judgement and evaluation? Is it possible to place a value on something without judging it? How does one determine wholesome from unwholesome without a judgement being made? Nhat Hanh suggests 'mindfulness illuminates what we are doing … with the light of mindfulness present, we recognize which actions are beneficial and which are harmful' (2007f: 32), in which case one would automatically adopt the wholesome and leave the unwholesome, or be aware one is deliberately choosing the unwholesome if that is the case.

A difference between judgement and evaluation could be understood in that judgement is reactive, whereas evaluation is responsive. Dreyfus intimates a variance between judgement and evaluation by indicating the reactive patterns of the mind from which one habitually behaves, '... clinging to pleasant experiences and rejecting unpleasant ones ... most of our judgements are dominated by this unbalanced pattern' (2011: 53). Dreyfus is not indicating that the interpretation of mindfulness as non-judgemental, present-centred awareness is wholly flawed, merely that it is partial, because it has no recognition of the cognitive and evaluative aspects of mindfulness to be readily found in early Buddhist teachings (2011: 53). However, these cognitive and evaluative aspects can be easily misconstrued as judgements and it is non-judging as an aspect of Mindfulness that Nhat Hanh emphasises, as the mind habitually leaps to judgements and opinions quickly, whereas Mindfulness provides the opportunity to put a space between experience and reaction. He accentuates the '... inclusive and loving' (Nhat Hanh 1999d: 64) qualities that arise when non-judging is allowed to occur, '... like an older sister looking after and comforting her younger sister in an affectionate and caring way' (Nhat Hanh 1995: 57).

Kabat-Zinn indicates he does not find Dreyfus' definition necessary or useful to a Western definition 'given how cognitive we tend to be already, and how little we experience the domain of being' (2011: 291) which concurs with Nhat Hanh's pedagogy of the being aspect of mindfulness, '... allowing change to happen naturally, without struggle, without the usual resistance and judgement that cause us to suffer more' (Nhat Hanh & Cheung 2010: 68). This can only take place once one has accepted a situation as it is. Judgements tend to put a particular filter on the way one views circumstances therefore the lens of judgement needs to be removed before one can see clearly. The Five Mindfulness Trainings (5MTs) to be discussed in Chapter 6 offer a prime example of a non-judgemental approach which can open up the perspective and allow one to appreciate the judgements one holds. They demonstrate an interbeing approach that can be problematic for Westerners used to considering, as Alden describes, the individual as superior to the collective (2006: 39). This could be a reason Kabat-Zinn refutes Dreyfus' argument and also why the questions posed at the beginning of this section can be difficult for a Westerner to answer. Nhat Hanh teaches one has to give up judging in order to be mindful, 'when we are mindful touching deeply the present moment, the fruits are always understanding, acceptance, love, and the desire to relieve suffering and bring joy' (Nhat Hanh 1999d: 24). Understanding and acceptance can only arise once judging has been dropped.

2:1:3 Bare attention

So it is also with bare attention, '... no value judgements are made' (Gunaratana 2002: 126). '... Mindfulness is kept to a bare registering of the facts observed, without reacting to them by deed, speech or by mental comment which may be one of self-reference (like, dislike, etc.), judgement or reflection' (Nyanaponika 1996: 30). This sounds similar to the discussion on non-judgement, and the difference between this and non-judgement appears to be minimal, as non-judgemental awareness could be interpreted as '... bare of labels' (Nyanaponika 1996: 32). However, Williams & Kabat-Zinn and Bodhi question the fullness of this definition as it precludes discernment (Williams & Kabat-Zinn 2011: 15) and implies spontaneity rather than cultivation (Bodhi 2011: 28). For those who use the term bare attention, which seems to be a *Theravadin* term, it is mindfulness as pure awareness, '... that flowing, soft-focused moment ... before you conceptualize [a] thing' (Gunaratana 2002: 138). Likewise it is the '... bare cognizing of an object, before one begins to recognize, identify, and conceptualize [because] one of the central tasks of *sati* is the de-automatization of habitual reactions and perceptual evaluations' (Analayo 2006: 59& 267). These definitions indicate the job of Mindfulness is to provide space in the mind before judging or conceptualizing comes in. Furthermore, it is '... both bare attention itself and the function of reminding us to pay bare attention if we have ceased to do so' (Gunaratana 2002: 143), that is both the means and the practice of being mindful. Whilst Nhat Hanh does not use the term bare attention his teaching reflects the term as '... the capacity of being aware of what is going on in the present moment' (Nhat Hanh 1992e: 101) which concurs with Henepola Gunaratana, '... noticing things exactly as they are without distortion' (2002: 145). I suggest the term bare attention can be used with an understanding it includes non-judgement as a faculty.

The above definitions demonstrate one cannot easily take one aspect of Mindfulness apart from others as this would be partial. *Sati* can be understood as beginning with bare attention in which objects, whether material or mental, are cognised without any label or definition. Then non-judgement allows one to see what is in front as a reality instead of a construed mental formation and finally one chooses the wholesome due to clarity of perception unadulterated by thinking or rumination. The wholesome choice comes about through discernment due to memory or remembering. Although these appear to be proceeding one after the other they take place instantaneously, and are continuously taking place as long as one is mindful.

The understanding of *sati* can be further deconstructed into four characteristics (Nyanaponika 1996: 30-44; Gethin 2001: 44; Kuan 2008: 41-56; Grossman & Van Dam 2011: 221) indicating the depth of its application.

2:1:4 Four characteristics of *Sati*

These scholars each indicate a systematic practice of gradual refinement (Grossman & Van Dam 2011: 221) as denoted in the Pali canon and early Buddhist literature. Whilst Nyanaponika does not enumerate the four characteristics I propose his discussion of bare attention is comparable with the other scholars and therefore is included in this discussion. These four characteristics of *sati* can be categorised as simple awareness, restraint of the senses (non-judgement), introspective awareness (recognising wholesome from unwholesome states), and insight (Kuan 2008: 41-56) and I now investigate these further according to the four scholars.

Although similar in many respects, Gethin's in particular reflects Dreyfus' claim for *sati* as memory and its retentive quality. Whereas Kuan begins with non-judgemental, simple awareness, Gethin denotes remembering and not losing what is before the mind; Nyanaponika conveys simple bare attention and Grossman & Van Dam indicate '... deliberate, open-hearted awareness of moment-to-moment perceptible experience'. Although Nhat Hanh does not discuss these particular four aspects of *sati* in one place it can be discerned from his writing that he concurs with each element. His indication that, 'in Buddhism, the most important precept of all is to live in awareness, to know what is going on' (Nhat Hanh 2007a: 65) reflects the open-hearted, non-judgemental awareness identified by three of the scholars. At this first stage only Gethin brings in the aspect of memory.

Throughout, Gethin emphasises the cognitive aspect of guarding what comes before the mind, recognising wholesome from unwholesome, knowing the value of each object of Mindfulness and thereby seeing things as they are. Kuan likewise denotes a requirement for moral discernment and introspection in the second and third aspects, whereas Nyanaponika translates this as slowing down the transition from thought to action, allowing Mindfulness to *mind the gap*, thus enabling one to move from reaction to response. Here these three each indicate a quality of evaluation whereas Grossman & Van Dam continue to emphasise the non-judgemental characteristic, '... sustained by such qualities as kindness, tolerance, patience and courage'. Nhat Hanh likewise uses the analogy of the guard, or sentinel '... at each of our sense doors to protect ourselves' (1999d: 34) as it is through this awareness '... of things as they are [that prevents] ... exaggeration and imagination' (2009a: 23-24).

Nyanaponika in the third aspect and Gethin in the second allude to analogies of Mindfulness from the Buddhist canon. There are references to *sati* as the gatekeeper (*Kimsuka Sutta*), King's treasurer (*Milindapanha*) and post to which six animals bound together (the six senses) are tethered (*Dukkhadhamma Sutta*). Nhat Hanh also uses the simile of the mindful guard, '... who is aware of every face that passes through the front corridor' (2008e: 38). Whatever arises is viewed with Mindfulness, yet still through a '... nondiscursive, non-analytic investigation of ongoing experience' (Grossman & Van Dam). The emphasis here is that Mindfulness does not miss anything and does not judge anything. The 'nondiscursive, non-analytic' aspect of Mindfulness further denotes that it is experiencing rather than thinking about whatever comes into one's awareness.

Grossman & Van Dam concentrate throughout on this non-judgemental characteristic and conclude simply with '... an awareness markedly different from everyday modes of attention', whereas the other three specifically indicate a process of moving towards perception, wisdom and insight (*vipassana*). Nhat Hanh often lists Mindfulness, concentration and insight together (1999c: 87; 2002a: 59; 2007c: 78; 2010b: 44) as '... with the support of concentration, conscious breathing, and looking deeply, [it] becomes a power that can penetrate deeply and directly into the heart of things' (Nhat Hanh 2007c: 81-82).

In summation, these four characteristics of *sati* signify a relaxing of mental activity to allow Mindfulness to experience rather than think about present occurrences on a moment-by-moment basis, acknowledging its shifting nature through acceptance and not trying to hold onto or reject particular feelings, thoughts, emotions or situations. This affirms the fullness of the *Buddha*'s teaching which can at times be understood merely as present-centred, non-judgemental awareness. Whilst this gives an idea of the current translation, *sati* in early Buddhism had a much richer understanding as has been demonstrated above. I propose this was why Nhat Hanh chose to put Mindfulness at the centre of his teachings, which whilst present in his books, the depth of meaning is not immediately apparent until one uncovers the complexities of this word.

These aspects of *sati* as simple awareness, restraint of the senses (non-judgement), introspective awareness (recognising wholesome from unwholesome states), and insight (Kuan 2008: 41-56) are readily detectable within Nhat Hanh's teaching. Absent from Kuan's list, however, is the aspect of memory or remembering which Gethin identifies and Nhat Hanh also references. Whilst Grossman & Van Dam stay with non-judgement and do not refer to evaluation their understanding of the four aspects are similar to Nhat Hanh's by emphasising the emotive and experiential side of open-heartedness, kindness, tolerance, patience and courage. I propose Nhat Hanh brings out the fullness of *sati* that can be seen as a combination of the descriptions discussed here, and outlined next.

2:1:5 A summation of Thich Nhat Hanh's elucidation of Mindfulness

As concluded above the term Mindfulness encompasses bare attention, non-judgement and choosing the wholesome or remembering properly, through which insight can be achieved. Choosing the wholesome indicates the moral or ethical dimension that is evident in Nhat Hanh's teaching, particularly the 5MTs. Although choosing the wholesome may initially appear to be judgement-forming I propose instead it is simple recognition of reality, such as being offered a rotten apple and a healthy one. There is no need for concerted deliberation, it is evident which to choose. This is reflected in the use of Mindfulness as Right Mindfulness, as one of the steps on the Noble Eightfold Path. I suggest the aspect of memory, which is debateable according to some scholars, recognises, 'your knowledge and experience of the practice of mindfulness is crucial; it lies at the heart of your ability to take Right Action and engage with the world' (Nhat Hanh 2003a: 102). Here Nhat Hanh brings in a further dimension of Mindfulness which has not been apparent so far in the discussion, the necessity of using Mindfulness as a means of engaging with the world. This quality will be readily perceived throughout his teaching in later chapters. Mindfulness is not a solitary practice for one's own enlightenment alone but one that affects, and can benefit, others. Nhat Hanh's exposition of Mindfulness can be described in diagrammatic form as,

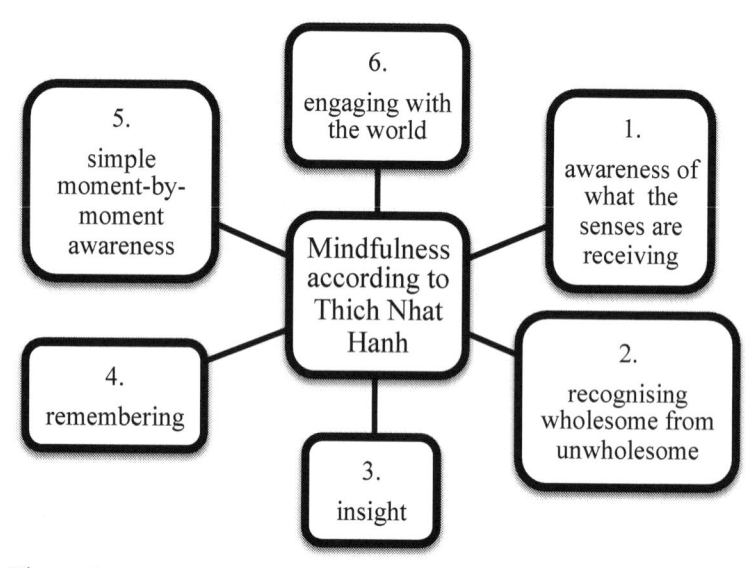

```
          ┌─────────────┐
          │     6.      │
┌──────┐  │ engaging    │  ┌──────────┐
│  5.  │  │ with the    │  │    1.    │
│simple│  │ world       │  │awareness │
│moment│  └─────────────┘  │of what   │
│ -by- │    ┌──────────┐   │the senses│
│moment│    │Mindfulness│  │are       │
│aware-│────│according │───│receiving │
│ness  │    │to Thich  │   └──────────┘
└──────┘    │Nhat Hanh │   ┌──────────┐
  ┌──────┐  └──────────┘   │    2.    │
  │  4.  │                 │recognising│
  │remem-│                 │wholesome │
  │bering│    ┌──────┐     │from      │
  └──────┘    │  3.  │     │unwhole-  │
              │insight│    │some      │
              └──────┘     └──────────┘
```

Figure 1

This diagram, whilst by no means a succinct definition of Mindfulness, incorporates all of the aspects discussed above. Relating each point to Nhat Hanh's own words can further elucidate this.

1. 'The essential thing is not to let any feeling or thought arise without recognizing it in mindfulness' (2008e: 38).
2. 'To recognize each seed as it comes up from the storehouse and to practice watering the most wholesome seeds whenever possible, to help them grow stronger' (1992e: 25).
3. 'The key that allows us to discern and act wisely, to respond appropriately, to know what to do and what not to do in a dangerous situation in order to bring about the best result' (2008g: 175).
4. 'Remembering to come back to the present moment' (1999d: 64).
5. 'The capacity to recognize what is there without being attached to it or fighting and suppressing it. That is called simple recognition' (2009a: 26).

6. 'We will create less suffering for ourselves and for other people. ... if we practice and become happy, we can inspire others to practice' (2009a: 65).

The first five aspects are recognisable within the discussion above on *sati* and it is in the area of engagement with the world (number 6) that Nhat Hanh brings his own innovation to an understanding of *sati*, as will be further examined throughout the book. These aspects are particularly relevant to the 5MTs discussed in Chapter 6. This is based upon a thorough study of the *Satipatthana Sutta* which informs much of his teaching, and will be discussed next.

2:2 The Satipatthana Sutta

As indicated above the practice of Mindfulness originates mainly from the *Satipatthana Sutta* of the Pali canon. It was delivered by the *Buddha* to a group of monks, but is now readily available to laity as well. It '... describes how to arouse and apply this faculty [*sati*] in a number of different situations' (Shaw 2006: 76) namely, of the body, feelings, mind and objects of mind (*Dhammas*). These categories are '... four areas where mindfulness has to penetrate in order for us to be protected, for joy to be nourished, for pain to be transformed, and for insight to be obtained' (Nhat Hanh 2012a: 118). The first section on the body is the longest, perhaps because of the usual attachment to the body and the belief in it as reality. The teaching here emphasises getting to know the body and its different parts intimately, therefore one meditates on the whole body (from the toes up and from the hair down) and its different impurities (thirty internal and external aspects), knowing each aspect individually, like sorting a sack of mixed rice and grain (Nhat Hanh 2006c: 18). Furthermore one is aware of the body when breathing and in any bodily position as well as recognising the presence of the four elements earth, water, fire and air (Nhat Hanh 2006c: 16-19). The section on the body concludes with a detailed consideration of the corpse in nine stages of disintegration until all that is left is dust, with the awareness that 'this body of mine is of the same nature, it will end up in the same way. There is no way it can avoid that state'

(Nhat Hanh 2006c: 19-21). The middle two sections on the feelings and the mind are comparatively short, concentrating on knowing what state the feelings or mind are in, '... for instance, confused, full of hatred, or constricted'(Shaw 2006: 78-79).

The final section of the *sutta* concludes with the Five Hindrances, the Five Aggregates of Clinging, the six sense organs and six sense objects, the Seven Factors of Awakening and the Four Noble Truths (Nhat Hanh 2006c: 24-31). The list is a comprehensive collection of the *Buddha*'s main teachings allowing one to recognise both those aspects that can hinder understanding (and thereby liberation) and those that lead towards it. The phrases used within each section of observing 'the body in the body ... the feelings in the feelings ... the mind in the mind [and] ... the objects of mind in the objects of mind' (Nhat Hanh 2006c: 15-16) are the means of penetrating the heart of things, as indicated at the beginning of the chapter. With each aspect 'he is mindful of the fact that "there is a body here", until understanding and full awareness come about. He remains established in the observation, free, not caught up in any worldly consideration' (Nhat Hanh 2006c: 18-19). The emphasis throughout the *sutta* is to become intimately acquainted with all aspects of body, feelings, mind and objects of mind as the '...most wonderful way to help living beings realize purification, overcome directly grief and sorrow, end pain and anxiety, travel the right path, and realize nirvana' (Nhat Hanh 2006c: 15). Each of these aspects can be easily recognised in Nhat Hanh's core teachings.

The four aspects of *sati* explicated in the previous subsection are developed further here as Nhat Hanh has expanded the *sutta* into twenty exercises as a means of realising '... the three basic observations of Buddhism, impermanence, selflessness and interdependent origination' (Nhat Hanh 2006c: 52). These three qualities permeate his teachings with particular emphasis being given to interdependent origination, which he terms interbeing, previously discussed in Chapter 1.

Much of his pedagogy is rooted in the *Satipatthana Sutta* and whilst he references it directly in some books (1999d: 67-68 & 215-216; 2008e: 40; 2012a 99-215) in others it is the basis of guided meditations (2009b) and *Dharma* talks. At the beginning of the *sutta* the *Buddha* indicates a monk[26] '... establishes mindfulness in front of him' through awareness of the breathing (Nhat Hanh 1999d: 16). Here, a cross-reference is already made to the *Anapanasati Sutta* (Mindfulness of breathing) which is also the basis of many of Nhat Hanh's teachings. Furthermore, the *Satipatthana Sutta* features in the daily programme at Plum Village in the particular practice of Deep Relaxation (which focuses on the body) as well as the general direction from the *sutta* of practising Mindfulness whilst walking, standing, sitting and lying down (Nhat Hanh 2012a: 105). All aspects of Plum Village practice are deeply rooted in the *Satipatthana Sutta*, embracing it as '... a way of developing awareness in all spheres of life and in various activities during the day' (Shaw 2006: 78). This is more fully explicated in Chapter 5.

2:3 Conclusion

Inherent in Nhat Hanh's teachings is the understanding that the *sutta* is not an ancient historical document but one that is entirely relevant to today's society and he accentuates, '... we have to read with the eyes of a person of today and discover appropriate ways to practice based on the teachings of the sutra' (2006c: 10). As has been deliberated above and continues to be so in the Journal of Contemporary Buddhism (vol. 12, 2011) *sati* is a complex construct of many meanings that have been examined here in order to understand its fullness in current society as Mindfulness. I have emphasised why Mindfulness cannot easily be translated as one simple definition due to this complexity although I have produced a diagram reflecting the fullness of Nhat Hanh's teachings.

---

[26] Nhat Hanh translates this as practitioner to signify it is not just a monastic practice.

This chapter demonstrates these intricacies and allows one to appreciate more fully why Nhat Hanh chooses to embed the *sutta* into his pedagogy as well as exhorting, 'this is one of the sutras to keep under your pillow, always with you' (2006c: 13). The understanding gained from this elucidation avails one to realise a richer comprehension of Mindfulness than could otherwise have been the case. In examining the *Satipatthana Sutta* as it relates to Nhat Hanh's teachings I have emphasised that whilst his pedagogy is seemingly simplistic it can belie the depth on which it is based, firmly rooted in the *Buddha's* teachings yet continually being reassessed in order to make them relevant to a modern audience.

The richness of Mindfulness that Nhat Hanh imparts is explored in the next chapter by uncovering the circumstances in which he learnt Mindfulness as a young novice monk and employed it as a crucial aspect of responding to the conflict situation in Vietnam.

3. Learning Mindfulness in Vietnam: the Formulation of Thich Nhat Hanh's Teachings

My aspiration [for Vietnam] remains very much the same, confronting the situation in which Buddhism has to be renewed in order to continue its service - the country under poverty, discriminating foreign control - and practising in such a way that you help your country, your nation, renew the tradition (Nhat Hanh, Q&A 2010).

Introduction

Having examined Mindfulness through the teachings of the *Satipatthana Sutta* in the previous chapter, I now discuss how Thich Nhat Hanh learnt and developed Mindfulness as a novice monk. At the Nottingham Retreat (2010) Nhat Hanh mentioned more than once the aspirations he had at the age of sixteen to renew Buddhism in order to help Vietnam and in a Q&A he emphasised his aims have not changed in this regard. Both here and in his writings he hints that Buddhism in 1940s Vietnam was not addressing the imperative issues of poverty brought about by foreign control and was therefore unable to help the country (1999c: 139). He realised Buddhism at this time had become separated from society and perceived it could be a social service and support to Vietnam, but was not doing so because its practice had moved away from the *Buddha's* teachings. In order to redeem Vietnam from its situation of poverty, foreign control and war Nhat Hanh proposes Buddhism had the answer at previous periods of Vietnamese history (see subsection 2:3:1). Earlier dynasties closely integrated Buddhism with political, economic and social life and it was from these paradigms that he was convinced both Buddhism and Vietnam could be 'renewed'. In this chapter I discuss Buddhism and Vietnam as two separate entities although I propose that Nhat Hanh sees them as intimately connected. It was this recognition of Buddhism as a social as well as spiritual support for Vietnam that helped him elucidate Engaged Buddhism, as I demonstrate throughout the chapter.

The key argument for this chapter is that Nhat Hanh's teaching of Engaged Buddhism was a contextual response to Vietnam in the midst of occupation and war and that Mindfulness was the means of implementing Engaged Buddhism. His inspirations and aspirations combined to formulate an Engaged Buddhism appropriate to helping Vietnam out of the malaise and despair into which it had fallen. His aspirations did not come out of a vacuum but were nurtured and practised in the extreme situations of war and occupation in Vietnam. Concurrently he began to inculcate Mindfulness into daily life in the way it had been introduced to him at the monastery. His particular prominence of Mindfulness as the spiritual basis underpinning the means of addressing suffering gave people a process for not only surviving war, but being optimistic and hopeful about a future beyond it. Without desiring prominence or recognition, his voice became the one that epitomised a peaceful alternative to war. He wished to prove that 'pain is inevitable, but suffering is optional. You may choose not to suffer even when the pain is there' (Plum Village Online Monastery 2011). The 'pain' was brought about by the continual wars in, and occupation of, Vietnam; occupation by France at the time he was born, the Indo-China War when he was a young monk, closely followed by the Vietnam/American War.

I will examine the circumstances in 1940s Vietnam and discuss the areas Nhat Hanh considered needed revitalising. However, to understand this one needs an overview of the historical context, demonstrating how Vietnam had become a country riven by wars as detailed above. I will, therefore, briefly discuss the history of

Vietnam before examining the situation into which Nhat Hanh grew up. Having considered the issues as they related to Nhat Hanh I will examine the inspirations and influences that assisted his formulation of Engaged Buddhism. These are the Ly and Tran dynasties who demonstrated Buddhism as integral to society, Mahatma Gandhi, Martin Luther King Jr. and Thomas Merton whose practices helped Nhat Hanh elucidate nonviolence as a means of achieving peace in Vietnam, and finally, two moments of personal revelation that clarified his path. Nonviolence was important to Nhat Hanh as the path the enlightened *Buddha* chose after practising austerities and realising they did not work (2012a: 185).

In section 3:4 I will examine the ways in which he implemented Engaged Buddhism in Vietnam. These are the monastery *Phuong Boi,* the School of Youth for Social Services (SYSS) and *Tiep Hien,* the Order of Interbeing. Each of these demonstrates that Nhat Hanh was able to execute practical living examples of Engaged Buddhism at various times in the 1950s and 60s by taking Buddhism out of the monastery and into the villages to physically aid people. The chapter concludes with a reflection on his methodology. I begin by showing that war and conflict are closely bound up with Vietnam's history.

3:1 The historical context of Vietnam

The history of Vietnam is one riddled with war and struggle for the greater part beginning with a millennium of occupation by the Chinese whose influences Vietnam has struggled to shrug off ever since (Corfield 2008: 4). The period after Chinese occupation is heralded as a peaceful oasis and a time of stability and outstanding leadership (Lockhart & Duiker 2006: 223 & 373). It is this period from the 11th to 14th centuries that Nhat Hanh uses as an inspiration because he suggests it was the influence of Buddhism that helped create peace and prosperity (see subsection 3:3:1). Throughout its turbulent history Buddhism has been a constant factor in Vietnam arriving by sea from India and by road from China as early as the second century CE (Nhat Hanh 1967: 12; Nguyen 2008: 9). Northern

Vietnam adopted *Mahayana* Buddhism from the Chinese (SarDesai 2005: 13) whereas southern Vietnam retained its Indian influences and *Theravada* Buddhism (Topmiller 2002: 10). This acceptance of both forms of Buddhism is consistent with Vietnam's melding of religions, also incorporating Confucianism and Taoism alongside indigenous practices including animism, superstition and ancestor worship (Karnow 1997: 294). The Vietnamese incorporated these worldviews as each played different parts in society; Confucianism provided a code of conduct and respect for elders, Buddhism nurtured the inner being and Taoism amalgamated existing beliefs and practices of magic and animism (Nhat Hanh 1967: 21) in 'accord with the universe' (Topmiller 2002: 12). Due to this mutual respect and acceptance of each religion Catholicism was initially received in the same regard (see subsection 3:2:2).

From the end of the Tran dynasty in the 1400s Confucianism gradually replaced Buddhism as the official religion (Irons 2008: 546) at a time when Vietnam was involved in many wars with its close neighbours for land and territory before succumbing to occupation again, this time by the French in the 1800s. However, 'Buddhism remained popular as a devotional faith in all strata of society and coexisted with Confucian beliefs rather than being replaced by them' (Lockhart & Duiker 2006: 50).

Vietnam fell to the French in the Western colonial sweep of the nineteenth century as part of a French empire to rival the British (Corfield 2008: 19), but the French were mainly concerned with access to China through the Mekong (SarDesai 2005: 38) or Red Rivers as viable commercial routes (Tucker 1999: 30). Although Vietnam had natural resources and several seaports (Corfield 2008: 19) these were secondary compared to France's desire to get into China. The French demonstrated a lack of concern towards Vietnamese citizens by not offering the same democratic freedoms that were available in France (Tucker 1999: 50; SarDesai 2005: 50). The imposition of Catholicism upon Vietnam highlights another way in which the Vietnamese considered themselves to be poorly treated by the French, as 'Christian missionaries in the colonies sought to replace what they considered to be inferior modes of religious belief with Christianity' (Tomalin 2006: 95). Vietnamese nationalism was stirred by France's aggression prompting civil rebellion and dissidence turning into war (SarDesai 2005: 38). The French took the strategy of divide and rule to successfully invade Vietnam retaining the separate names of Tonkin, Annam and Cochinchina for the north, central and southern parts of Vietnam 'in order to perpetuate the notion of a divided country' (Tucker 1999: 22). They highlighted the differences between north and south by playing upon previous divisions from the 1630s when 'the Nguyen rulers built a wooden wall ... ironically not far from the 17th parallel[27] division of 1954' and divided the country for the next 150 years (Tucker 1999: 14). Having annexed Laos and Cambodia as well by 1887 French Indochina was created comprising these two plus Cochinchina, Annam and Tonkin (Corfield 2008: 25). When Nhat Hanh was born in 1926 French occupation of Vietnam resulted in much discontent among Vietnamese citizens looking for a way to remove their aggressors.

The French-Indochina War (1946-54) effectively divided Vietnam into two with the Communist Viet Minh holding the north and the French supported by anti-Communist Vietnamese in the south (Corfield 2008: 51-52). It did so literally by the end of the Indochina War with the partition of the country at the 17th parallel (Corfield 2008: 54-5). As this war metamorphosed into the Vietnam/American War (1955-75) France was increasingly backed by America with the Viet Minh boosted by the powerful Communist countries of USSR and China; the second half of the war 'became part of the worldwide struggle between Communist and "free world" forces' (Tucker 1999: 62-63). When the French were defeated America took its place in supporting South Vietnam against the Communist North. The Vietnam/American War 'was really no different from any of the others in Vietnam's war-ridden history, that of ridding its country of

---

[27] The provisional military demarcation line drawn up by the Geneva Accords in 1954 between North and South Vietnam (Britannica).

hostile foreigners' (Tucker 1999: 50). Inevitably war led to more war with little abatement or end in sight.

3:2 Thich Nhat Hanh's experience of Vietnam in the 1940s – 1960s

Nhat Hanh's concern in the conflicts discussed above was directed towards the Vietnamese peasants who had no influence over proceedings yet still constituted over eighty per cent of the population by the 1940s (Tucker 1999: 38). They endured severe poverty, hunger and political suppression with no economic resources to adequately provide for them. Furthermore, by the 1960s, the napalm that the Americans initially used to clear vegetation was used on the Vietnamese people themselves (Corfield 2008: 89&95) and with more high explosive being dropped on the country 'than had been used in the whole of the Second World War' (Hobsbawm 2002: 217) it was the ordinary people who suffered most. Nhat Hanh was most concerned about helping these people who had no support from elsewhere. Their suffering was great and to him it was apparent that 'these kinds of sufferings called for action, called for practice in order for us to liberate ourselves and the desire to shine the Buddhist insight on the situation was very strong' (Nhat Hanh, Peace is Every Step 1997). Whilst there appeared to be an apparent inevitability to war, Nhat Hanh was able to propose a different approach of nonviolence based on the concept of interbeing and prompted by the desire for unity and peace.

Division and strife were palpable in both Buddhist practice and Vietnamese society during Nhat Hanh's formative years. He wished to address this division by offering a Buddhism that would provide unity. As well as civil war due to French occupation, Vietnam was battling with the growing threat of Westernisation and what its response should be. This was particularly relevant to Nhat Hanh who concluded the older monastic generation were not willing to engage or incorporate Western philosophies, as discussed in subsection 3:2:1. He and others of his generation, having received a Western education, had a different perspective and wanted to assimilate new ideas. Whilst the turbulent situation in Vietnamese society was the foundation of his formulation of Engaged Buddhism it was within Buddhist society that he encountered apathy, animosity and resistance to his proposals.

Using perhaps his most condemning language from his early diaries, Nhat Hanh indicates a situation in Vietnam where
> high-ranking Buddhist monks were so blinded by the respect and admiration people gave them that they had fallen into a state of complacency [and] ... intellectuals and students became increasingly disillusioned with Buddhist hierarchy. Vietnamese Buddhism, two thousand years old, was not offering a way out of the noose that was strangling Vietnamese society (1999b: 139).

Although Nhat Hanh had clear ideas as a novice about how Buddhism could help Vietnam he discovered the Buddhist hierarchy archaic and not ready for change and therefore unwilling to hear his fresh ideas. Nhat Hanh continually presses his point that 'every tradition has to renew itself from time to time to address the pressing needs of the day' (2008c: 21) and he found it difficult to accept the reluctance of the Buddhist hierarchy. This aspect of renewal is now practised at Plum Village where Nhat Hanh indicates the practices need renewing every twenty years (*Dharma* Talk 2009). He admits to being a revolutionary monk (2004a: 110) and inevitably caused trouble by not towing the line. Whilst some teachers at the Institute liked his refreshing and stimulating ideas others considered him to be dangerous and banned a magazine *Voice of the Rising Tide* in which he and fellow monks put forward their new ideas (2004a: 110-111). As these young monks resisted the hierarchy in calling for change they were accused of '... sowing seeds of dissent when we challenged anything traditional' (Nhat Hanh 1999b: 50).

Gethin indicates that in the *Buddha's* time there formed a distinction
> ... between two kinds of monastic duty: that of books and that of practice ... The former is concerned with the study of

the theory as preserved in Buddhist writings. The latter is the straightforward attempt to put the Buddha's system of training into practice, to live the spiritual life as prescribed by the Buddha and his followers. Although this formal distinction is found in the writings of a particular Buddhist school, the point being highlighted holds good for Buddhism as a whole (1998: 38).

It will be seen throughout this chapter that this was a tension Nhat Hanh wrestled with by wanting to promote the practitioner path and coming into conflict with Buddhist scholars who were text-based. Gethin further denotes this tension led to the arising of the Ch'an (Zen) school of Buddhism '... whose well-known suspicion of theoretical formulations of the teaching is summed up by the traditional stanza,
    A special tradition outside the scriptures;
    Not founded on words and letters;
    Pointing directly to the heart of man;
    Seeing into one's own nature and attaining Buddhahood.[28]
(1998: 38).

As Nhat Hanh's spiritual ancestors are from the Zen tradition it is not surprising that he has adopted this path of practice. Whilst Nhat Hanh is not rejecting scholastic work, and is himself a renowned scholar as indicated by the translation of many Buddhist texts he has undertaken[29], it will become clear here as in preceding chapters that it is the practical rather than theoretical application of the *Buddha's* teaching that he espouses and to 'live the spiritual life as prescribed by the Buddha'.

---

[28] Verse attributed to Nan-chuan P'u-yuan (748-834); see Heinrich Dumoulin, *A History of Zen Buddhism* (London 1963: 67).
[29] *Prajnaparamita* Heart *Sutra* 1988; Discourse on Living Happily in the Present Moment 1990; *Anapanasati Sutta* 1992a; *Prajnaparamita Diamond Sutra* 1992b; *Sutra* on Knowing the Better Way to Catch a Snake; 1993b; *Satipatthana Sutta* 2006c.

3:2:1 Buddhism in the 1940s – 1960s

The state of Buddhism at this time as Nhat Hanh saw it was dualistic in the sense that there was a distinct difference between the practices of the monastics and laity. This in itself is not unusual, but he felt there could be more parity and in particular he wanted to introduce Mindfulness to the laity rather than it remaining a monastic practice. He could not comprehend why there should be such a difference in practice between them. After its peak period in the 11th to 14th centuries Buddhism had gradually been reduced to a popular practice for the laity and intellectual study in the monasteries. '... The masses, through ignorance, had gradually converted Buddhism into a religion filled with superstition ... [whereas the monks] debased Buddhism' by seeking to enhance their material fortunes (Harris 1999: 267). By the 1940s the lay practices were ritualistic and empty of meaning and the monastic practices heavily doctrinal. The monastics practised *Thien* (Zen) Buddhism 'a discipline that teaches that the key to liberation can be attained through meditation on a seemingly incongruous statement or question' (Topmiller 2002: 10). Their practice was intellectual in a theoretical sense but not in the way Nhat Hanh denoted when he later instigated a Buddhist University in Saigon.

In contrast to the practices of the monks the laity observed a Pure Land[30] practice which encouraged them to look after the monks in order to gain merit for the next life (Topmiller 2002: 10) and in return the monks offered *Dharma* talks as a reward for the service. Laypeople were encouraged to practice the Five Precepts, serve the monks and attend the temple twice a month at the time of the new and full moon (Nhat Hanh 1967: 14). The temples had large gold *Buddha* statues which were worshipped without meaning (Nhat Hanh, Peace is Every Step 1997) and animal sacrifices were a regular

---

[30] 'The Pure Land School is currently the most popular school of Buddhism in China, Vietnam and Japan. Pure Land Buddhism is based on the faith that there is a Land of Happiness (Sukhavati)' in the West (Laity 2003 : 7). For more information read Laity 2003 : 7-12.

part of the practice (IC, Person E 2009). The lay practice had become one of looking for salvation outside of oneself and was full of superstition (Do 1999: 225 & 267). Laypeople were not encouraged to meditate as this was seen as a stringent monastic practice only. The lay practices were ritualistic and too concentrated on the outer forms of symbol rather than inner experience, there was no focus on practice for enlightenment in the here and now. Nhat Hanh's assessment of both monastic and lay situations was that in each case they continued as had been practised for many years without any mindful distinction as to whether this was now useful or appropriate to meet the current needs of Vietnam. He questioned if it was necessary for monastic and lay observances to be so disparate.

Nhat Hanh had desired becoming a monk from the age of nine (Nhat Hanh 2008b: 11) and as a novice at the age of sixteen he was convinced Buddhism could help Vietnam out of its desperate situation 'in order to improve the lives of the ... poor peasants' (Nhat Hanh 2003a: 94). Yet he discovered the Buddhist hierarchy had no interest in social practices as denoted above; instead it was conservative (Nhat Hanh 1999b: 6-7) and the teachings had not changed for centuries (Nhat Hanh 2008b: 21-30). He found the practices in the monastery had no connection with the suffering of the laity and this went against his 'deep desire to bring Buddhism into every walk of life' (Nhat Hanh 2003a: 94).

This situation was exacerbated by a lack of Buddhist leadership with an awareness and understanding of current social issues. Some Buddhist leaders had studied abroad in the 1930s, were thus knowledgeable of the latest intellectual and political currents and upon returning to Vietnam established centres as focal points for other intellectuals (Tucker 1999: 82). This upsurge of youthful energy provoked many 'to resist the foreign invaders, and protect their nation and native religion [and led to] ... arrest, torture, imprisonment and execution' for many Buddhist leaders (Nguyen 2008: 263). Intellectuals, students and young people alongside Nhat Hanh were enthused by this renewal of Buddhism (Nhat Hanh 1967: 56), but the arrest and imprisonment of the leaders led to problems as the passionate young people were left with poor leadership (SI, Sr Chan Khong 2009). Into this vacuum others set themselves up as leaders claiming to be Buddhist monks when they were not and who believed in the superstitions and cult practices (Nguyen 2008: 269) associated with Taoism and other indigenous beliefs. These false leaders turned people away from what Nhat Hanh believed to be the true path of Buddhism laid down by the *Buddha*. Here, Nhat Hanh distinguishes between Buddhist leaders from the previous generation who had been imprisoned due to their involvement in social issues and the Buddhist 'hierarchy' that replaced them who concentrated on theoretical knowledge and would not engage with 'the pressing issues of the day' (Nhat Hanh 2008b: 21). The Buddhist hierarchy could not understand let alone assist Nhat Hanh with the reforms he wished to introduce.

His generation was the first in Vietnam to receive a Western education and many had a different outlook to the Buddhist hierarchy. In the monastery Nhat Hanh found to his disappointment the teaching was restrictive and unwelcoming of a novice who demanded studies beyond those offered at the Buddhist institute (Nhat Hanh 2003a: 8-9) and the attitude complacent (Nhat Hanh 1999b: 139). He 'was critical of the conservatism of monastic life, especially in its failure to pursue new knowledge and its non-involvement in contemporary social issues' (Fernando 2007: 20). He and his friends were looking beyond Vietnam and engaging with the wider world for knowledge and intellectual stimulus. Whilst not accepting Western views wholesale, to replace the traditional Vietnamese ones, they were willing to engage with Western ideas, philosophies and literature 'because we were convinced that these subjects could help us infuse life into the practice of Buddhism in our country' whereas their teachers would not address such needs (Nhat Hanh 2008b: 21-22). Nhat Hanh felt he was not given the support or guidance he required from his superiors.

His argument for the renewal of Buddhism in Vietnam parallels the introduction of the *Mahayana* tradition. His critique of *Theravada* Buddhism at the advent of *Mahayana* is that 'the practice of the

Dharma had become the exclusive domain of monks and nuns, and laypeople were limited to supporting the ordained Sangha with food, shelter, clothing and medicine' (Nhat Hanh 1999d: 16). There arose an equivalent situation in 1940s Vietnam and Nhat Hanh was determined the *Dharma* should not be exclusive or only for the few, it should be available to everyone. From his point of view although the monks were well-educated they were cut off from society and therefore not interested in addressing social issues. It was a key issue for him that Buddhism should engage with society rather than withdraw from it and be able to offer practical assistance to ease suffering. He also objected to the rigidity he met with in keeping to the tradition of what had been laid down previously. Whilst traditional values are valuable, when they become dogmatic or inflexible there is no opportunity to question or re-evaluate and it was this inflexibility that he reacted against.

One particular aspect that Nhat Hanh objected to was the undue Chinese influence in the monastic studies of Buddhist texts and *sutra*s. Monastics had initially learnt Chinese in order to be able to read the *Tripataka*, Buddhist texts introduced during the early years of Buddhism coming to Vietnam from China (Nhat Hanh 1967: 15). These had remained in Chinese long after the occupation of Vietnam had ceased, an indication of the wider Chinese influence still palpable in many aspects of Vietnamese society (Tucker 1999: 10). A further key point of reformation for Nhat Hanh as he became a novice was that Buddhist chants should be sung in Vietnamese rather than Chinese (SI, Sr Chan Khong 2009). Although these may appear to be minor points it was indicative of a wider lethargy that had descended upon Buddhism and Vietnam in general and particularly from the Buddhist hierarchy who, according to Nhat Hanh, were unwilling to assess whether practices were still relevant to current society. His point reflected wider calls for renovation that had been stirring from the 1920s which would allow the Vietnamese peasants to become literate by using the national language to produce newspapers and magazines, which was easier to learn, read and reproduce rather than the antiquated Chinese (Nguyen 2008: 271). For Nhat Hanh, the Chinese here represented an outside power being forced unwillingly upon Vietnam, something they have tried to resist throughout their history. Yet even after the Chinese had relinquished Vietnam their impact was still recognisable and I suggest his intention was that for Vietnam to regain stability these influences had to be removed; 'during the Vietnamese history there were times when Buddhism had been able to help defeat the Chinese invasions ... When the Chinese came and occupied the country for many years, we were able to win our independence because we were united' (Nhat Hanh 2004a: 109-110).

Furthermore, Nhat Hanh was surprised to discover the levels of disunity and discord that pervaded the monastery. Whilst he was convinced that Buddhism should become more socially active and be of service to the Vietnamese people he was disappointed with the complacency he detected the Buddhist hierarchy had fallen into (Nhat Hanh 1999b: 139), as discussed earlier, who were 'not ready to provide the kind of practice and answers that could satisfy our personal and social needs' (Nhat Hanh 2004a: 110). This was not an easy discrepancy to resolve. He spent seven years in the monastery learning the valuable lesson of Mindfulness, which he later used as the basis of Engaged Buddhism, and studying to become a monk. Once he became ordained, however, he chose to leave the monastery and pursue academic studies that he felt were more relevant to helping Vietnam. This will be further discussed in section 3:5.

3:2:2 The Buddhist response to occupation and war

Buddhist groups, by which I mean particularly the younger generation who were resisting war and foreign intervention, made a valuable contribution to the Vietnam/American War and I will assess the effectiveness of this here. Their response was to create a Unified Buddhist Church (UBC) in 1963 that would amalgamate different sects of Buddhism in Vietnam. The UBC, known as the Struggle Movement, became the voice of the antiwar movement (King 2009: 76). With the country divided into Communist north against Capitalist south the UBC wanted to present a third viewpoint that expressed a peaceful and nonviolent solution. Nhat Hanh exclaimed

'I am from the center' in his efforts to disassociate himself with either north or south and free people from their notions that one had to be for one side (1999d: 55) and therefore against another. He further reiterates this in one of the many poems written during the early 1960s in Vietnam 'help us remember we are just one family, North and South' (1999a: 36) conveying unity rather than separation. The UBC responded particularly to the exploits of the South Vietnamese government (GVN) whose actions 'created conditions for Christianity to develop at an inordinate pace and encroach upon and replace native religions' (Nguyen 2008: 263). A 'private' status was imposed upon Buddhists 'requiring its adherents to obtain official permission to conduct public activities' (Karnow 1997: 294). Whilst the Buddhist associations preferred to maintain neutrality from both sides, neither praising nor condemning, they chose to react against the GVN when the French government 'blatantly acted against the Buddhists in 1963' (Tucker 1999: 83) as this was seen as deeply affecting the peasantry in Vietnam, most of whom were Buddhist. Nhat Hanh and others felt the union of Buddhist groups throughout Vietnam would give strength to their calls for neutralism and peace.

Previously, Buddhists had been stirred into action when the French invasion led to the French colonizing Vietnamese land which they equated with 'loss of freedom, loss of independence ... loss ... of their own value system' (Nguyen 2008: 263). The French occupation is intimately intertwined with the imposition of Catholicism which had initially been introduced peacefully by missionaries in 1615 (Tucker 1999: 22) with thousands of conversions (Karnow 1997: 71) because it was believed it could sit alongside Buddhism, Confucianism and Taoism as another of several religions practised in the country. However, the evangelistic attitude of Christians 'who showed contempt towards what Buddhists believed and practised' (Harris 2010: 119) in other colonial sweeps likewise created tensions between the indigenous population and the French. Once 'the missionary fathers attacked the traditional religious beliefs and customs of Vietnam ... the Emperor and the mandarins declared

Roman Catholicism to be wrong and harmful to their country's traditional culture' (Nhat Hanh 1967: 23-25).

Thus religious persecution gave France the excuse it was looking for to invade Vietnam (Nhat Hanh 1967: 29; SarDesai 2005: 35; Tucker 1999: 27). In doing so they promoted Catholicism as the primary religion aware that the inferior status of Buddhism affected 'over 80 percent of the populace' (Topmiller 2002: 1-2). Nhat Hanh was not against Catholicism personally, but what it came to stand for in Vietnam, introduced to replace indigenous cultural practices of ancestor worship and to become the primary religion of Vietnam (Nhat Hanh 1967: 25-26). He did not see Catholicism in itself as a threat to Buddhism only in the way it was utilised by the French as a means for weakening Vietnamese society. As the majority of the peasant population were Buddhist it was Buddhism that the French attacked by reducing it from a religion to an association. As mentioned earlier, this meant they had to obtain permission to conduct public activities that had been previously practised for many years. The underhand way in which Catholicism was imposed upon the Vietnamese and used as the method of occupying Vietnam impressed upon Nhat Hanh the necessity of reminding people that they already had a strong belief system that could permeate every aspect of society and daily life. Buddhism was deeply inherent in Vietnamese life and aspects such as interbeing and reincarnation indicate differences between the American and Vietnamese worldviews that produced different reactions to war.

To counteract the imposition of Catholicism the UBC formed in 1963 in order to project a united voice by combining elements of eleven different sects as well as *Theravada* and *Mahayana* streams of Buddhism (Topmiller 2002: 6-7). Whilst Nhat Hanh was supportive of the amalgamation of the different sects he resisted all attempts to engage politically because he saw their strengths as monks and not politicians (Nhat Hanh & Berrigan 2001: 89). Indeed, he neither approved of nor took part in many of the aspects of social activism advocated by the UBC, whilst not judging those who did (King 1996: 349). His intention was to seek for a peaceful solution and as events like the demonstration outside the radio station in Hue at the time of *Wesak*[31] indicated peaceful demonstrations do not always end peacefully. In this situation eight people died (Tucker 1999: 84; Chan Khong 2007: 33-34). However, others within the UBC did not have the same intentions as Nhat Hanh and saw it as an ideal opportunity to make a political stance.

Topmiller indicates the in-fighting that arose within the UBC has deep roots throughout Vietnamese history in the disagreements between 'those who saw work for social justice and peace as proper for Buddhist clergy and those who emphasized religious values and removal from the world' (2002: 7). In the particular instance of the UBC the disagreements were between political or non-political actions. Whilst it wanted to present a strong and united force during the War this did not happen. Within the leadership Thich Tam Chau 'advocated a progovernment, antineutral stance' whereas Thich Tri Quang supported neutralism and promoted the notion of a coalition government (Topmiller 2002: 7). Nhat Hanh's apolitical stance could have been thrown into doubt by his association with Thich Tam Chau, however, these three leaders collectively were a forceful movement within the UBC (King 1996: 326)

It was not unknown for Buddhist monks to take a political stance as in the late 19th and early 20th centuries they encouraged political resistance of the 'feudal colonial regime' (Nguyen 2008: 263). The idea of Buddhist monks protesting against social injustices and, in this case, the opposition to religious oppression was therefore not a new idea. It came to the fore, however, in 1963 firstly in the self-immolation of Thich Quang Duc and secondly in the role the Buddhists played in deposing the pro-Catholic leader Diem from the GVN. Both actions in their different ways brought the UBC into the political arena.

---

[31] Wesak is the main Buddhist festival in April or May commemorating The Buddha's birth, enlightenment and *parinirvana*.

The wholly unexpected self-immolation of Thich Quang Duc took the world by surprise, and 'photographs of the burning monk dominated the front pages of U.S. newspapers the next day stunning the American public' (King 1996: 327). This marked the time the West began to seriously take notice of America's involvement in Vietnam (Nhat Hanh 1967: 9). Self-immolation was not intended as suicide but an action to awaken the world to the suffering caused by the War and the persecution of the Buddhists (Amore & Ching 2002: 299-300; Nhat Hanh 1993: 43) because 'to burn oneself by fire is to prove that what one is saying is of the utmost importance' (Nhat Hanh 1967: 118). Nhat Hanh proposes it is not sacrifice (Nhat Hanh & Berrigan 2001: 65), but the action of a *bodhisattva* who had 'realized a level of non-fear and non-attachment, no birth and no death' (Nhat Hanh 2008g: 160). He personally knew both Thich Quang Duc and Nhat Chi Mai (Nhat Hanh & Berrigan 2001: 65) who was one of several monastics copying Quang Duc's example. She was one of the six original members of *Tiep Hien*. Sr Chan Khong recounts the details leading up to the self-immolation of Sr Mai and whilst these deaths were clearly upsetting there was recognition that in severe circumstances one has to take drastic action (2007: 93-104). Nhat Hanh, who was out of the country on both occasions, indicates from the letters both left behind that they were fully in control of what they were doing (Nhat Hanh & Berrigan 2001: 65). Self-immolation demonstrates another area where American and Vietnamese viewpoints were dissimilar. It was something that the Americans could not understand and whilst this was the action of individuals rather than any orchestrated action by the UBC it was effective because it compelled people to re-evaluate their position regarding the War.

Moreover, it forced Americans to reconsider how they viewed the Vietnamese people rather than simply regarding them as 'the enemy' (Thomas 2006: 15). As far as the UBC were concerned the self-immolations were the beginning of a shift in perspective that 'radicalized the Buddhist public of Vietnam' (King 1996: 327) leading to demonstrations and outright civil disobedience which culminated in the GVN abolishing the celebration of *Wesak* (Nhat

Hanh 1967: 37) in 1963. The reaction was to draw out thousands in support of the UBC who, by this time, 'carried so much weight, that for a short time they gained the ability to bring down governments ... and call thousands of followers into the streets' (Topmiller 2002: 4). The outcome was a coup culminating in the assassination of Diem and his brother-in-law (Nhu). Whilst the Buddhists wished to remove Diem they would not have approved of the violence used to achieve it. Furthermore, the removal of Diem played into American hands who were also 'actively seeking to force Diem to sack Nhu, and oust both of them if Diem refused' (Corfield 2008: 69). Whilst the death of Diem led to a relaxation of the laws demoting Buddhism, which was the intention of the UBC, it also led to an increase in American forces, entirely the opposite of what the UBC were looking for (Topmiller 2002: 4-5).

At this peak moment when the UBC had maximum support it led to their virtual demise as they were not ready to cope with the influx of young people looking for guidance and leadership which they could not offer. 'The number of monks and laymen with sufficient ability and experience to exercise leadership was small, while the need for responsible leaders became pressing' (Nhat Hanh 1967: 56). As discussed in subsection 3:2:1 many Buddhist leaders were currently imprisoned after earlier attempts to bring together intellectual groups to initiate change and therefore the masses were ready for action with few who could adequately guide them. The surge in support for the UBC 'resulted more from the weakness of the GVN than from their own power' as they were effective at forming resistance, but ill-prepared to lead a government (Topmiller 2002: 27). As a group they were not ready for the flood of interest which required organisation and leadership (King 1996: 338). It appears that in responding to what they perceived as social injustices the UBC had no strategies in place for what would follow on. They were good at practical social action such as rescuing villagers caught in the crossfire between North and South (Nhat Hanh 1993: 59), rebuilding bombed villages, sometimes several times after each new destruction (Chan Khong 2007: 85), and using 'literature and the arts as "weapons" to challenge the oppression' (Nhat Hanh 1993: 41) but they were not politically minded enough to enter the public arena. Indeed, this was not an area Nhat Hanh wished to join.

Nhat Hanh hoped the 'history-making unification [of the UBC] ... may well serve as an example for a World Unified Buddhist Church in the future' (1967: 13), however, the internal disputes and battles to control the organisation 'hurt the movement badly ... making it easier for the GVN to suppress the UBC' (Topmiller 2002: 8). Whilst they continued to operate in the social sphere they 'ceased to be a major political force since their role in the overthrow of ... Diem in 1963' (Corfield 2008: 122). Furthermore, when the Communists came to power at the end of the Vietnam/American War they established 'a government-sponsored and –controlled Buddhist church that became the only recognized Buddhist religious association in the country' (Topmiller 2002: 150-151). The UBC was outlawed and the work of the SYSS in 'orphanages, dispensaries, schools, and resettlement centers were all shut down or taken by the government' (Nhat Hanh 2007c: 19). Although it may appear that all the work of the UBC and SYSS was for nothing this was not the end of the matter as far as Nhat Hanh was concerned. He continues to ensure charities in Vietnam are provided for, especially promoting the Hungry Children's Fund from Plum Village. In this respect, as indicated earlier, his aspiration for Vietnam has not changed. The final impetus that the UBC had was to nominate him as the Buddhist representative in the Paris Peace talks at the conclusion of the Vietnam/American War. Once more giving him an official role, whilst in exile in France.

Whilst the Buddhists took action against the GVN because of their backing from external forces they did not actively oppose the Communists. Although the Buddhists did not agree with Communist policies Nhat Hanh's argument was against the GVN which appears to make his neutralist stance questionable. Whilst he advocates not taking sides he did not actively condone the Communists because they were Vietnamese. Instead he became a voice for the majority of the peasants who had none of their own. He would not take either side in the conflict and in many respects the peasants were outside of the War yet unwillingly involved.

> You don't hate anyone, you try to embrace all warring parties, you want reconciliation, you don't want to continue with the war. That is a difficult stand to take because in a situation of conflict if you align yourself with one party you are protected at least by that party, but if you do not align with any warring party you are exposed to the attack of both warring parties (Nhat Hanh, Q&A 2010).

This attitude was not one the Americans in particular could understand; 'those who stood in the middle and attempted to steer a course between the two ideologies appeared more dangerous than anyone else. The idea of rejecting both seemed incredible since American logic said one is either with us or against us' (Topmiller 2002: 14). Even these dangerous situations, which put the lives of his friends and associates at risk, could not deter Nhat Hanh from his stance. 'In a situation of war, practitioners of peace do not take sides ... We were a nonviolent army that carried only love and our intention to help as our weapons, but we suffered casualties just like other armies' (Nhat Hanh 2003a: 103-104). Whilst this may seem a naïve attitude to hold amidst such heavy fighting he was convinced it was the appropriate path to take given that Vietnam's history of conflict had proven that war did not provide long-term resolution. The Buddhist response was to call for 'a negotiated political, rather than military, solution to the war' (Mitchell 2002: 293). Why did they choose to participate in the war at all? They did so because the suffering of the peasants was so great they could not keep silent and do nothing. Nhat Hanh demonstrates Edmund Burke's (Thinkexist) words that evil triumphs when good men do nothing. Even whilst taking actions against the French and Americans the Buddhists did not hate them they merely wanted them out of Vietnam.

3:3 Thich Nhat Hanh's inspirations and influences

Nhat Hanh's concepts were informed by inspirations and influences both from people he met as well as ideas that had been developed previously. The insight for Engaged Buddhism comes from Vietnamese leaders in the 11th to 14th centuries; Gandhi informed the concept of nonviolence as well as meetings with Martin Luther King Jr., and Thomas Merton; and the aspect of Mindfulness was introduced to him as a novice in the monastery. I conclude this section with two personal experiences in Nhat Hanh's life which I propose demonstrate key moments when his theoretical understanding was informed by practical insights and these are *meditation in action* and *being peace*.

3:3:1 Prosperous and flourishing Vietnam[32]

Nhat Hanh's vision for both Vietnam and Buddhism is based on the paradigm of the Vietnamese leaders in the 11th to 14th centuries (Nhat Hanh 2002b: 19) kings who were not only able to keep Vietnam secure from hostile invaders, but also promoted economic expansion and development by taking care of the internal growth of Vietnam from a Buddhist perspective.

The Ly and Tran Dynasties (1009-1400) were 'a golden era' (Nhat Hanh 1967: 15) in which the prosperity of Vietnamese Buddhism reached its zenith (Minh Chau 1994: 2-3). It provided a peaceful epoch of stability (Lockhart & Duiker 2006: 223) after the Chinese had finally been dismissed from Vietnam and Mongol invaders, 'the most powerful military force in Asia' (Duiker 1998: 242), were kept at bay. The Ly Dynasty (1009-1225) 'developed the political and social institutions that would provide stability for the Vietnamese empire ... and place it on a firm footing for the next several hundred years' (Duiker 1998: 142). After one thousand years of Chinese rule and attempts at removing them Vietnam finally 'enjoyed a thousand years of freedom from alien rule' (SarDesai 2005: 19) developing the

---

[32] Nhat Hanh 1967: 16.

country economically and politically. The kings were devout Buddhists who promoted Buddhism as the official state religion and accepted the advice of Buddhist monks (Woods 2002: 41-42). 'Buddhist monks were part of the national administration ... [and] worked to unify the disparate local cults under the Buddhist umbrella, and aided in the unification of the country' (Keown 2003: 327). At this time Buddhist monks were an integral part of governance.

In the Tran dynasty the relationship between monks and monarchy continued and Tran emperors abdicated to become Buddhist monks, delegating reign to adult sons (Lockhart & Duiker 2006: 373; Nhat Hanh 1967: 19). The kings and emperors venerated Buddhism (Nguyen 2008: 89) and actively supported it as a worldview (Irons 2008: 546). It was the Buddhist influence in the sociopolitical dimension which had been so apparent in the Ly and Tran dynasties but had since dissipated (Nguyen 2008: 262) that particularly appealed to Nhat Hanh.

There are two people in particular from this era that Nhat Hanh esteems, the Buddhist master Van Hanh and King Tran Nhan Tong. Van Hanh (938-1025) was renowned for his 'extraordinary wisdom [as well as] his practice of nonviolent action' (Laity 1991: 32). He heavily influenced the first king of the Ly dynasty, who 'organised political and cultural life in the spirit of openness, fearlessness and non-dualism as taught by Zen Master Van Hanh' (Plum Village4). Nhat Hanh later named the University he established in Saigon in the 1960s after Van Hanh. His qualities of 'openness, fearlessness and non-dualism' are exactly the traits Nhat Hanh advocates; directly relating to Engaged Buddhism and Mindfulness they could be analogous for Nhat Hanh's key teachings. King Tran Nhan Tong of the Tran dynasty became the founder of the Truc Lam [Zen] sect (Nguyen 2008: 125) of which Nhat Hanh is of the forty-second generation (Hunt-Perry & Fine 2000: 37).

What was it about these examples that Nhat Hanh wanted to replicate? They provided a holistic view in which Buddhism was not restricted to the temple or to monastics, but was apparent in and applicable to every aspect of society[33] which is how he terms Engaged Buddhism. Indeed, he credits this 'period of peace and prosperity' (Lockhart & Duiker 2006: 223) directly to the practice of Buddhism and he saw his task as a monk to 'keep Buddhism alive and ... to engage Buddhism with everyday life like it used to be during the Ly and Tran dynasties' (Nhat Hanh 2002b: 19). He uses this paradigm to denote a time where Buddhism was integral to the growth and development of Vietnam, something that he felt was missing from 1940s Vietnam. The Ly and Tran dynasties were Nhat Hanh's primary source of inspiration, yet he also looked to more contemporary figures to guide his thinking, such as Gandhi (1869-1948) who demonstrated a nonviolent approach.

3:3:2 A nonviolent approach

The significant Buddhist principle of *Ahimsa* (harmlessness) intimates nonviolence and Nhat Hanh was devoted to finding a solution to war that would not involve more fighting because of the suffering it caused; 'we realized that the means and the end are one, and we never employed any kind of action that betrayed our commitment to nonviolence' (Nhat Hanh 1993: 43). His paradigm in this respect was Gandhi whose implementation of *Satyagraha* (holding onto truth (Monier-Williams 1990: 372 & 1135)) in India demonstrated that a nonviolent approach was possible. Nhat Hanh denotes he was initially influenced by the success of Gandhi's endeavours, but came to realise 'you cannot judge the value of an

---

[33] This was not an entirely new idea as King Asoka of India is acknowledged as one of the most renowned practitioners of Engaged Buddhism, although he himself would not have used such a title. In the third century BCE., ' in his devotion to Dharma [he] built hospitals and public wells and tree-lined roads for the "welfare of all beings"' (Macy, 1988: 173). His conception of Buddhist kingship is cited as a model 'of political virtue and concern for every member of the social order' (Swearer, 1996: 213).

action based on whether or not it brings success' (Nhat Hanh 2003d: 89). This in itself was a lesson for Nhat Hanh. One can pursue a course of action based on whether one judges it to be truthful and most accurate and not on its outcome. He imitated Gandhi's advice to hate the sin and not the sinner (Gandhi 2001: 254). Furthermore, Gandhi's influence is palpable within the SYSS and Plum Village itself, where Nhat Hanh retained the idea of a village as the most effective means of living and working as a community.

This path of nonviolence took him to America in 1966 both as an appeal to the Americans to stop the Vietnam/American War but also to bring the realities of life in Vietnam to the wider public. For this discussion, however, it is important to consider the meetings he held in America with both Martin Luther King Jr. and Thomas Merton. Although a Baptist minister and a Trappist monk, they were nonetheless sympathetic to Nhat Hanh's cause. As with Gandhi, it mattered not that these men were not Buddhists but that they spoke the same language in calling for nonviolent action as a means of achieving peace.

In the cases of King and Merton there was an immediate recognition of kindred spirits. Nhat Hanh's enthusiasm convinced King to speak out opposing the Vietnam/American War against the advice of his own colleagues (Nhat Hanh 2003d: 87). Nhat Hanh was influenced by King's understanding of nonviolence '... not through his words. His enthusiasm, his sincerity, his presence made me believe in the path of nonviolent action' (Nhat Hanh 2003d: 87). Although he and Merton only met once it was likewise fortuitous resulting in Merton's exclamation that Nhat Hanh was his brother; 'I have far more in common with Nhat Hanh than I have with many Americans' (King 2001: 19). He also wrote the Foreword for *Vietnam: Lotus in a Sea of Fire* (Nhat Hanh 1967). These meetings with people whose faith brought them to a mutual understanding of each other rather than a separation gave Nhat Hanh the opportunity to see a different side to Christianity other than the encounter with Catholics in Vietnam. It also greatly encouraged his convictions that this was the correct approach.

King was so impressed by Nhat Hanh that he nominated him for the Nobel Peace Prize in 1967 noting

his ideas for peace, if applied, would build a monument to ecumenism, to world brotherhood, to humanity ... conferring the Prize on Nhat Hanh would itself be a most generous act of peace. It would remind all nations that men of good will stand ready to lead warring elements out of an abyss of hatred and destruction. It would re-awaken men to the teaching of beauty and love found in peace. It would help to revive hopes for a new order of justice and harmony (Hartford 1996).

King's nomination denotes that Nhat Hanh is not alone in his endeavours, but he stands as an exemplar that others can follow. Unfortunately, as the nomination was made public it did not result in the Prize being awarded but, for Nhat Hanh, public recognition of his work would not have made any difference to its continuance. It could be that this nomination was too politically sensitive coming as it did in the middle of the Vietnam/American War for it to be seriously considered. There was no Peace Prize awarded that year and ironically in 1973 Henry Kissinger (American) and Le Duc Tho (North Vietnamese Communist) were jointly awarded the Prize for bringing about the Paris Peace Accords although Tho declined (Nobelprize). King's nomination demonstrated that whilst Nhat Hanh's articulation of nonviolence was relevant to Vietnam it also had wider ramifications. As Gandhi's *Satyagraha* influenced many people Nhat Hanh's example could likewise benefit others with its approach of not taking sides and standing for reconciliation rather than victory. As well as these meetings with remarkable people Nhat Hanh's elucidation of Engaged Buddhism was further informed by two moments of revelation which for him indicated the particular path he should be taking. These two aspects will now be considered.

3:3:3 Meditation in action

As a young novice monk in the 1940s Nhat Hanh experienced a moment of realisation during meditation in the temple when the way forward became obvious. *Meditation in action* (Nhat Hanh, Peace is Every Step 1997) is the term he uses to explain the combining of two disparate activities. Having heard bombs dropping whilst he was meditating he could not justify staying in the temple knowing that his own countrymen and women were being killed or injured (Nhat Hanh 2003a: 95). He was inspired by compassion to go out and help those in need having prepared himself with years of meditation practice. It was no longer a question of taking one path or the other, the meditative temple monk or a kind of social worker offering assistance, but 'how to engage without losing the contemplative life' (Kraft 1999: 80); how to assist people from '... the state of consciousness ... attained in ... meditation, that is, mindfulness' (Irons 2008: 502). *Meditation in action* is crucial to understanding his practice of Engaged Buddhism in that both aspects are equally vital.

This was a poignant moment for him acknowledging that his path was not cloistered behind monastery walls but out in the world. For him it was an obvious step as 'in our tradition, monasteries are only a kind of laboratory to spend time in, in order to discover something. They're not an end, they're a means. You get training and practice of the spiritual life so that you can go elsewhere and be with other people' (Nhat Hanh & Berrigan 2001: 125). This did not mean reverting to a lay life, but how to bring the practices he found so useful in the monastery out to also be of use to the laity. He further illustrates this with the analogy of a nursery garden growing seedlings; 'when those seedlings have grown strong enough, we have to bring them out and plant them in society ... So our training and our practice in the monastery are a preparation to go into the world' (Nhat Hanh 2010c: 7). Here he suggests it is a natural step to retain the monastic training and position whilst engaging in the world. Although his ideas met with a lot of resistance from the Buddhist hierarchy as discussed in subsection 3:2:1 he was not put off pursuing this path. He was determined to follow a path of engagement through peaceful means and for him this meant awareness in every aspect of daily life, or Mindfulness. He realised this path was not going to be fulfilled in the monastery at the current time so he resolved instead to pursue *meditation in action* as the means for achieving his aspiration towards Vietnam.

Engaged Buddhism was not a new path as discussed earlier. Vietnamese monastics in the 1930s had been inspired to form a revival movement (Hunt-Perry & Fine 2000: 36) but Nhat Hanh's particular emphasis on Mindfulness as the necessary foundation of social action was innovative, as will be further discussed in Chapter 4. An additional point that for him clarified the path of Engaged Buddhism came during his tour in America.

3:3:4 Being peace

Nhat Hanh made a valuable discovery in America in 1966, that many people campaigning for peace were doing so fired by anger. In one example, an American lambasted him for even being in America instead of Vietnam suggesting he should go home (Forest 2008: 102-103; Nhat Hanh 1995: 114). His response was, 'if you want the tree to grow, it won't help to water the leaves. You have to water the roots. Many of the roots of war are here, in your country. To help the people who are to be bombed, to try to protect them from this suffering, I have come here' (Forest 2008: 103). In the midst of being personally attacked for his actions he realised that in order to speak about peace one had to be peaceful within oneself (Nhat Hanh, Peace is Every Step 1997). Although he could no longer implement this directly in Vietnam, as it was after this tour that he was exiled and refused re-entry to Vietnam, he was able to clarify a teaching that became a focus of Plum Village. As discussed in later chapters in teaching Mindfulness he emphasises *being peace* before *doing peace*.

I suggest this is one defining moment in Nhat Hanh's formulation of Engaged Buddhism that helped to shape what he now teaches. He concluded that the movement in Vietnam had not been more effective because it was motivated by anger and therefore it could never succeed (Nhat Hanh 2007c: 12). He sees anger as a form of violence and not an appropriate starting point for seeking peace. He now emphasises using loving speech even towards an aggressor and I propose this is because he recognised 'the peace movement often is filled with anger and hatred and does not fulfill the role we expect of it. A fresh way of being peace, of making peace is needed' (Nhat Hanh 1995: 111). *Being peace* denotes that one begins by practising oneself, one cannot attempt to help others without realising that change comes from oneself first. *Being peace* echoes the emphasis he places on Mindfulness. It is the state of one's being that needs addressing before any doing takes place and is a way of creating a sustainable approach to meeting the needs of those who are suffering.

His formulation of Engaged Buddhism was inspired by these two aspects of nonviolence and Mindfulness. His path was clarified in this respect by both living and historical examples as well as practical experience. The Ly and Tran dynasties served as effective examples because they clarified for him that it was possible to imbue Engaged Buddhism in every dimension of life. He had concrete experience himself that infusing society with Buddhist concepts was valuable and useful as will be discussed in the next section. His meetings with King and Merton as well as the palpable influence of Gandhi in his thinking demonstrated that the nonviolent struggle in Vietnam might not have succeeded 'not because it was not wrong, but because it did not have all the conditions needed' (Nhat Hanh 2003d: 89). Here Nhat Hanh recognises that the conditions were not yet right in Vietnam for a peaceful solution as the two sides were intent on war, and on holding their own position. For this reason Nhat Hanh encourages not being dogmatic or being attached to views (1st MT). This did not, however, deter him from a nonviolent path as he was convinced this was the only way forward for Vietnam. People do not stop advocating nonviolence because Gandhi and King were killed, conversely it makes the call for nonviolence all the more imperative. In spite of the fact that the nonviolent approach may have had little effect in the eventual outcome to the War Nhat Hanh was convinced it was an apposite path to take not only as a Buddhist monk, but also for the many that followed his lead. The next section examines the means he had of affecting an Engaged Buddhist approach in Vietnam.

3:4 Theory into practice through engagement and Mindfulness

Previously I have discussed why Nhat Hanh did not have the support of the Buddhist hierarchy, yet here I examine the practical means by which he was able to engage Buddhism within Vietnamese society despite the objections and lack of support he received from many in the Buddhist hierarchy. He endeavoured several times to build communities where mindful living could be practised, the first one being *Phuong Boi*.

3:4:1 *Phuong Boi,* Fragrant Palm Leaves

In 1957 Nhat Hanh and the five monks with whom he had departed his root temple for Saigon built a monastery in the mountains of Dai Lao Forest northeast of Saigon. The aim at *Phuong Boi* was to create a retreat monastery away from the trouble-torn cities, towns and villages. Not a place to run away to, but 'a place for us to heal our wounds and look deeply at what happened to us and to our situation ... sheltered from the harshness of worldly affairs' (Nhat Hanh 1999b: 3 & 19). It was a place to recover from illness as far as he was concerned and also a place to heal and become whole again after the resistance to his ideas experienced in Saigon which will be discussed in section 3:5.

Phuong Boi was the first prototype of a monastery practising Engaged Buddhism. As it was an experiment there were no rules or disciplines because they were exploring how an engaged monastery should be. As with *Tiep Hien*, which came later, *Phuong Boi* accepted laity as well as monastics 'because the people who came

there had the same kind of need' although it was still based in monastic tradition (Nhat Hanh & Berrigan 2001: 126). Nhat Hanh had discovered it was more important to work with friends who shared a common aim than insist on monastics only. As the 1st MT indicates, his elucidation of the *Buddha*'s teachings is,
> not to be idolatrous about or bound to any doctrine, theory or ideology, even Buddhist ones. Buddhist teachings are guiding means to help us learn to look deeply and to develop our understanding and compassion. They are not doctrines to fight, kill or die for (Nhat Hanh 2007b: 103).

I propose *Phuong Boi* was the means of finding out what this teaching meant in practice. It was an important phase in his life, even though it did not last beyond a few years, because it was his first experience of a fourfold community working together with a shared mutuality and desire without any stipulations to be ordained. It was the original mindful community that he instigated and the forerunner of Plum Village (see Chapter 5). It gave Nhat Hanh a chance to practise the ideas he had of bringing Mindfulness into every aspect of daily life. This kind of community is the one he has continued with since, rather than insisting on a purely monastic setting. *Phuong Boi* was short-lived because 'it seemed that the authorities had been watching us for some time, perhaps to retaliate for the articles and books I'd written opposing their policies' (Nhat Hanh 1999b: 56) and it was closed down. With the end of *Phuong Boi* he returned to Saigon. Although this manifestation came to an end his vision for a mindful community was kept very much alive waiting for the moment when it could manifest again.

Through the monastery at *Phuong Boi* Nhat Hanh was able to not only articulate but also bring to realisation his concept of Engaged Buddhism despite being criticised by the Buddhist hierarchy and investigated and hampered by the Vietnamese governments. This is important because his rejection of the monastery was due to his critique of it not engaging with society and, in the examples discussed here, he demonstrated exactly how his ideas could assist the Vietnamese peasants. The most successful experiment was the

SYSS, due to the support he had at grassroots level from young and energetic students who were enthused by a vision of renewing and revitalising Vietnam.

3:4:2 The School of Youth for Social Services (SYSS)

One of the 'primary vehicles of Engaged Buddhism during the war in Vietnam' (King 1996: 323) was the SYSS. In initiating it, Nhat Hanh was able to realise Engaged Buddhism as he had conceived it as a novice monk based upon a three-point proposal, calling for
> *a cessation of hostilities in Vietnam, ...*
> *an Institute for the Study and Practice of Buddhism to train the country's leaders to practice the tolerant, open-minded spirit taught by the Buddha and surely needed for the nation [and] ...*
> *a center for training social workers to help bring about nonviolent social change based on the Buddha's teachings*
> (Chan Khong 2007: 48-49 italics in original).

The second point brought about the Van Hanh University (originally the Institute of Higher Buddhist Studies). The third point eventually instigated the SYSS although ironically it was initially rejected by the UBC as unrealistic, yet it became the most successful achievement to emerge from the UBC. The University was 'the first Buddhist university [in Vietnam] organised along Western lines' (Nhat Hanh 1967: 57) where Nhat Hanh and others taught programmes that led to 'bachelor's, master's, and Ph.D. degrees in Buddhist Studies' (Chan Khong 2007: 50). The idea was to move beyond merely an academic institution to one that gave practical experience as well as theoretical knowledge, a social type of programme he had been endeavouring to initiate for over twenty years since he first became a monastic. Despite the lack of encouragement he received from his elders in the Buddhist hierarchy he never gave up on his concept of a university offering practical as well as theoretical teachings that would be entirely relevant to Vietnam at war. Such was his conviction on this being the way forward that he 'almost single-handedly set up the University raising money from friends and acquaintances' (Minh Pham 2001: 228).

The SYSS was developed to produce and train young people equipped with practical knowledge to go out to the war-torn villages in Vietnam now further overwhelmed by flooding (Hope & Young 1977:203). Kibbutzim in Israel and communities in India and the Philippines were studied as examples of communal living that could be copied in Vietnam (Nhat Hanh 2003a: 95-96) to express the concept of interbeing.

> The SYSS represented the culmination of Thich Nhat Hanh's belief in the importance of socially engaged Buddhism ... Despite the war going on all around them, graduates of the SYSS opened schools, built hospitals, fed the hungry, housed the homeless, cared for refugees, arranged for local truces during natural disasters, worked for peace and tried to end the suffering of the innocent victims of the war (Topmiller 2002: 137-138).

The young people assisted communities by living with them in order to help rebuild their lives and homes, working together to identify the needs of each village and helping create schools and health services. Nhat Hanh wanted to do away with the notion of charity as something one person offers to another who is in need, but instead 'would cultivate the understanding that they and the poor peasants were partners in a common task' (Chan Khong 2007: 49). The students worked voluntarily on the understanding that their remuneration was merit, something normally associated with attending the Temple, but here the *bodhisattvas* came out of the Temple to care for those that no-one else cared for (Nhat Hanh 2003a: 100). The SYSS and the Van Hanh University were both ramshackle affairs to begin with, instigated with no money other than donations and no buildings (Nhat Hanh 1999b: 156), but lots of goodwill and a desire to be part of a great vision. When the training for the SYSS was first advertised 1,000 people applied for 300 places (Chan Khong 2007: 70).

Whilst his nonviolent approach to an early settlement of the Vietnam/American War had no obvious impact, the SYSS was demonstrably successful in helping to rebuild physical and spiritual lives for thousands of villagers who were the unseen victims of war. For Nhat Hanh, it was not enough to practise Buddhism in the meditation hall. He felt this was cut off from the realities of life especially when those realities were full of suffering for the Vietnamese peasants. He teaches 'we must be aware of the real problems of the world. Then, with mindfulness, we will know what to do and what not to do to be of help' (1995: 91). He had no doubt that his path lay in the Vietnamese countryside literally rebuilding broken lives rather than in a monastery. As far as he was concerned the vital aspect in ensuring the continuance of the SYSS was Mindfulness, the spiritual support that nurtured the social action, and for this reason he established *Tiep Hien* in 1966.

3:4:3 *Tiep Hien*, the Order of Interbeing

Tiep Hien began as a 'spiritual resistance movement, based completely on the teaching of the Buddha' (Plum Village1). As a continuation of all the practicalities of the SYSS it began in 1966 as a means of observing peace in the midst of war by requiring practitioners to observe sixty Days of Mindfulness (DoM)[34] a year. For those surviving the horrors of war having days set aside in which to retreat from the usual activities of life and to have no other requirements than to be mindful was a necessity. The prerequisite for sixty DoMs indicates the importance Nhat Hanh placed upon balancing the efforts of social action with an inner nurturing, again emphasising that Engaged Buddhism and Mindfulness interrelate in his teachings and that in caring for others spiritual nourishment is needed.

He decided *Tiep Hien* should be open to monastics and laity working together on an equal basis. The first six members could choose

---

[34] See Chan Khong 2007: 79-80 for details of how the DoMs were practised.

whether to live as 'formal monastics or as laypersons' (Chan Khong 2007: 77). He instigated *Tiep Hien* without the support of the UBC because 'the image of an ordained monk who was also a married man was just too much for the conservative Sangha at that time' (Minh Pham 2001: 227). It was innovative because 'the concept of an order that included both monks and laypeople, who would work for peace and social reconstruction on an equal footing, was bold' (Brazier 2001: 72). Brazier, however, later questions whether this egalitarianism has continued at Plum Village and the other monasteries.

When it first began in Saigon, *Tiep Hien* was a crucial means for people to avoid getting caught up in the horrors of war and 'an important instrument for responding to difficulties and anguish of the world' (Hunt-Perry & Fine 2000: 40). It inaugurated with only six members, the leaders of the SYSS, and a decision was taken that no new members would be invited to join until *Tiep Hien* had practised deeply for fifteen years (Eppsteiner 2000: vii-viii). It was apparent that a new Order for young people was necessary (Nhat Hanh & Berrigan 2001: 126) yet due to the War in Vietnam and exile of Nhat Hanh it was not until 1981 that the seventh member finally joined and the period of experimentation was over (Nhat Hanh 2000a: viii). The original intention to support those practising within the SYSS in Vietnam could not be fulfilled yet the Order continues to grow and thrive.

Tiep Hien has since grown into a worldwide organisation, the Order of Interbeing,[35] with approximately 2,000 members currently. It is a bridge between the monastics and society in general. *Tiep Hien* was Nhat Hanh's final act of nonviolent protest of the Vietnam/American War before his exile in 1966 and was his ultimate demonstration that there was another way besides the aggressive ideologies of America and the Communists. *Tiep Hien* was the culmination of his implementation of Engaged Buddhism which demonstrated the

---

[35] See footnote 7 for more details of the Order.

necessity for a supportive and harmonious community of people practising together.

The SYSS in particular was a manifestation of Engaged Buddhism that incorporated both aspects Nhat Hanh denoted, which is social action from a basis of mindful contemplation. Whilst it may seem that social action was the most important part it was effective because of its foundation of Mindfulness. Otherwise, practitioners would have eventually succumbed to burnout, disillusion and despair. Even though the government discontinued each endeavour they remain as viable and concrete examples of Engaged Buddhism in practice, and have led to Nhat Hanh's recognition worldwide as an Engaged Buddhist leader (see Chapter 4).

3:5 Reflections on Thich Nhat Hanh's Engaged Buddhist methodology

In some respects Nhat Hanh was fortunate in being able to instigate these mindful communities because his forthright declarations opposing the Vietnam/American War brought him to the attention of the Buddhist hierarchy as well as government authorities on both sides throughout his life. As discussed in subsection 3:2:1 he was unable to equate the Buddhism he found as a novice with the one he read about in the 11th to 14th centuries.

For this reason once he was ordained as a monk he and five friends left the root temple and lived in Saigon (Nhat Hanh 2003a: 9). Here, they were able to pursue the academic studies incorporating Western philosophy and literature as well as the Buddhist studies (Rothberg & Senauke 2008: 24) he had requested in the monastery which had been rejected. Although academia was important to Nhat Hanh it was more important for him to learn how to effectively combine Mindfulness and social action as a Buddhist monk, therefore academic pursuit was only a means to this end. It was underpinned by the belief that the Vietnamese people needed to 'acquire an understanding of every kind of culture if they were to survive the threat of westernization' (Hope & Young 1977: 194). Indeed, he did not see Westernisation as a threat as there were aspects such as democracy which could benefit Vietnam. His motivation behind the academic studies in Saigon was engaging with 'Western philosophy and science, because we were convinced that these subjects could help us infuse life into the practice of Buddhism in our country' (Nhat Hanh 2008b: 22). For this reason he not only studied himself, but also helped to found the An Quang Buddhist Institute to teach novices in 1949 (Nhat Hanh 2008c: 5), ensuring that the younger generation had access to a broad and modern education. In this way he began to nurture students who would later help to implement the SYSS.

From his academic studies Nhat Hanh produced a series of articles offering 'insight as to the spiritual direction we should take in order to deal with the great confusion in the country' which, he suggests, was mainly due to the aftermath of the French-Indochina War (Nhat Hanh 2008c: 5)[36] and he recommended that Buddhism, which was latent in many Vietnamese, could provide an answer. This writing provided much-needed funds for the six monks to live on (Nhat Hanh 2008b: 21-22), but it also gave him a medium for articulating his concept of Engaged Buddhism to a wider audience.

It was, however, this writing that alerted the governments to the stance he was taking. He wrote about Engaged Buddhism to demonstrate how it could help Vietnam, but his writings did not initially receive approval from the Buddhist hierarchy, especially when he suggested unifying the various Buddhist groups (Nhat Hanh 1999b: 6-7). Furthermore his articles drew the unwanted attention of the governments due to the forthright way he declared ideas that were not in line with governmental official approach. He had to use several pseudonyms in order to continue publishing (Nhat Hanh 2008c: 5-6). It was more important to him that his ideas were being broadcast than that they were recognised as his. Recently Robert

---

[36] Partition in the country necessitated the relocation of approximately one million people.

Buswell cites Nguyen Lang as a reference for his Encyclopedia without apparently realising this is one of Nhat Hanh's pen-names (2004: 883).

As he and his friends strove to organise themselves into a co-ordinated movement to speak out against the War they were infiltrated by police agents posing as monastics 'damaging our prestige and sowing seeds of fear. They excited extremists and fanatics to overturn and destroy the leadership and members of the movement' (Nhat Hanh 1993: 46). Minh Pham suggests both sides chose to vilify Nhat Hanh personally as a means of undermining his efforts and those of the UBC towards peace as the Communists recognised the Buddhists could 'win over the hearts and minds of millions of ordinary Vietnamese, the real victims of war', whereas the southern government opposed the Buddhists' call for a democratically elected government (2001: 252-253). As discussed in subsection 3:2:2 the Buddhists were capable of rallying thousands of people onto the streets. Both governments were afraid the Buddhists 'were trying to seize power, but we had no interest in power. We only wanted to stop the slaughter' (Nhat Hanh 1993: 43). It was at this point Nhat Hanh and his friends retreated to *Phuong Boi*. A necessary step because his writing was provocative and caused much attention from the governments who were unwilling to listen to a neutralist stance.

In a similar manner, he deemed it appropriate to remove himself from Vietnam in 1962 at a time when government officers were questioning his writings and trying to impose controls. He followed his aspiration for academic study in America where he broadened his perspectives with Comparative Religion re-instigating the academic pursuits begun in Saigon. This initial foray into America led to the tour in 1966 that thrust Nhat Hanh and his teachings into the limelight at a pertinent moment when he was becoming an embarrassment to the Vietnamese government. Whilst these journeys had legitimate reasons behind them the situation with the Vietnamese government had become untenable, so rather than risk arrest he took the opportunity to travel to America and Europe in order to present the Vietnamese case to those who had a one-sided view of the War. It was not the path he had foreseen taking, but seemed to be most apposite at the time. He thought his trip to America would be a few months at most and not result in permanent exile.

These are several instances where Nhat Hanh appears to retreat in response to close examination by the government of his activities and particularly his writing, initially to *Phuong Boi*, two trips to America and when he initially settled in France in exile. Whilst there are justifiable motives for taking these steps it could also be seen that he was running away from potential threats to his life. Clearly his life was in danger and the attempts to get rid of him would only have increased had he stayed in Vietnam. He could have been easily silenced had he remained in Vietnam as 'anyone viewed as a threat to national security could be arrested without trial' (Minh Pham 2001: 249). So he followed the advice of his elders and went to America. Although it could appear he was running away from a difficult situation he had more than himself to consider as the UBC and the SYSS were also under suspicion through his connections. Indeed, five members of the SYSS were deliberately killed in one incident because 'such a school, in such a time, became a mortal threat to some of those for whom weapons were the indispensable means of survival or liberation' (Berrigan 1993: 5). He undoubtedly avoided death by leaving Vietnam and going to America, but it was not an easy situation or a particularly safe place for him to be as he met with criticism and hostility there as well. The risk in going to America was comparable to staying in Vietnam. Not until he settled in France and the Vietnam/American War finally ended did the risk to his life abate, yet here he was in exile cut off from family and the majority of his friends. I propose his response of retreat, by which I mean withdrawal in order to consider his next step rather than flight from danger, indicates his teaching which is reflected in the 6th MT that one consider carefully before speaking or acting. Indeed, it is apparent that Nhat Hanh's exile has been of great benefit to the West and one questions whether he would be as well known in the West as he is if he had remained in Vietnam.

A further question for consideration is did his nonviolent approach help Vietnam? There is no evidence to suggest that his approach made any difference to Vietnam in the short term. It did not help resolve the War any sooner nor did it apparently have any effect on the outcome. As a political movement the UBC failed as 'the war continued for another nine years after the defeat of the Struggle Movement'; Vietnam at this time was not a land for pacifists (Topmiller 2002: 151). Yet Nhat Hanh denotes this is a long-term problem, and also a worldwide problem, not restricted to Vietnam; 'I think we may fail in our attempt to do things, yet we may succeed in the correct action when the action is authentically nonviolent, based on understanding, based on love' (Nhat Hanh 2003d: 89). One cannot measure the effects of a nonviolent stand in terms of the success or failure of one war, indeed, for Nhat Hanh, success is an end to war not a victory for either side. In this respect, the UBC and the Struggle Movement demonstrated 'great examples of courage, altruism, and activist spirituality' (King 1996: 355). 'Even if what you said or did failed to stop the war, what is important is that you tried, using your insight and compassion' (Nhat Hanh 2007c: 10). It is one's intentions behind an action that determine their apparent success or failure and, as discussed earlier, if conditions are lacking as it appears they were in Vietnam for a nonviolent resolution to the War one can only continue in the hope that conditions will change.

Nearly forty years after the end of the Vietnam/American War Nhat Hanh believes conditions are changing in Vietnam, yet still the work is not complete; 'we need several decades more in order to completely renew the teaching and the practice of Buddhism, to offer them to the younger generation'; he hopes the members of the Order and CoI will take this on in his stead (Q&A 2010). This demonstrates the great patience needed in implementing a quality such as nonviolence. One cannot assume changes will take place quickly because as he discovered one meets with ferocious opposition when people's dearly held beliefs are challenged.

Nhat Hanh offers a different path that is not guided by belief in the binary opposites of right and wrong, good and evil. He asks people to look beyond beliefs that may change to a path that is not guided by convictions that *I am right therefore my opponent is wrong*. From an interbeing perspective there is no opponent, no-one to stand against. Whilst it may be easy to surmise that his actions failed because Vietnam did not listen to his suggestions his own reflections demonstrate a wider view; 'in our struggle for Vietnam, we did our best to remain true to our principles. We never lost sight that the essence of our struggle was love itself, and that was a real contribution to humanity' (Nhat Hanh 1993: 47).

3:6 Conclusion

In this chapter I have discussed the main themes relating to Nhat Hanh's formulation of Engaged Buddhism which are, the context of Vietnam in the midst of occupation and war, the inspirations and influences that led to his elucidation of Engaged Buddhism and the practical means by which he instigated it. I have demonstrated that for him Mindfulness is the foundational principle from which the social action of Engaged Buddhism takes place.

Hostile foreign control and war were the fuels that ignited his articulation of Engaged Buddhism as a peaceful means of benefiting Vietnam. Also, his introduction to Mindfulness at sixteen unlocked a wakefulness that was already inherent within him and I suggest it was for this reason that he had such clarity with regard to a peaceful solution for Vietnam. Whilst it is natural for young people to criticise or want a fresh approach from the older generation, I propose he responded in the way he did because he was able to clearly visualise an answer to the problems of both Buddhism and Vietnam. Guided by his Buddhist teachings and the inspirations from the Ly and Tran dynasties he was convinced a nonviolent approach was the only solution, yet this was a new suggestion in the midst of war and not one that was accepted by the warring parties.

For Nhat Hanh, 1940s Vietnam and Buddhism were inextricably linked; Buddhism could assist in the crisis of poverty and suffering in Vietnam, but not in the way it was practised, it had to be a social practice such as had been demonstrated previously. He highlighted the shortcomings of Buddhism at that time, as he saw it, not in order to criticise but to offer a different approach. When his elders did not take this up he resolved to implement it himself and removed to Saigon where it could be put into action. He took a concept that had been developed previously and made it his own by the practical application of the ideas that were relevant to Vietnamese society. He combined the essential inspirations from previous eras in Vietnam along with current practices of nonviolence demonstrated by Gandhi, King and Merton and melded them with his own understanding that a peaceful and mindful basis from which to begin any action was imperative. He thus integrated previous practices but adapted them to suit the particular situation in Vietnam. Having realised 'that my path was the path of nonviolence' (Nhat Hanh 2004a: 113) his stance was unequivocal in this respect. He was able to offer people hope and practical solutions to better the experience of their daily lives.

The practical methods by which Nhat Hanh instigated Engaged Buddhism were each a contextual response to the immediate situation of suffering in Vietnam. When the An Quang Buddhist Institute in Saigon came under scrutiny from the authorities he and his friends retired to *Phuong Boi*. As this was closed down he took the opportunity to study in America in order to let things calm down at home. On his return to Vietnam, however, he immediately developed the SYSS which in many respects was the culmination of his conception of Engaged Buddhism, demonstrating the need for mindful contemplation as the foundation of any social action. This was further developed through *Tiep Hien* which has since become a worldwide organisation. Whilst the development of these schemes undoubtedly contributed to his exile Nhat Hanh does not deem them to be a failure as they were the seeds of other engaged practices which will be discussed in following chapters. The practical application of Engaged Buddhism was imperative for him and in subsection 3:4 I have demonstrated how he turned the theory into praxis by instigating the social institutions that were vehicles for Engaged Buddhism. It was through the Van Hanh University rather than the monastery that he was able to instigate his concept of Engaged Buddhism. Furthermore, it was through academic pursuits in America that he was able to create a network of contacts who shared his outlook and were able to encourage his implementation of Engaged Buddhism. The two most influential men he met were not Buddhist but Christian, giving him the opportunity to discard any misgivings he may have had about Christianity after its evangelical representation in Vietnam.

The aspect of Mindfulness that he learned as a novice served him well in assisting his formulations of Engaged Buddhism and it is probable that he would not have come to these conclusions alone. The active quality of incorporating Mindfulness into all aspects of daily life, as opposed to the rigid and antiquated ideas he also met in the Buddhist Institute, has become his pedagogy; developed and clarified in his formative years at the monastery and in the years that followed before his exile.

Despite Vietnam's combative history he was able to articulate and propose a peaceful, nonviolent path that could bring an acceptable end to the Vietnam/American War for all parties. As both sides were bound to combative ideologies they were unable to hear his suggestions as anything other than a threat to their way of being. Although neither side took them up Nhat Hanh did not waver in his recommendations and did everything in his power to help people understand his proposals. It is important to acknowledge that he was able to pursue his vision of making Buddhism engaged and relevant to the people of Vietnam despite the politics of the era. He may have been restricted in his activities and movements, watched at every stage and his motives questioned, but there is no doubt he was effective in getting his message across to many people who were willing to follow his lead. The imposition of the government 'sowing seeds of fear' (Nhat Hanh 1993: 46) and being condemned by the Communists for being the landowner of *Phuong Boi* (Nhat Hanh 1999b: 9) may have provided the tension that encouraged him to pursue his aspirations.

Nhat Hanh has the ability and charisma to make people want to follow him and to do what he is doing not through rhetoric or manipulation, but by being a living example, by demonstrating through his actions what he is teaching through words. Although he took on this mantle of leadership within Vietnam it was finally in France at Plum Village that the vision became a reality. In the next chapter I examine the key teaching of Engaged Buddhism that Nhat Hanh took forward as the main aspect of everything that had developed in Vietnam.

4. 'Entering into Life'[37]: The Development of Engaged Buddhism

We need a Buddhism that will help us when we need it. When we teach the Four Noble Truths, the Noble Eightfold Path ... all these teachings have to be applied in our daily life. They should not be theory. We can teach the Lotus Sutra very well, but we have to ask ourselves: how can we apply the Lotus Sutra to resolve our difficulties, our despair, our suffering? This is what we mean by applied Buddhism. If you are a Dharma teacher, as a monk or nun or a lay person, your life has to be an example of the teachings. You only teach what you yourself practice (Nhat Hanh 2010c: 8-9).

Introduction

This teaching above indicates Thich Nhat Hanh's emphasis on the practical aspect of Buddhism as opposed to the theoretical philosophising that he came into contact with as a novice. He was interested in Buddhism as it can be applied to daily life in order to transform suffering into happiness. Later in the chapter I discuss his new use of the term Applied Buddhism. Nhat Hanh is widely acknowledged as the instigator of the term Engaged Buddhism and is called 'the father of Engaged Buddhism' (Toms 1998: 29; Tricycle 1995: 37) originating from articles written during the Vietnam/American War in 1954 (Nhat Hanh, 2008c: 5). He does not claim to be the instigator of Engaged Buddhism, however, he insists

---

[37] Nhat Hanh 2008d: 5.

'Buddhism is already engaged. If it is not, it is not Buddhism' (Hunt-Perry & Fine 2000: 36). He further insists it is not a new movement, as identified in the previous chapter and these points form significant facets of the following discussion.

The key arguments for this chapter are that Nhat Hanh's definition of Engaged Buddhism centres on *being peace in order to do peace* and that social action rather than social activism is the basis of his teaching. I will examine how these statements compare with scholars' viewpoints as well as the interviews undertaken. Further discussions in the definition focus on Jones' continuum of Engaged Buddhism and where Nhat Hanh can be placed upon this spectrum, as well as questioning whether Engaged Buddhism is a new *yana* (movement). In examining Engaged Buddhism from the interviewees' data I will draw out the key aspects that form this discussion before considering some critiques of CoI practice.

I wish to highlight a difference between social activism and social action because whilst Nhat Hanh took part in social activism in Vietnam I argue his teachings focus on social action. Social activism 'refers to action for social and environmental change, particularly radical, long-term social changes ... [and] must inevitably be involved in questions of power and conflict, confrontation and partisanship' (Jones 2003: 175-176) whereas social action concerns one's relationships within human society and I propose it is this aspect that Nhat Hanh emphasises rather than 'radical confrontation'. He seeks to actively promote reconciliation over conflict and harmony as opposed to confrontation. This is the stance he has taken by accentuating *being peace* before *doing peace* and not approaching social questions from an angry point of view. As discussed in Chapter 3, many of the peace campaigners Nhat Hanh met in America were fired by anger and this prompted him to take a different path with the emphasis on peace, both internally and externally. Whilst not all social activists are driven by anger his personal experience was that many were, and although anger can be a motivational force it also causes a lot of suffering for both parties as one of the mental formations '... described by the Buddha as poisons' (Nhat Hanh 2001: 2). Rather than basing one's actions on the shifting sands of anger in which a lot of emotion can be involved one uses an approach based on mindful practices in which understanding and compassion can be present (Nhat Hanh 2001: 3). Therefore, Nhat Hanh's emphasis as he began teaching in the West was to use Mindfulness (i.e. being peace) as the solid foundation from which to act (i.e. doing peace).

In the previous chapter I addressed Nhat Hanh's situation in Vietnam and examined the specific examples of how he implemented Engaged Buddhism into society. The purpose here is to investigate both Nhat Hanh's interpretation of Engaged Buddhism counterbalanced with other views. I will compare his interpretation with that of other scholars as well as his students. I also intend to determine whether there is one definition of Engaged Buddhism. Truong (2006) terms Engaged Buddhism a new *yana*; literally meaning vehicle in Sanskrit, it describes the paths taught by the *Buddha* (Keown 2003: 339) and I will examine whether this denotes a new direction for Buddhism.

4:1 Thich Nhat Hanh's definition of Engaged Buddhism

As addressed in the previous chapter, for Nhat Hanh, Engaged Buddhism was a response to the spiritual direction the Vietnamese people needed as an antidote to their confusion (Nhat Hanh 2008c: 5) brought about by a war which, on the whole, they did not wish to partake in. 'Buddhism is a very ancient tradition in Vietnam, and most of the people have a Buddhist seed in them' (Nhat Hanh 2008c: 5) yet the attempts to side-line Buddhism and promote Catholicism (see Chapter 3) stirred up confusion in the minds of the Vietnamese populace as Nhat Hanh saw it. In order to revitalise both Vietnam and Buddhism he proposed Mindfulness would present a practical solution for the laity to whom it was a new concept. They needed to find the means to not only survive but live through the war without being consumed by hopelessness. 'We wanted Buddhism to be present in every walk of life – not just in the temple, but also in society, in our schools, our families, our workplaces, even in politics and the military' (Nhat Hanh 2009a: 95) and the means of applying this was the practice of Mindfulness. Mindfulness should not be merely appropriated for the temple, but could be available to laypeople as well. Although I discuss Mindfulness and Engaged Buddhism as two separate factors Nhat Hanh equates the two as one practice.

What is Engaged Buddhism? Nhat Hanh's seemingly simplistic response is 'it is applying Buddhism in every aspect of your daily life, cleaning your teeth, looking after your child etc. Buddhism is there' (Nhat Hanh, Q&A 2009). What is meant by Buddhism here? I suggest an understanding of the *Buddha*'s teachings on suffering and its cessation, the intimate connection of body and mind, combined with interbeing, impermanence and Mindfulness. All these aspects together incorporate Nhat Hanh's formulation of Buddhism which has Mindfulness at its heart. By being mindful in any and every activity throughout the day one is aware of what is and is not needed in each situation. As will be further discussed in Chapter 5, one practises Mindfulness in everyday situations as an on-going process so that when it is needed in a particular crisis it is available (Nhat Hanh 2007c: 13). Nonetheless, Engaged Buddhism is not only Mindfulness; it is the balance of the inner practice of Mindfulness with the outer practice of social action that will be examined here.

As highlighted above and discussed in the next section, social activism has been considered to be the driving force behind Engaged Buddhism. This was often in specific areas such as free medical care and the training of nurses in Taiwan as undertaken by Venerable Shih Cheng-Yen ((King 2005: 2), empowering villages and communities to contribute to the betterment of the social situation in Sri Lanka as implemented by Dr. A T. Ariyaratne (Tricycle 2008) and re-establishing Buddhism after it had virtually been wiped by the Khmer Rouge in Cambodia (Weiner 2003: 115), which Maha Ghosananda assumed. These examples are merely a sample of the type of work Engaged Buddhism can address. Yet for Nhat Hanh the more relevant aspect was slightly at a variance with the others, which is awareness in daily life.

This holistic approach, with Nhat Hanh's placement of Mindfulness (awareness in daily life) as the primary characteristic of Engaged Buddhism, indicates his emphasis of *being peace* before *doing peace*. Nhat Hanh clarifies that Mindfulness, or meditation, does not only take place *on the cushion* i.e. during periods of sitting meditation. Whilst these periods are necessary to support any action it is the incorporation of Mindfulness in every aspect of daily life whether it appears to be directly relevant to social activism or not which will ultimately be the firm foundation for any activity one wishes to engage in.

The praxis begins with the so-called individual and then permeates out into wider society,
> how can we practice at the airport and in the market? That is engaged Buddhism. Engaged Buddhism does not only mean to use Buddhism to solve social and political problems, protesting against the bombs, and protesting against social injustice. First of all we have to bring Buddhism into our daily lives (Nhat Hanh 2007a: 53-54).

Nhat Hanh argues Engaged Buddhism is more than social activism, going out and saving the world, indeed it need have no connection to social activism because one practises Mindfulness on a daily basis in order to know how to respond in any situation or crisis. He teaches 'once there is seeing, there must be acting. We must be aware of the real problems of the world. Then, with mindfulness, we will know what to do, and what not to do, to be of help' (Nhat Hanh 1995: 91) denoting that the practice of Mindfulness comes before any action but is fed by the recognition of suffering in the world and that action is required as a response. I propose this quotation demonstrates Nhat Hanh's definition of Engaged Buddhism which depends on how one interacts with one's children, partner, family and work colleagues but begins with the details of whether one cleans one's teeth mindfully. This concentration on the minutiae in one's daily life is where Nhat

Hanh differs from other Engaged Buddhists who place social activism at the forefront of their practice. This distinct portrayal of Engaged Buddhism is now compared with scholars' academic views.

4:2 Defining Engaged Buddhism

In seeking to define Engaged Buddhism I begin by briefly examining scholars' interpretations of the term, and how their emphasis diverges from Nhat Hanh's before identifying two areas that will form subsequent discussions. Queen begins his exploration of *Engaged Buddhism in the West* by distinguishing three characteristics, 1) awareness (i.e. Mindfulness), 2) '... a deep identification of the self and the world – a sense of oneness, nondualism, interdependence' and, 3) action (2000: 6). These three aspects agree with Chappell's definition,
 ... this new Buddhism is based on inward calmness, mindfulness, and compassion that is (a) aware of the interdependence of self, others, and the environment, and (b) based on the impermanence of self and others, has compassion for others, that is free from ego (1999: 78).

It is from an awareness of the relationship between oneself and others that compassion and therefore Engaged Buddhism can arise. This relationship is recognised by several scholars (Macy 1988: 172; Jones 2003: 6; King 2005: 19; Henry 2008: 4) as being one of the key areas defining Engaged Buddhism. It suggests the main emphases for some Engaged Buddhists are interdependence with the world and action, whereas for Nhat Hanh it begins with Mindfulness. Henry's discussion on Socially Engaged Buddhism in his thesis (2008: 3-7) picks up the point of the social interaction between self and other that these scholars have indicated. Whilst this aspect is also true for Nhat Hanh he nonetheless begins with the individual and the application of Mindfulness before investigating how this relates to others. Furthermore, both Queen (2000: 3) and Henry indicate the *Mahayana bodhisattva* as providing an '...ideal or the icon for the activist' (Henry 2008: 5). However, this can infer that only *Mahayana* Buddhists practise Engaged Buddhism, which is refuted by the paragraph in section 4:1 indicating some of those involved with Engaged Buddhism, and further discussed in subsection 4:2:3. Finally, Chappell above and Queen both use the term new (2000: 24) in relation to Engaged Buddhism, which will be addressed in subsection 4:2:1.

There are difficulties in achieving one definition of Engaged Buddhism (Queen 2000: 7) due to 'disagreement about the precise meaning and implications of the term engaged Buddhism' (Bell 2000: 400), and I shall address these before reviewing the continuum by which Engaged Buddhism can be assessed. 'As efforts to define Engaged Buddhism continue' (Puri 2006: 147) it is difficult to characterise due to the diverse nature of areas in which Engaged Buddhists apply themselves which can include 'social work, anti-poverty and development programs, political activism, human rights agitation etc.' (Powers 2000: 75). As is demonstrated by this list (and discussed in section 4:1) a common understanding of Engaged Buddhism is external, addressing issues of social injustice rather than an internal practice for the individual. Some scholars also consider Engaged Buddhism to be a nascent subject (Puri 2006:1; Kraft 1992: 12) about sixty years old and because it is still evolving, particularly in the West, it has yet to settle into a particular formation or pattern. The concept of Engaged Buddhism as nascent is itself debatable as indicated by Nhat Hanh's comment that it has always been engaged.

Part of the problem in assessing the meaning and application of Engaged Buddhism is that it can be described as a spectrum (Batchelor 1994: 363) or continuum which has individual ethical practices at one end, progresses to a wider awareness of conscious living aligned to Right Livelihood and culminates in social activism and nonviolent resistance (Jones 2003: 175). This spectrum encompasses many different activities which can be called Engaged Buddhism from personal engagement to social activism (Jones 2003: 175). These have been alluded to as 'soft' and 'hard' ends (Jones, as quoted by Bell 2000: 405) or 'conventional' and 'ultimate' (Kraft 2004: 158-9) both of which suggest that true engagement in social activism takes place at the hard or ultimate end of the continuum.

This continuum places Nhat Hanh's work in Vietnam at one end of the scale whereas his more recent emphasis on Mindfulness within one's family and immediate society moves to the other end of the scale. Here little is apparently being done within a social context to lighten suffering because of the emphasis on the individual. Whilst the end product from both is the same Jones in particular suggests it is only at the hard end of social activism that Engaged Buddhism takes place (2003: 175).

In considering the continuum as a framework one can debate whether Engaged Buddhism only appears at the 'hard end' which is concerned with political, social activism or can it also include Nhat Hanh's description of it as awareness in daily life? There is a question here about visibility. Does Engaged Buddhism have to take place on a public stage, or is it also engaged within the home, workplace or local community? I propose that both are necessary in that the effectiveness of both is multiplied manifold by their joint application. It could be that the invisible work taking place at the soft end of the continuum is the foundation for the visible profile of Engaged Buddhism in social activism.

A further debate surrounding Engaged Buddhism is, in what ways it is different to Buddhism. For some, and Nhat Hanh is included in this, it can be dismissed as tautology (Bell 2000: 400), which makes the statement somewhat redundant (Jones 2003:178-179). Likewise, the term can be problematic as it implies 'Buddhism is normally disengaged from society' (Harris 2001: 99). Thomas Yarnall denotes opposing sides as traditionists and modernists (2003: 286-303) in this argument. Traditionists, such as Nhat Hanh, hold that a spiritual life and social engagement are co-existent whereas modernists propose the social side has been latent in Buddhism until its recent encounter with the West (Yarnall 2003: 286-287). A viewpoint of Yarnall's 'modernists' is that 'socially engaged Buddhism is the product of the interpenetration of Euro-American and Asian cultures and has arisen in Asia in response to the material forces of modernity, industrialization and urbanization' (Deitrick 2003: 256). Whilst it is apparent that a new form of Engaged Buddhism arose in Asia from the 1940s, as discussed in the previous chapter, there are other examples of Engaged Buddhism preceding this era.

In trying to define Engaged Buddhism some scholars (Kraft 1988: xii; Chappell 1999: 76) term it a new *yana* or new 'turning of the wheel', also termed 'a fourth vehicle, *Navayana*, ... *Lokyana* or Global Vehicle' (Truong 2006: 285) and this aspect will be considered next.

4:2:1 A new *yana*?

A new *yana* would be a fresh interpretation of spiritual practices introduced by the *Buddha*. As with the origination of *Mahayana* Buddhism, which did not wish to supercede everything from the *Theravada* tradition, a new *yana* scaffolds on the centuries of Buddhism that have been practised previously.

The 'new' aspect of Engaged Buddhism could be the technological and organisational means by which the global community have instant and easy access to each other 'more concerned than ever before to move society towards nonviolence, justice, truthfulness, and peace' (Chappell 1999: 76) and thereby engaging with all modern means available to pursue this aim. Certainly from the latter part of the twentieth century, technology has enabled Buddhists to engage with one another worldwide on an unprecedented scale. Technology has been embraced rather than rejected at Plum Village and the *Dharma* talks Nhat Hanh offers are recorded and streamed live onto the Internet. There have been apps developed offering bells of Mindfulness for computers and phones and the Plum Village website has a Mindfulness software page (Plum Village7), encouraging students to engage mindfully with technology and be aware of its addictive qualities.

Responding to the needs of a changing society may be another way of viewing the apparent sudden growth of Engaged Buddhism throughout the world, which would include a response towards technological advances. This is a viewpoint Nhat Hanh promotes;

'Buddhism, in order to be Buddhism, must be suitable, appropriate to the psychology and the culture of the society that it serves' (2007a: 84) which also means changing and adapting to the current needs of society as it evolves. As discussed in Chapter 3, this is something Nhat Hanh tried to address in Vietnam with the introduction of Engaged Buddhism as he identified the conditions in Vietnam during the War produced more suffering rather than alleviating it. Whilst the question of suffering was not a new one to consider it indicates Nhat Hanh's belief that Buddhism should be responding to addressing their suffering. In the same way he suggests the 5MTs should be regularly updated, about once every twenty years, to ensure they focus on the present needs of society (as discussed in Chapter 6).

Furthermore, the debate on whether Engaged Buddhism is nascent or not falls into two categories depending on whether one holds the view that the recent surge was influenced by the meeting of Asian and Euro-American cultures or a reinterpretation of the *Buddha's* teachings. At the commencement of his teaching the *Buddha* indicated the need to serve humanity by going 'forward for the benefit of many people, for the happiness of many people, out of compassion for the world, for the good, welfare, and happiness of gods and men' (Kloppenborg 1973: 43)[38]. This is perhaps why Nhat Hanh insists Buddhism has always been engaged as it draws upon the *Buddha's* teachings, which from the beginning were concerned with teaching and demonstrating how to live a happy and compassionate life, and has moved with the times, reinterpreting itself in accordance with historical situations (Bond 1996: 121).

Conversely, Queen argues that Engaged Buddhism is '... unprecedented, and thus tantamount to a new chapter in the history of the tradition' (2000:1). Queen particularly identifies three aspects that have '... emerged in the context of a global conversation on human rights, distributive justice, and social progress' (2000: 1). This statement seems to ignore the aspects of Engaged Buddhism that informed Nhat Hanh's work in Vietnam and others, including

---

[38] Catusparisatsutra.

King Asoka (see footnote 33). Whilst it is apparent that engagement is an aspect of the *Buddha's* teachings this particular aspect was brought to the forefront of Buddhism from the 1940s onwards with more emphasis than had been demonstrated recently. Why did it take until the 1940s to emerge in the way that it did? As has been discussed in the previous chapter Engaged Buddhism has been practiced at various points throughout its history but was often overtaken by more dogmatic practices. Yet it would appear that the meeting of Euro-American and Asian cultures along with the '... forces of modernity, industrialization and urbanization' (Deitrick 2003: 256) was the catalyst to bring forth a more Engaged approach to Buddhism as has been discussed above.

I suggest the prefix *new* is misleading as it denotes a rejection of what has gone before which is inaccurate. Buddhism is flexible and ready to recreate itself into different forms in the transplantation process, as will be discussed in Chapter 7. This adaptation requires deep looking and a lack of dogmatism. Nhat Hanh seeks to make Buddhism appropriate to current daily life and by updating or reviewing the practices regularly in order to ensure this is still the case (*Dharma* Talk 2009).

As demonstrated in the previous chapter Engaged Buddhism is a reinterpretation of the *Buddha*'s teachings utilising aspects that were already present in Buddhism in a fresh and innovative way, particularly the practical application of the *Buddha's* teaching as opposed to theoretical study. Joanna Macy interprets this as a 'fresh reappropriation of the *Buddha's* central teachings [which is] ... our essential nonseparateness' (2009a). In this respect Nhat Hanh is accurate in deeming Engaged Buddhism is not new as it is re-examining existing teachings and re-presenting them in a way more apposite to the current time. It is apparent, however, that this 'fresh reappropriation', also termed the Third Turning of the Wheel (Macy 2009b), requires one to look deeply at what the *Buddha's* teachings are saying rather than blindly accepting what has gone before. In this respect I submit it is correct to propose Engaged Buddhism is an upsurge of particular global forces in terms of 'the meeting of Euro-

American and Asian cultures' that came together from the 1940s onwards allowing a revolution, or 'fresh reappropriation', to occur. By this I mean a transformational change rather than a rebellious rejection of all that had preceded. It was transformational in terms of individuals working in their particular situations (as proposed in section 4:1) who on reflection were all demonstrating Nhat Hanh's definition of *being peace in order to do peace*. I suggest only time will tell if this is a new *yana* or not, yet given the changes that have occurred in Nhat Hanh's lifetime through his teaching in bringing thousands of Westerners to a new understanding of Buddhism (as will be discussed in later chapters) I propose it is.

Some critics of Nhat Hanh's work suggest that his form of Engaged Buddhism does 'not give enough emphasis to traditional notions in Buddhist practice' (Hunt-Perry & Fine 2000: 61) reflecting the criticism he encountered from the Buddhist hierarchy in Vietnam, but one has to question what these 'traditional notions' are and whether they are keeping Buddhism alive or fossilizing it. This critique may arise from those preferring a textual-based approach who find Nhat Hanh's practical application and introducing monastic practices to laity inappropriate. Criticism, however, is not a bad thing as indicated by Cheng-Yen's example in Taiwan. She was stirred into action when criticised by Catholic groups for not being concerned in charity work (Huang 2003: 138). The new *turning of the wheel* may be an active rather than passive response to criticism as demonstrated by Cheng-Yen. Furthermore Nhat Hanh seems to have thrived on the criticism he has received, firstly in Vietnam, in America and more recently in the accusations of quietism and it has not deterred him from his approach. There may also be critics who will condemn his latest adaptation, from Engaged Buddhism to Applied Buddhism as will be discussed next.

4:2:2 Applied Buddhism

For Nhat Hanh, the new *yana* could also be Applied Buddhism, something that has arisen out of the transplantation process. He has recently begun using this term instead of Engaged and has set up two Institutes of Applied Buddhism, one in Germany (European, EIAB) and a more recent one in Hong Kong (Asian, AIAB). Although he initially said Applied Buddhism 'is just another way of referring to Engaged Buddhism' (2008c: 9) he has more recently indicated Applied Buddhism is a step on from Engaged Buddhism (2010c: 8). Although there is no essential difference between the adjectives *engaged* and *applied* it could be that the new term has been taken up because there is no consensus of the definition of Engaged Buddhism. *Applied* has the sense of being practical and pragmatic whereas *engaged* suggests being involved or even engrossed. Does this mean Nhat Hanh is using *applied* to suggest detachment? However, *applied* could also be understood as intellectual and the term Institute instead of monastery or practice centre denotes a specifically educational establishment. These issues will be further discussed in Chapter 7.

He recently denotes Applied Buddhism indicates a practical step that can offer the essence of Buddhism to a secular audience rather than theoretical knowledge. 'You can be fluent in Pali, Sanskrit and Tibetan and in all the different teachings of the two canons, but if you get into difficulties and don't know what to do, your Buddhism doesn't help you' (Nhat Hanh 2010c: 8). The Buddhism that Nhat Hanh offers is '... the Buddhism that will help us when we need it' (Nhat Hanh 2010c: 8) as indicated at the beginning of this chapter, because of its practical nature. Whilst the Institutes clearly have Buddhism as a foundational basis the emphasis is on providing teachings that are secular in approach and therefore open to anyone. People do not need to be Buddhist to understand the teachings of Mindfulness or practise compassion. The important aspect here is that Nhat Hanh is implementing a holistic teaching, combining practical elements with theory, as he first instigated in Saigon.

I propose he is now coming full circle in creating Institutes of Applied Buddhism which aim to replicate the Van Hanh University he founded in Saigon. Therefore 'new' is not an appropriate adjective, yet this is a different *yana*, scaffolding on what he has previously practised. It appears he has outgrown the term Engaged Buddhism and wishes to drop the title in order to release any previous connotations, particularly those associated with social activism. I propose in this respect Applied Buddhism is a step on from Engaged Buddhism, particularly in engaging in the secular side of society, as will be further examined in Chapter 7. The new Institutes offer not only mindful living, but also short courses focussed on particular aspects of applying Mindfulness, and encouraging and helping lay people to become *Dharma* teachers (Nhat Hanh 2010c: 8). This is a variance to Plum Village whose retreats are all of the more general type promoting mindful living. EIAB (further examined in Chapter 7) denotes a practical application of Buddhism that Nhat Hanh is eager to present, addressing social issues, as will be discussed next.

4:2:3 The social dimension of Engaged Buddhism

Several scholars (Eppsteiner 1988: ix-x; King 2005: 17; Puri 2006: 11, note 3) indicate traditionally Buddhism has been regarded as a practice of removing oneself from the world in order to attain *nirvana* on a personal level. As Henry discusses, Engaged Buddhism is a particularly social dimension that is in opposition to this erroneously held view of Buddhism as 'passive and aloof, emphasising meditation and withdrawal' (2008: 5) which is rooted in Max Weber's stereotype of Buddhism as other-worldly rather than this-worldly (1966: 169-171). Engaged Buddhists deliberately choose to associate themselves with the concerns of suffering in the here and now whilst recognising that they are impermanent, as discussed at the beginning of this section. There is a decision to engage with social problems by addressing them directly rather than negating them, as is suggested here, or merely accepting them as having no substantial reality.

It appears a Western understanding of Buddhism is taken from an idea of the *Theravada* tradition where 'Buddhism is only for deep meditation and personal transformation' (Sivaraksa 1988: 12) and is otherworldly and not at all concerned with social issues. This idea may have been deliberately promulgated by 'British officials and Christian missionaries [who] ... used it as an argument for promoting Christianity and Christian schools' (Bond 1996: 124). Christian missionaries in their first encounters with Buddhism reported on practices that they perceived were nihilistic, without God and without hope (Harris 2006: 103-104). Buddhism as individual and passive is perceived to stem from the *Theravada* tradition which suggests enlightenment is not for all but for the few *Arhats* who create a 'spiritual elite ... [and] did not care to share their knowledge with others' (Chhaya 2007:211). Conversely, Engaged Buddhism is influenced by the *Mahayana* ideal of the *bodhisattva* who puts off his or her own enlightenment to assist all sentient beings towards *nirvana*.

Richard Gombrich proposes in *Theravada* the 'Pratyekabuddha ('Enlightened singly') ... seeks Nirvana for himself alone [whereas] the Bodhisattva ... preaches his wisdom to others to save them' (1998: 17-18). The distinction here is somewhat muddied by the idea of an individual being enlightened or even choosing to put off enlightenment. At this level of practice interbeing is no longer a concept but a way of life and the notion of an individual does not exist. Furthermore, Sid Brown recently complained about the pro-*Mahayana* anti-*Theravada* stance continually being taken in Western Buddhist journals, and objected to the suggestion that the *Arhat* is selfishly seeking only for personal enlightenment (2008: 9). As discussed in Chapter 1, the stereotypes that have arisen suggesting *Theravadin* monastics are withdrawn and passive whereas *Mahayana* ones are engaged and concerned with the enlightenment of all beings does not reflect actual practice. These rather simplistic viewpoints refute the understanding that 'despite doctrinal differences between *Theravada* and *Mahayana* Buddhism, both streams place the concept of compassion and nonviolence at the center of their ideology' (Topmiller 2002: 5) suggesting that both traditions recognise the need for social action. It could be understood that *Theravadins* do not practice Engaged Buddhism yet this is not the case as demonstrated by King (2009).

Nonetheless, several interviewees specifically identified Nhat Hanh's teachings as being more out in the world than some Buddhist traditions which are understood to take a '... relatively isolative and introspective stance' (SI, Person 28 2011). By this they mean going out into the community (SI, Person 6 2010) and actively engaging in a mindful way with those one meets or relates to, rather than just sitting *on the cushion* and meditating (SI Person 7 2010; Person 9 2009; Person 10 2010; Person D 2011; Person 24 2010; Person 27 2010); '... taking Buddhism outside the monastery and into the world' (SI, Person 1 2009). The mistaken division of Buddhist practice into those who merely sit and meditate and those who go out and interact with society (see Chapter 1) is a prevalent viewpoint within the CoI. In this situation it is based on Nhat Hanh's experiences of his Buddhist elders who did not want to leave the monastery and help Vietnam in the social way that was evident to him (see Chapter 3). It is also informed by his emphasis on the *Sangha* as an important aspect of practice and that one engages with others on the path as well as focussing on one's personal practice. I now move onto examine the interviewee's interpretation of Engaged Buddhism in order to compare this with Nhat Hanh's teaching.

4:3 The interviewee's understanding of Engaged Buddhism

In this section I examine how Nhat Hanh's students understand Engaged Buddhism, specifically the interviewee set, for whom it is an important part of their practice. Nhat Hanh indicates,
> Peace must begin with ourselves: with the practice of sitting quietly, walking mindfully, taking care of our body, releasing the tension in our body and in our feelings. That is why the practice of being peace is at the foundation of the practice of doing peace. Being peace comes first. Doing

peace is something that comes from that foundation (2009a: 95-96).
As discussed previously, Nhat Hanh denotes that the basis of any action must be informed by the practice of meditation and Mindfulness and also that both aspects of being and doing are necessary. For the interviewees the question of being is likewise important, going 'beyond practising for myself' (Person 2 2010). An apt answer, because engaging suggests how people formulate their appreciation of Mindfulness with the larger world beyond themselves. Person 7 concurs with the quotation; 'I think the quality of being is essential to inform the doing ... but I think Engaged Buddhism is important because we can get stuck in just being ... bliss out on the being and there's plenty of stuff that needs doing in the world' (SI, 2010). One has to be skilful in melding the two aspects together and Person 7 suggests the Quakers are a good example of 'effective and quiet and skilful doing over the years ... [showing] a sense of integrity' (SI, 2010). The 'quiet' way of responding is important to Person 7, rather than '... being agitative or aggressive in the world' (SI, 2010), reflecting Nhat Hanh's approach in Vietnam of social action rather than activism.

The interviewees recognise a tension between going inward and '... manifesting our values in the world and doing that every day in a thoughtful and compassionate way ... the two aspects are really important, the inner quest and the outer activity in the world' (SI, Person 22 2011). What is the outer activity that is expressed here? For the CoI it is not necessarily political action, this is steered away from for most of the interviewees. Person 20 is in the minority by suggesting Engaged Buddhism is '... not ... shrinking away from political engagement' (SI, 2010). As discussed above, social activism was not part of Nhat Hanh's teaching so much as social action, which entails practising with your family as well as the wider environment (Person 2 2010). Although Nhat Hanh deliberately chose not to engage politically in Vietnam this does not exclude his students from choosing this option if it is appropriate for them, however, the majority adopt a less socially active approach by focussing on the family and their immediate social circles.

For fourteen interviewees family is where the practice starts, whether at home or attending a retreat with family members as well (SI, Person 1 2009; Person 15 2009; Person 25 2009; Person 2 2010; Person 4 2010; Person 6 2010; Person 10 2010; Person 17 2010; Person B 2010; Person C, 2010; Person 27 2010; Person D 2011; Person 23 2011; Person 28 2011). This concurs with Nhat Hanh's teaching as expounded by Sr. Chan Khong; 'Thay say that "my Engaged Buddhism is twenty-four hours with yourself, with people around you in peace, in harmony" and we have to resolve the little conflict in the heart of each one [It is rarely on a large scale] ... but right away today, in each house' (SI, 2011). As discussed earlier (section 4:1) Nhat Hanh himself teaches Engaged Buddhism starts 'in our daily lives' (2007a: 53-54) rather than in large scale actions of protest and the interviewees have taken this on board. Person D discussed sitting to meditate outside prisons in America where prisoners are being executed but continued,

> it doesn't have to be so flamboyant as that, it can also be ... practising with your family ... bringing your difficulty, being able to express it ... it's not about focussing inward it's about engaging with the things that are going on around us, that's my understanding (SI, 2011).

For the CoI the practice comes back to social action rather than activism and working on Mindfulness within one's family is central to the practice whereas the activist approach of sitting outside prisons or being involved in overt political action is not so apparent. Person 17 concurs with this. As a *Dharmacharya* his engagement is '... through Sangha-building, visiting Sanghas and leading retreats and Days of Mindfulness, but actually those things in many ways are less important than what I do in my everyday life and how I live my everyday life' (SI, 2010). This closely reflects Nhat Hanh's teaching.

In an informal conversation during the Facilitators' Retreat the majority view was that people who join Units tend to be already engaging in some aspect due to the nature of their work such as teachers, counsellors or prison chaplains. Therefore they do not require their Unit to be engaged in a specific way; instead they seek nourishment and refreshment from it. One suggestion was the question should be 'how are we *being*?' rather than, 'what are we *doing*?' (IC, Facilitators' Retreat 2010). This rather gentle approach to the practice as opposed to direct action reflects Nhat Hanh himself. Whilst his words are direct his demeanour is quiet due to many years of practising meditation and mindfulness and letting this inform his actions.

Some interviewees felt it was addressing questions such as 'action needs to be taken, and how to take that action?' (SI, Person 25 2009); 'how could you not act? How could you not contribute to making the world a better place?' (SI, Person 15 2009); 'if you want peace in the world, how do you bring that to the world?' (SI, Person 25 2009). These questions are not easy to answer, especially in considering an approach that is non-agitative, yet the fact they are being addressed indicates a communal rather than individualistic worldview. I propose Nhat Hanh's answer could be, 'peace in oneself, peace in the world' (the title given to the 2008 Nottingham retreat). It is one of his many quotations that people use as reminders like the Mindfulness *gathas*, and actualising this in one's daily life is how the CoI practise Engaged Buddhism. For them it is not an organised activity as it is with other Buddhist groups (Henry 2008: 201). It is 'a way of being in the world ... being mindful of what you're doing and what's going on around, trying to maintain a sort of stability within yourself, within whatever's happening' (SI, Person 12 2009), succinctly described by Person 14 through the poem 'If' (Kipling 1996: 9). This replicates his teaching,
> Sometimes if we don't do anything, we help more than if we do a lot. We call that non-action. It is like the calm person on a small boat in a storm. That person does not have to do much, just to be himself and the situation can change ... not talking, not teaching, just being' (Nhat Hanh 2007a: 25).

The quality of being is important so that one understands one's motivation for engaging; being 'peaceful and calm in a stressful situation' can help others without them having to know there is anything Buddhist about it (SI, Person 9 2009). Whilst this may appear to be a naïve approach to take it is a path Nhat Hanh has walked for many years since first adopting it in Vietnam. As discussed in Chapter 3, he is adopting a long-term approach that needs gentle and patient nurturing for the seeds of Mindfulness to take affect. A gardener does not give up if seedlings do not appear and take fruit immediately and likewise Nhat Hanh is following a slow-growth that will nonetheless have a stable foundation of being peace at its core.

Engaged Buddhism is finding a mode of relating to the world around one in a way that is satisfactory to oneself. In this respect it is individual as well as communal because 'it invites you to be present in life, not withdrawn from life' (SI, Monk A 2010). The aspect of remaining calm in a difficult situation is something I suggest is not brought out in the earlier discussion about Engaged Buddhism (section 4:2), and it emphasises the being aspect of his teaching. Here one is mindful in each and every aspect of one's daily life, whether it is what one might consider something important or more mundane activities like brushing one's teeth. Although it is approached at the level of the individual, it addresses the question of that individual's relationship to society and how much the individual does to affect that society; 'it's by practising as an individual within a society, within a community' (SI, Person 6 2010). This leads on to the interbeing aspect of Engaged Buddhism.

In this respect Engaged Buddhism is '... less individualistic' (SI, Person 20 2010) and instead acknowledges, 'everything I do can affect not only myself but others' (SI, Person 13 2010). It is an appreciation of interconnection (SI, Person 3 2011) and '... recognising interdependence and the realisation that we are not separate, if someone suffers we all suffer' (SI, Person 4 2010). Although each person is working from the basis of an individual there is also awareness of a connection with the wider world; 'you realise that you don't have inherent independent existence, your existence is a result of so many things' (SI, Person 15 2009). This includes animals, plants and minerals as well as other humans. The illustration of Indra's Net[39] is pertinent here with each individual being one jewel on an interconnected mesh and I would suggest this is how the CoI view society and the world at large although no one used the term specifically. To see oneself as part of a larger whole rather than an insular individual is the foundation underpinning Engaged Buddhism, where one's personal ideas are secondary to addressing the needs of others. 'It's when the separation between the self and others breaks down, and you start to do things for others ... because you have identified yourself as being part of something larger' (SI, Person 16 2010) which underlines *my happiness lies in the happiness of others.* Person 16 clarifies this with examples of people helping in small ways, washing teacups at work, handing out books at school etc., '... they've done what a mother does in her family ... she doesn't make food for the children because she's being altruistic, she makes food for the children because she is the children' (SI, 2010). This recognises doing a job or task because one perceives it needs doing rather than for any result or how one may appear to others.

This can be equated with making the world a better place, another interpretation of Engaged Buddhism that several interviewees discussed (SI, Person 1 2009; Person 15 2009; Person 24 2010; Person 27 2010). Here Engaged Buddhism is seen as '... the way of reminding us that we should share what we gain with people and environment around us to create a better more harmonious and a loving community and to alleviate the suffering of people and animals, nature around us' (SI, Monk B 2010). It is about working as an individual to reduce the suffering in the world around one in a '... very practical' way (SI, Person 29 2009). Four interviewees (SI, Person 11 2009; Person 14 2010; Person 3 2011; Person D 2011) further equate Engaged Buddhism with Christian or Catholic engagement that they were brought up with, i.e. '... running

---

[39] Indra's Net is a concept in the 'Digha Nikaya [DN1] of the Pali Canon ... according to which all phenomena in the universe are interrelated' (Keown 2003: 119), depicted by a vast cosmic net, strung with jewels at each intersection and in which all of the other jewels are reflected.

orphanages ... running credit unions that ... comes from a sense of interconnection' (SI, Person 3 2011) rather than a condescending or superior attitude. Although these aspects closely reflect the work that Nhat Hanh and the SYSS undertook in Vietnam they do not generally reflect the current work of the CoI, as discussed earlier.

I put forward that a dilemma for Nhat Hanh's students is whether one initiates action or responds to what is in front of one. Person 1's statement that one is 'looking for areas of suffering' (SI, 2009) is a minority viewpoint within the interviewees; for most the emphasis is on responding to what one meets in the world at large rather than going out on a mission to seek for the socially disadvantaged. Yet the 4th MT calls for one to 'be with those who suffer' which seems to suggest a proactive rather than passive stance. This point is discussed in the next section, addressing whether Nhat Hanh has adopted a quietist approach in the West somewhat different from the perceived activism he undertook in Vietnam.

As has been discussed in this section, some interviewees referred to Engaged Buddhism meeting the needs of social injustice whereas for others it is in more general terms of accepting that everyone suffers as that is part of the human condition. In this case there is no need to go in search of suffering because one begins with oneself by addressing the suffering within. The suffering '... helps us to understand ... it nurtures our compassion, and ... for this reason it is vitally necessary for us' (Nhat Hanh 2004b: 69-70), which is quite a different understanding of suffering. Furthermore, as soon as one interacts with another being there is another possibility of addressing suffering. And if one realises the suffering within oneself is the same as the suffering of others 'because of our insight we are capable of practicing real peace and reconciliation' (Nhat Hanh 1992e: 32). If one can demonstrate being happy and peaceful in any situation this will help others realise it is also possible for them; 'it's about using the practice for the benefit of others' (SI, Person 16 2010). This is not to deny that suffering exists or to avoid addressing it but to recognise the usefulness of suffering as a means of awakening compassion. This relationship between suffering and happiness is further discussed in Chapter 6.

The understanding of the CoI with regards to Engaged Buddhism emphasises the simplicity of the everyday practice rather than political or organised activities that other Buddhist groups may undertake. Person 1 denotes Nhat Hanh '... tells you that the flower's there, but he always goes back to the roots' (SI, 2009) meaning that he continually brings the practice of Engaged Buddhism back to any and every activity however mundane. From the evidence of the interviews, as discussed above, there is no one cohesive way that the CoI have developed in which to practise Engaged Buddhism as it depends on the individual's nature and their preferences. It could be addressed to the family, the environment, one's everyday life and all the aspects therein. There is a sense of creativity as to the ways in which people integrate Engaged Buddhism within their lives. Although there may be a current consensus within the CoI that it is not necessary to initiate any proactive engagement it is also accepted that this is not a fixed position and the question will be addressed periodically (IC, Facilitators' Retreat 2010). However, there are criticisms on what is perceived as the CoI's lack of social engagement from Brazier (2001: 72-74), Henry (2008: 202-230) and Minh Pham (2001: 66-67) which I will now examine.

4:4 Critiques of Community of Interbeing practice of Engaged Buddhism

Brazier argues that with the exception of a few Units in the USA
> few of his [Nhat Hanh's] white supporters ... have any real enthusiasm for engaged Buddhism ... what many want is a form of religion that teaches mindfulness and gentleness in daily life and offers them freedom from stress and anxiety. They want their spiritual disease ameliorated without the trouble of attending to its social causes. Many Westerners are so alienated from the political process that they no longer

see any connection between spirituality and society. Though radical by sentiment, they are effectively conservative in practice (2001: 72).

Here, Brazier suggests a point that Van Minh Pham raises questioning whether 'the meaning of engagement has become ambivalent [for Nhat Hanh's students who] ... nowadays consider mindfulness as the ultimate goals of their practice' (2001: 66-67). Furthermore, Henry suggests the CoI adopts a 'conservative' attitude towards Socially Engaged Buddhism (SEB) demonstrated by the fact that 'individual social action in overt protest or campaigning, is, with a few exceptions, largely avoided, as they [the CoI] emphasise the notion that they will, by living mindfully, beneficially 'Inter-be' with society' (2008: 205). Whilst these three critiques acknowledge that the practice of the CoI is very different to the social activism undertaken by Nhat Hanh in Vietnam I propose this is in line with Nhat Hanh's own teachings, this is not the role that he himself wished to present (as discussed in Chapter 3). It was Mindfulness in responding to a situation rather than activism that Nhat Hanh put forward.

Although it may be accurate, as Brazier suggests, that some members of the CoI are seeking amelioration from their individual suffering, this does not acknowledge the aspect that many interviewees have reported in which the process begins with recognising one's individual suffering in order to then be of use to the wider community. I suggest Nhat Hanh did not approve of some of the overt social activism with which the UBC became recognised in Vietnam (See Chapter 3) and, furthermore as discussed above, he denoted *being peace* as the foundation of *doing peace* after recognising the anger that motivated some of the so-called peacemakers in America. He proposes Mindfulness is the primary key for any action and one could question what he means by action in exclaiming 'once there is seeing, there must be acting' (1995: 91). This can be answered from one of Nhat Hanh's guided meditations 'taking action to transform' (2009b: 55). Here the action is '... breathing, smiling, and walking mindfully, and no longer to do things like judging, blaming, comparing [indeed anything that can] ... water the seeds of happiness, tolerance, compassion, forgiveness, openness, bringing joy to people' (Nhat Hanh 2009b: 55). I put forward the action Nhat Hanh speaks of is not the social activism that Brazier, Minh Pham and Henry discuss in comparing the CoI with other Buddhist groups. Instead it is action that the interviewees demonstrate in terms of applying Mindfulness to one's daily life in order to be awake to suffering in the world (both in oneself and in others) and thereby live a compassionate life.

Henry, however, acknowledges that within the CoI SEB is 'primarily an individual-to-individual influence, despite Nhat Hanh and the wider monastic community's more coherently individual-to-collective influences within Vietnam and elsewhere' (2008: 204). This suggests Mindfulness is principally an individual action, but does not recognise the intention is for it to affect the wider society. Nonetheless, Henry appreciates a tension, which the CoI would do well to address, between the perceived lack of social action from themselves compared to the activities Nhat Hanh has undertaken in his life.

> His [Nhat Hanh's] focus is to transform society through individual transformation - with an "individual-to-collective influence", but the interpretation of many within the UK C of I is for a more "individual-to-individual influence", based on an uncertainty of approach towards overt transformations of the collective (society). The UK community seem content to see transformation born out of peace within, without recourse to direct social action, hence the critique leveled at the group of it being quietist (Henry 2008 229-230).

Henry has recognised a caution and an uncertainty within the CoI as to how to engage socially, but I propose this is because the perception of Nhat Hanh's teachings is slightly askew. The social activism with which he was recognised in Vietnam was due to Mindfulness rather than a desire to protest. As discussed in Chapter 3 the work of the SYSS arose out of compassion rather than political reasons or dissent. Furthermore, the autonomy encouraged and perpetuated from Nhat Hanh down through the monasteries and the CoI means each Unit has its own way of responding to the teachings which may be considerably different to another Unit. It is up to each individual Unit to decide how or whether it wishes to engage in a formal or organised way based on how they respond to Nhat Hanh's teachings. In this respect one cannot look for uniformity of response throughout the CoI UK. As discussed previously, Nhat Hanh does not encourage political action or any sort of activism motivated by anger. In 1973 he deliberately chose to disassociate from any political party and reaffirm his standpoint coming from a religious community (Nhat Hanh & Berrigan 2001: 88-89). Instead he promotes Mindfulness as a way of living and once that is incorporated into one's life it matters not what action one undertakes because it will be founded in Mindfulness. This is not to say that one can behave without thought for the feelings of others, quite the opposite, one begins to act as a *bodhisattva* with compassion and caring towards all beings without discrimination.

It is legitimate for Brazier, Minh Pham and Henry to question the CoI's engagement with society because there is no tangible evidence that Nhat Hanh's teaching on Mindfulness is having an effect in society other than speculation discussed in Chapter 6. Furthermore, I propose Minh Pham's critique that Nhat Hanh's teachings have become ambivalent for his students who 'nowadays consider mindfulness as the ultimate goals of their practice' (2001: 66-67) is justified in the uncertainty that Henry perceived from his interviews. In this respect the CoI would benefit from greater clarity in its aims and purpose. The ethical issues of the 5 and 14MTs seem to require one to stand up and be counted in a way that appears not yet to be happening with the CoI and it is this tension that Brazier and the others address. However, to this I would answer that patience is needed as inner processes such as Nhat Hanh proposes take time to establish and one cannot tell how many lifetimes Nhat Hanh has been preparing for this manifestation as a Mindfulness teacher.

Given that over eight hundred people attended the Nottingham retreat in 2012 if each went home and affected a change within their family of compassion and appreciation it could ripple out into society. This is not to suggest that one is looking for a mass wave of mindful compassion but that it is possible to slowly achieve a change in thinking by teaching Mindfulness in the same way that drop by drop water can imperceptibly wear away stone. Once again, it comes back to the question of whether engagement has to be visible to be effective (see Chapter 3) and the inner work of practising within one's family, that is not so visible, may be more important than loud protestations that may actually be ineffectual as all they could achieve is to water the seeds of otherness and opposition instead of interbeing. It reflects what Nhat Hanh calls non-action, as discussed earlier. A person being mindful may not have to say very much as their actions speak louder. Nhat Hanh denotes it is easy to write letters of condemnation to governments, criticising their actions, but how often does one write 'love letters' that they will want to read? Again, he comes back to the question as to whether one can be peace in order to do peace; 'it would be wonderful if we could bring to the peace movement our non-dualistic way of looking at things. That alone would diminish hatred and aggression' (1995: 111).

When the question of Engaged Buddhism was addressed to someone from Asia they did not understand because for them the term was irrelevant, it is a Western term; 'Buddhism is about your life, the whole thing ... not ... something that you think about but it's something you live with and it's inside you' (SI, Person A 2009). It is this understanding of Engaged Buddhism that Nhat Hanh encourages his students to accept and incorporate into their lives, for it to become a personal practice that is integral to one's way of being and goes beyond a dependence on the Unit. Whilst Engaged Buddhism as denoted by the interviewees may not be the social activism that was apparently prevalent for Nhat Hanh in Vietnam, as I have argued, this is a partial understanding of Nhat Hanh's Engaged Buddhism. It is not a separate section that can be compartmentalised; Engaged Buddhism is about looking at one's life in holistic terms and applying Mindfulness to every part of it; there is nowhere in one's life that Mindfulness cannot touch. Engaged

Buddhism is not an add-on or something else to try and incorporate into one's already busy life, it is one's life.

4:5 Reflections on the definition of Engaged Buddhism

In this chapter I have indicated the difficulties in assessing the phenomenon Engaged Buddhism due to its many facets. Is Engaged Buddhism only concerned with social activism or does it contain a wider understanding of social action including the relationships within a family, workplace and community, as the CoI demonstrate? Whilst there is a intimation that every practice along the continuum is engaged there is an implication that only those at the 'hard' end are truly Engaged Buddhists. Furthermore, there is the suggestion that Engaged Buddhism is directly related to the *Mahayana* paradigm of the *bodhisattva* (Henry 2008: 5) which discounts *Theravadins*. Yet Engaged Buddhists are found in all paths of Buddhism. There is also the argument of 'traditionists' versus 'modernists' in assessing whether Engaged Buddhism has always been part of Buddhism or is a new phenomenon. Given that Nhat Hanh is viewed as the 'Father of Engaged Buddhism' one could conclude that his practices are the archetype of engagement, yet, as has been discussed here, his practices have altered over the years. Has the social activism through which he was known in Vietnam been superceded by Mindfulness as an individual practice? With all these variables one could conclude there is no one definition of Engaged Buddhism. I propose, however, there are key aspects that can be applied to all Engaged Buddhists despite the varied circumstances particular to their situation or location. These are, the balance of being and doing, participation in the world, and interbeing. These elements are particularly evident from the CoI interviews. Whilst these aspects are relevant to other practices of Buddhism as well, it is the sum of the parts together that I propose brings about what can be called Engaged Buddhism, which will be indicated by a diagram at the end of this section.

4:5:1 The balance of being and doing

A key aspect in Engaged Buddhism is the balancing of inner and outer peace i.e. equilibrium between the cultivation of a spiritual practice and active social compassion which mutually support each other (King 2005: 27; Jones 2003: 173). As Nhat Hanh discovered (see Chapter 3) *being peace* was an imperative foundation of *doing peace*. Another way of describing these seemingly disparate aspects is wisdom and compassion, key terms informing Buddhist practice which I equate with Mindfulness, or meditation, and action. Wisdom is the inner practice 'cultivated through the practice of insight meditation or similar forms of mental training' (Keown 2003: 218) that becomes the foundation for the outer practice of compassion directed towards others. Indeed, as Nhat Hanh emphasises, they are not disparate at all, but necessary as two sides of the same coin.

In *Mahayana* Buddhism compassion is equated with wisdom as the 'two wings with which one flies to the island of enlightenment' (Keown 2003: 138). This metaphor indicates the equal necessity of both aspects as 'compassion without wisdom can cause great suffering [and therefore] ... wisdom and compassion must walk together' (Ghosananda 1992: 35). If one has wisdom alone it remains theoretical as it is not offered to be of use to anyone, but if one has compassion alone without the wisdom of insight meditation one can become disillusioned in putting all one's energy into a project without the spiritual foundation to support it. 'We know that without a spiritual practice social engagement tends to burn us out because it is emotionally stressful and exhausting' (Loy 2004). 'Action without the physical inaction of meditation can be flawed' (Harris 2010: 98) and therefore in the practice of Engaged Buddhism wisdom and compassion sit side by side as equal partners.

Nhat Hanh likewise suggests that social action without recourse to inner nurturing can lead to a lack of potency because people whose 'hearts are filled with compassion' may not be aware that all the subtle energy they are putting into addressing issues of suffering needs recharging; 'real strength is not in power, money, or weapons, but in deep, inner peace' (2000b: 87). It is a detached insight accomplished from many years of meditation practice which allows for 'a lucid understanding of social problems and social change, [rather than] ... the burning energy of compassion' (Foster 1988: 60) running out of control. In order to maintain the equilibrium of wisdom and compassion Nhat Hanh denotes 'we must be careful not to take in too much. Any remedy must be taken in the proper dosage. We need to stay in touch with suffering only to the extent that we will not forget, so that compassion will flow within us and be a source of energy for our actions' (2007c: 9). He again demonstrates the delicate balance between being and doing that is required for engagement to be effective in the world. Compassion needs to be detached to the extent that it can be a source of energy rather than a sentimental desire to remove suffering and this is achieved through the foundational practice of meditation or wisdom. Compassion alone cannot achieve the aims of Engaged Buddhism because, as Loy has identified, this can easily lead to burnout. The balance of being and doing naturally leads to participation in the world, the next aspect to be considered.

4:5:2 Participation in the world

As Jones' continuum suggests, participation in the world involves social, political and economic affairs as well as every aspect of daily activity thus placing 'greater stress on world engagement rather than on world abandonment' (Puri 2006: 1). Engaged Buddhism is seen as being different from other Buddhist practices precisely because it engages with the social issues of this lifetime and presents this as the primary focus rather than the release from *samsara*; in part it is a response to the charge that Buddhism has emphasised 'meditation and withdrawal rather than reaching out to the mass of humankind' (Keown 2003: 86). Engaged Buddhism is the antithesis of withdrawal, focussing on recognition of the interbeing nature of all sentient beings which necessitates action. This does, however, suggest that to view Engaged Buddhism as suddenly switching from being 'passive, otherworldly, or escapist' (Kraft 1988: xii) to a social and political movement concerned with 'this-worldly liberation' (Queen 1996: 10) denies the fact that Buddhists have long been genuinely concerned in current affairs. Countries where Buddhism has been the main religion for centuries were underpinned by a Buddhist input into social and political affairs (Sivaraksa 1988: 12). It was in these very countries that Engaged Buddhist activities began, again, strengthening the argument that Engaged Buddhism is not a new movement.

Garfinkel suggests that once the balance of being and doing is established 'you don't take action: action takes you' (2007: 65). The action is one of assuaging suffering whether in oneself or another. Thus, Engaged Buddhists suggest the aim naturally moves from a wish for individual peace to 'a healthy, just and peaceful world [in which the] ... global community [becomes the area of concern, from a basis of] ... the universal truths of wisdom and compassion' (INEB). Yet, whilst this is apparent at the 'hard' end of the continuum it is not so obvious for Mindfulness practitioners who appear to be practising for themselves alone. If one accepts the concept of interbeing, however, one cannot practise for oneself alone because each action has an effect that ripples out beyond the individual. Therefore, I propose that those at the 'soft' end of the continuum are contributing to engagement by emphasising the easing of suffering in the here and now through the world.

4:5:3 The interbeing aspect of Engaged Buddhism

The third aspect of Engaged Buddhism is interbeing or interdependence. It is from this aspect that Engaged Buddhism emerges as a realisation of dependent co-arising or Indra's Net which invokes a 'sense of responsibility arising from our co-participation in all existence' (Macy 1988: 172). From an interbeing viewpoint 'the universe is experienced as an organic whole, every "part" affecting every other "part"' (Kraft 1999: xiii) providing the necessary compassion that stirs the individual to action. Recognition of interbeing is what makes Engaged Buddhism a vital practice, acknowledging that one's actions and behaviour affect others. Nhat Hanh calls this developing correct insight; by acknowledging that all things inter-are 'we will stop blaming, arguing, and killing, and we will become friends with everyone' (2007c: 11). It was this concept that led to his neutral stance in the Vietnam/American War because he could not conceive of standing on one side with an opponent on the other when in reality they are the same.

As discussed in Chapter 1, interbeing extends beyond an anthropocentric view of the world to include all sentient beings, animals, plants and minerals where 'every Buddhist practitioner should be a protector of the environment' (Nhat Hanh 2007c: 10). There is no preferential treatment for humans over and above other sentient beings. 'The recognition of our essential nonseparateness from the world' (Macy 2009a) becomes the foundation from which one proceeds. The concept of interbeing is one that I suggest can be difficult for Westerners to grasp living in a deeply individualistic society where the individual self is held to be most important. Interbeing teaches there is no separate self, everything is interconnected; 'we cannot be by ourselves alone. We have to inter-be with everyone else, with everything else' (Nhat Hanh 2010f: 58). I propose interbeing is a foundational aspect of Engaged Buddhism because it denotes the interrelatedness of all beings and therefore acknowledges that one cannot just be concerned with one's own welfare as if it has no effect on others. An awareness of interdependence leads to nonviolence, something that was key to Nhat Hanh's practice in Vietnam, as discussed in Chapter 3. Although this aspect is implicit in the interviews it did not come out as a significant factor.

4:5:4 A summation of Engaged Buddhism

Whilst I have not been able to draw out a concise definition of Engaged Buddhism, from the above discussion I bring together these three elements in the following diagram, which I propose form a portrayal of Engaged Buddhism.

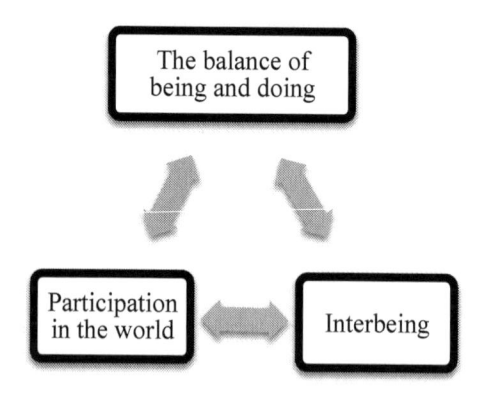

```
        ┌─────────────────┐
        │  The balance of │
        │  being and doing│
        └─────────────────┘
           ↗           ↖
┌──────────────┐   ┌────────────┐
│ Participation│ ⟷ │ Interbeing │
│ in the world │   │            │
└──────────────┘   └────────────┘
```

Figure 2
This depiction indicates it should not be perceived as progressive as all aspects are relevant and necessary to Engaged Buddhism. It does not present too narrow an explanation nor does it exclude an individual's interpretation to proceed in the world with whatever action they see fit and it therefore can be applied to any Engaged Buddhist practitioner. Being and doing indicates action as an outcome of inner spiritual practices although action is not constrained to social activism. I suggest this is where Engaged Buddhism has been limited in the past in its definition, if not its practice, by the assumption that it only applies to political social activism and therefore excludes social action. Through this inclusive definition all points of the continuum can be expressed as Engaged Buddhism without distinction or parameters.

4:6 Conclusion

In this chapter I have discussed the various aspects that contribute towards the development of Engaged Buddhism and indicated the difficulties involved in forming a consensus of its definition. Some in the West see Buddhism as a religion that is unconcerned with the problems of the world because its goal is to be free of the cycle of birth and death. It is not looking for a solution within the world it is seeking to attain freedom from it by reaching *nirvana*. However, Nhat Hanh's interpretation represents one by which *nirvana* can be attained in this lifetime, which is where the focus of his teachings lie and is why Engaged Buddhism was an imperative for him. His work in Vietnam was based in the social activism end of the continuum, yet he nonetheless indicates that awareness in daily life is an imperative aspect to Engaged Buddhism and it is this emphasis that sets him apart from others. Hence the circumstances in Vietnam and the application of Engaged Buddhism will be different to its implementation in Plum Village as will be discussed in later chapters. Like Buddhism itself it has to be fluid not static. Whilst Nhat Hanh himself negates the title of Father of Engaged Buddhism he has demonstrated admirable qualities that brought him to the forefront of an awakening throughout Southeast Asia from the 1940s. In this respect I have concluded from his immense efforts in bringing Mindfulness to many people's awareness in the West that Nhat Hanh has created a new *yana* with Engaged Buddhism, which he now terms Applied Buddhism. I have, however, argued that it is only new in terms of reinterpreting and re-emphasising certain aspects of the *Buddha's* teachings and bringing the aspects of participation in the world into focus rather than negation of it. It is not new in terms of offering a teaching that has not been explored before, but scaffolds on previous teaching.

There is a query about the effectiveness of the work undertaken and critics have questioned the 'lack of tangible results' (Weiner 2003: 114). However, looking for tangible results in an activity that is putting into practice Buddhist teachings seems to miss the point of responding to a need in the here and now and not searching for, or expecting, future outcomes. The practices of meditation as effective means of building one's resources of inner peace, which lead to a natural concern and wish for worldwide peace, do not stop they are continuous. The work proceeds on a step-by-step basis and the only desirable outcome that can be conceived of is peace; inner peace for the individuals concerned and outer peace in terms of effectiveness on a worldwide scale. One also has to hold a long-term view – Jon Kabat-Zinn holds a 1,000-year view (Public Talk 2010) – by patiently practising Mindfulness step-by-step without being concerned with a future outcome.

The relevant characteristics that stood out from the interviews are the balance of being and doing, participation in the world and interbeing and I have depicted these in diagrammatic form as a summation of Engaged Buddhism. I propose it is the combination of these aspects that together form Nhat Hanh's singular exposition of Engaged Buddhism as something that is equally relevant in the mundane parts of one's daily life as in the more visible facet of social activism. I have discussed some critiques of Nhat Hanh's and the CoI's practice in terms of quietism and lack of clarity as to their approach in Engaged Buddhism. From this discussion I conclude it would be helpful for the CoI to consider a more cohesive approach, particularly to the aspect of participation in the world. However, as will be discussed in Chapter 7, the vital autonomy of each CoI Unit may not make this achievable.

The key feature of Mindfulness in day-to-day activities is a prominent characteristic of Nhat Hanh's Engaged Buddhism. The mindful communities of *Phuong Boi*, the SYSS and *Tiep Hien*, which Nhat Hanh established, were all physical manifestations of Mindfulness and were practice grounds for studying and observing it from a collective energy. In Chapter 5 I investigate the means through which Mindfulness is implemented in Plum Village, a continuation of these early communities.

5. A Manifestation of Mindfulness: the Plum Village Meditation Practice Centre

I believe that the encounter between Buddhism and the West will bring about something very exciting, very important ... I would like to present to you a form of Buddhism that may be accepted here in the West. In the past 20 years we have been experimenting with this form of Buddhism, and it seems that it may be suitable for our modern society. It is called the Tiep Hien Order[40] *the Order of "Interbeing" (Nhat Hanh 2007a: 83-85).*

Introduction

Having developed Engaged Buddhism in Vietnam and been exiled because of his ideas, as discussed in Chapter 3, Thich Nhat Hanh settled in France in the late 1960s initially near Paris, before moving to Loubes-Bernac near Bordeaux where he and mainly Vietnamese friends bought farmhouses to inaugurate the Plum Village Meditation Practice Centre. The *Tiep Hien* Order was still active here and grew as Plum Village flourished.

The key argument for this chapter is that Plum Village demonstrates the evolution of Nhat Hanh's pedagogy of Mindfulness beyond Vietnam. Its inhabitants are living examples of aiming to dwell in Mindfulness, closely following the advice of the *Satipatthana Sutta*; 'when he walks, stands, lies down, sits, sleeps or wakes up, speaks or

---

[40] See Chapter 3 for a discussion on *Tiep Hien*.

is silent, he shines his awareness on all this' (Nhat Hanh 2006c: 18). The chapter will examine the key components of Plum Village that are intended to enhance mindful living by shining the light of awareness; the elements of the daily programme, the emotional connections with Nhat Hanh and the bell and the familial atmosphere designed to address conflict resolution and healing. All these aspects culminate in the Plum Village Model, creating not a blueprint but a guide of mindful living to be replicated in other situations. Throughout this chapter I will be establishing that Mindfulness is central to everything that takes place at Plum Village. Some sections are necessarily descriptive in order to convey the depth of the practices that formulate the Plum Village Model.

5:1 The instigation of Plum Village

Whilst still at the Sweet Potatoes hermitage near Paris Nhat Hanh had time to reflect on the events of the preceding years, his calls for a peaceful solution in Vietnam that went unheeded by the warring sides, the success of the SYSS which recruited tens of thousands of young volunteers who were able to make a positive difference to the lives of many peasants in Vietnam, and the failure of the rescue mission for the Boat people[41] who left Vietnam in the 1970s and 80s fleeing the harsh regime instigated by the Communist government after the end of the Vietnam/American War. Nhat Hanh's efforts towards peace seemed to be welcomed and condemned in equal measure. Although he had many supporters both in Vietnam and elsewhere he also had many critics, including both the Vietnamese and American governments, epitomised by the American who lambasted him for being in America when he should be helping in Vietnam (Nhat Hanh 1995: 114). Yet he used this criticism to realise the practice of *being peace* and it expanded his understanding that Mindfulness needed to be the foundation of any action as emphasised in the *Satipatthana Sutta*. In this new context the practices of Engaged Buddhism that had been implemented in Vietnam were not

---

[41] For details of Nhat Hanh's attempts to help people leaving Vietnam on un-seaworthy boats see *Love In Action* 1993a: 101-106.

relevant and Nhat Hanh had to elucidate Mindfulness in a way that met the needs of the Westerners he now connected with.

Plum Village was Nhat Hanh's second home in France after Paris and was established as a meditation practice centre in 1982. It currently comprises four main hamlets, two for monks and two for nuns; adjacent to these are four further hamlets which are used only during large retreats (Nhat Hanh 2003e: 71). The name *Plum Village* originates from an attempt to create income by planting plum trees which was not, however, successful; it involved planting 1,250 trees in recognition of the original *Sangha* practising with the Buddha (Nhat Hanh 2003c: 20). The original intention was to name it *Persimmon Village* after a practice centre they had envisioned for Vietnam which had not manifested. It was, however, more practical to grow plum trees that were already a local harvest and sell the plums dried (Nhat Hanh 2003c: 20). The use of *village* denotes the size of community where everyone knows each other (Nhat Hanh & Berrigan 2001: 42).

Plum Village began as a primitive rustic farmhouse setting with no proper beds, just planks of wood on top of bricks (SI, Person B 2010), where Nhat Hanh was the only monk and the visitors were mainly Vietnamese refugees (Chan Khong 2007: 216). Over time it developed its monastic practices and became a truly international community; when the numbers were still small there was much more access to Nhat Hanh and the other monastics (SI, Person 17 2010; Person B 2010). Now the established community has approximately seventy monks or nuns at each of the four hamlets, fewer laypeople and thousands of retreatants each year. It is from some of these visitors that my data has been collected alongside field notes and participant observation (see Chapter 1).

Whilst still in Vietnam Nhat Hanh established mindful communities which, I argue, were the forerunner of Plum Village. Having experimented in Vietnam, particularly in the situation of *Phuong Boi*, he had clarified what the essential qualities of a practice centre in which he wished to operate were. First and foremost was a fourfold

Sangha in which monastics and laity live together free from the rules and dogma that Nhat Hanh discovered were rampant in Vietnamese Buddhism and governance at that time. Whilst this freedom was possible among the handful of friends who inhabited *Phuong Boi*, some code of conduct is necessary for the large numbers of people who now stay on retreat in Plum Village which has developed as the 5 and 14MTs as well as an updated version of the monastic *Vinaya*[42] (Nhat Hanh 1997).

Although *Phuong Boi* and *Tiep Hien* did not succeed in Vietnam Nhat Hanh remained determined to institute such a centre, as his vision for its necessity remained undimmed. He pursued the same ideals of maintaining Vietnamese culture and tradition and Buddhist practices even as he settled in France. These 'home traditions' (Knott 1986: 10) have been, and still are, one of Nhat Hanh's main foci in sustaining Plum Village which will be further discussed in Chapter 7, exploring how the traditions, practices and customs of Vietnam are maintained in a way that was not possible at home. It is not, however, an Asian Buddhist practice transplanted in the West, but an integrated practice retaining aspects of both the original country as well as adopting ones from the country in which it is now flourishing. I suggest this aspect of transplantation is what has made Plum Village attractive to Westerners. It is not trying to entirely Westernise itself in order to appeal to a different audience, but is bringing a tradition that is based in over forty generations of Vietnamese practice and lineage and presenting it with an awareness of the differences in worldview. These can, however, also create adversities; 'when we bring plants from Vietnam and plant them in the West, they do not grow the way they would in Vietnam' (Nhat Hanh 2003c: 26). This means Nhat Hanh has had to adapt his teachings to respond to the new situation in which Plum Village flourished.

Plum Village offers 'buddhism with a small b' (Sivaraksa 1992: 68) by which I mean the practices, especially Mindfulness and centring

---

[42] *Vinaya* is a framework of rules for the Buddhist monastic community.

the attention on the breathing, are accentuated whereas the ritual and symbolism of Buddhism (that Nhat Hanh found so prevalent in Vietnam) are not. This is further demonstrated at retreats led by Nhat Hanh in the UK. Here there is no *Buddha* statue because he suggests it could be an obstacle (Q&A, Nottingham 2012) to people hearing the teachings if they get caught in symbolism or think the *Buddha* is a god to be worshipped.

The ethical teachings Nhat Hanh presents offer personal responsibility, compassion and loving kindness towards oneself and others with interbeing as a foundation. The teachings denote that happiness is possible and that life is more than suffering; they are aimed at transforming suffering into happiness. Therefore one has to meet and work with one's suffering, in whatever form it manifests, before being able to transform it. In this respect whilst a retreat can be enjoyable and the majority of retreatants feel they gain something and like to return (SI, Person B 2010) they can also be difficult yet, as Person 2 denotes, though '... I may not have a very easy time and I may have a lot to work with but actually I always come back inspired' (SI, 2010). The 'work' is in terms of bringing Mindfulness into every aspect of one's daily life and whilst this can be gratifying it also requires effort to maintain the practice.

Plum Village is the centre from which the teachings emanate now that Nhat Hanh is established in the West. It is the hub from which the satellite monasteries and the lay community[43] have sprung and in retrospect is seen as the realisation of his teachings in a way that was not possible in Vietnam.

5:2 Plum Village practice centre

> The Buddha was asked, 'What do you and your monks practice?' And he replied, 'We sit, we walk and we eat'. The questioner continued, 'but sir, everyone sits, walks and eats'. The Buddha told him, 'when we sit, we know we are sitting.

---

[43] See Chapter 7.

When we walk, we know we are walking and when we eat, we know we are eating' (Nhat Hanh 1996: 4).

This, in essence, indicates what takes place at Plum Village and is thereby offered to retreatants. The activities undertaken here are not different to daily life, instead it is the way in which they are carried out that is important in that all aspects of the programme are designed to inculcate and support Mindfulness from an experiential rather than theoretical perspective, as discussed in Chapter 2. In particular, it is the *simple moment-by-moment awareness* from Nhat Hanh's exposition of Mindfulness (subsection 2:1:5). 'Mindfulness in everything is central ... a very good way to ... underpin it all, it's the ... central focus of pretty much everything you're doing' (SI, Person 20 2010). Indeed it is not just the physical activities; mindfulness is 'to be aware and mindful in all activities and movements both physical and mental' (Rahula 2000: 89). It also introduces people to practices they can implement into their personal home situations,

> it's about the embodiment of the practice in the everyday activities ... there is nothing at Plum Village that isn't the practice ... the place is conducive to that and the presence of the brothers and sisters and people who are experienced in the practice ... all contribute to that (SI, Person 6 2010).

Mindfulness is something to be practised continuously throughout the day as it is a means not an end. Whilst mindful states can nurture well-being they do not bring a lasting end to suffering (Teasdale & Chaskalson 2011: 118). It is for this reason that Nhat Hanh suggests Mindfulness is a moment-by-moment practice that can be accessed twenty-four hours a day (Nhat Hanh 1999c: 96). Whilst seeming to be an easy activity it requires commitment to sustain the practice because of the mind's habit energy[44] of running away from the

---

[44] '... the energy that pushes us to do what we do not want to do and say what we do not want to say is the negative habit energy in us. In Sanskrit, the word is *vasana*. It is very important that we recognize habit energy in us ... We are intelligent enough to know that if we do this or say that, we will

present moment. A programme has been devised at Plum Village for a week's retreat, the minimum time recommended for a stay. These practices focus on present moment awareness in order to recognise what is taking place in body and mind. They also nurture healing and reconciliation by recognising that conflict can arise in any situation such as one's home life, work environment or social life. Beginning Anew has been instigated at Plum Village as a means of attempting to restore relations when communication breaks down and will be discussed in subsection 5:4:2.

The Plum Village community[45] attempts to practise Mindfulness continuously in order to illustrate that Mindfulness in any circumstance is possible. I say *attempts* because it is a difficult practice to maintain. Whilst it is easier for those living in a monastic setting where the community as a whole is working for peace, there are inevitably times when conflicts or dissonance will arise. Greater mindful awareness is a direction towards which people are moving (Nhat Hanh 1995: 108) not a claim that they are always a peaceful and harmonious society, therefore Plum Village is called a practice centre. It does not advocate that those living there have achieved Mindfulness they are still practising moment-by-moment as well, but in a more conducive situation than most of the retreatants find at home, because of the collective energy created by many people practising together. It is for this reason Nhat Hanh emphatically recommends the formation of *Sanghas* (Units) discussed in Chapter 7.

As mentioned earlier, Plum Village is a community aiming for 'harmony and awareness' by which harmony is expressed not as

---

damage our relationship. Yet when the time comes, we say it or we do it anyway. Why? Because our habit energy is stronger than we are. It is pushing us all the time. The practice aims at liberating ourselves from that kind of habit energy' (Nhat Hanh 2000MB).

[45] In using the term Plum Village community I am referring to all those who follow Nhat Hanh's teachings, which includes the satellite monasteries and the worldwide lay community, as well as Plum Village itself.

uniformity but 'it is always an interplay of a number of different motifs, each retaining its separate identity and sustaining the resulting melody through, and thanks to, that identity' (Bauman 2003: 94). There is thus recognition of both the individuals contributing to the whole and the cumulative community as a single entity which benefits from the individuals' efforts. 'As members of a sangha, we can develop our individual talent and our individual potential, and at the same time contribute to and participate in the talent and happiness of the entire group. Nothing is lost; everyone wins' (Nhat Hanh 2003a: 176). The Plum Village community is not seeking sameness or standardisation of response, but is approaching community from the standpoint of interbeing rather than individualism (see Chapter 1). Plum Village exemplifies what can be termed a 'cultural community' which operates through consensus (Clark 2005: 102-105). It is first and foremost a *Sangha* as a single unit and every decision is made on the basis of this unit; 'before making a decision or taking action, we consult with the Sangha to arrive at the deepest, collective insight' (Nhat Hanh 2003c: 253, note 3). Problems and needs are brought to the Sangha in the first instance with an awareness that the needs of the individual are automatically taken care of.

The key aspect in aiming to produce a harmonious *Sangha* is that the unique characteristics of human nature as displayed by different individuals, which Bauman terms identity (2003: 94), are acknowledged in order to appreciate the fullness of humanity. In suggesting Plum Village is a community of like-minded people this does not mean they all think the same things or speak with one voice; diversity within the unity cannot be ignored as this is also part of humanity post modernity. It is how one addresses the diversity that is vital, 'I always tell the monks, nuns, and lay practitioners at Plum Village that if they want to succeed in the practice, they have to find ways to live in harmony with one another, even with those who are difficult' (Nhat Hanh 2008b: 113). It is this key area of harmony that provides the field of practice in that one is learning how to relate to others in a nonviolent way without creating conflict and making assiduous attempts to heal when conflict does occur; 'if we don't have a happy, harmonious relationship with our family and our Sangha, helping others will be very difficult' (Nhat Hanh 2009a: 56). If this can take place within the monastic setting, an atmosphere conducive to practice, it becomes easier to address in the outside world. The Plum Village practices demonstrate how Nhat Hanh's teachings are brought out of the meditation hall into every aspect of daily life (Nhat Hanh 2007a: 54). Whilst they are easy to state it is recognised they are much more difficult to practise, as addressed above, which is why Beginning Anew, (subsection 5:4:2) is such an important and relevant practice that moves beyond violence and retaliation and seeks instead to offer nonviolent resistance. This may sound naïve but Nhat Hanh is convinced peace is possible through these practices, even in such fractured communities as Palestine and Israel (2004a: 109-119).

5:2 The mindful practices

As denoted in the previous section it is the way in which one sits, walks and eats that is paramount in Plum Village, which is to maintain '... observation, free, not caught up in any worldly consideration', shining one's awareness on everything one does, as directed in the *Satipatthana Sutta* (Nhat Hanh 2006c: 17-18). It is not that one is undertaking unusual or rigorous austerities in order to achieve Mindfulness. Nhat Hanh denotes 'meditation is not to get out of society, to escape from society, but to prepare for a re-entry into society' (2007a: 45) from a more mindful viewpoint and this is what all the practices are orientated towards, highlighting the aspect of *engaging with the world* from Nhat Hanh's exposition on Mindfulness (subsection 2:1:5).

Nhat Hanh further indicates that any practice can be a meditation if one applies one's attention to it rather than doing one thing whilst thinking of something else; 'if we want to fully enjoy life's gifts, we must practice Mindfulness at every turn, whether we're brushing our teeth, cooking our breakfast, or driving to work. Every step and every breath can be an opportunity for joy and happiness' (2009d: x).

For the Plum Village community these moments are underpinned by the basic practices of sitting, walking and eating which are framed within silence, and comprise the list of mindful practices discussed next. I shall examine each aspect in order to determine how they demonstrate a mindful practice that can be continued at home for the retreatants.

5:2:1 Sitting meditation

Here I will define meditation as practised at Plum Village before examining some of the tensions and challenges relating to meditation that became apparent during the interviews and my field research. Nhat Hanh denotes sitting meditation as having two aspects *shamatha* (stopping and calming) and *vipashyana* (looking deeply) where the stopping aspect relates to stopping 'our running, our forgetfulness, our being caught in the past or the future' and looking deeply pertains to seeing 'the true nature of things' (1999d: 209-210). The two aspects of *shamatha* and *vipashyana* are terms that are central to meditation practice from the earliest Buddhist traditions. They combine together in the practice of meditation, 'they touch each other and diverge' (Harris 2010: 84). Indeed, these two words can be compounded together indicating that *shamatha* is not a precursor to *vipashyana* (Bell 1991: 203). I propose Nhat Hanh would agree with this statement as he advises 'the practice of stopping and calming contains the practice of insight' (1992e: 19). However, as I shall discuss later in this section this does not always appear to be the case.

In Plum Village the practice of sitting meditation is one of becoming still in order to appreciate what is taking place internally rather than separating
> ourselves from the world of thoughts and feelings and return[ing] to a kind of pure state where the mind contemplates itself and becomes "true mind." It is a lovely idea, but it is basically misleading. Since mind is not separate from the world of thoughts and feelings, how can it leave and retire into itself? (Nhat Hanh 1992d: 62).

Meditation at Plum Village is not in order to achieve a trance-like state of going beyond the mind, but to examine mindfully what is taking place there. Mindfulness and meditation are synonyms according to Nhat Hanh (2003a: 5) and practising both *shamatha* and *vipashyana* allows one to see things more clearly; 'the cultivation of the two together enables us to develop a mindfulness that is characterized by calmness and clarity, ... meditation ... grants the mindfulness two powerful aspects: acceptance and transformation' (Batchelor 2011: 163-164). Batchelor indicates how *shamatha*, which she terms concentration, and *vipashyana*, inquiry, bring forth acceptance and transformation which are all necessary in the process of refining Mindfulness (Grossman & Van Dam 2011: 223).

Sitting meditation is meant to be a practice of coming to stillness and thereby appreciating the present moment, the here and now, and relaxing mind and body by allowing and recognising what is taking place; 'whenever a feeling comes up, recognize it. Whenever a thought arises, identify it and recognize it' (Nhat Hanh 2009d: 10). The acceptance of what arises is vital in order to dissipate any sense of struggle or trying to meditate. There is a difference here between effort and application. Effort is not required in meditation as that would indicate doing in order to lead to non-doing which would be nonsensical. However, application is required in returning again and again to Mindfulness once one has noticed the mind has slipped away from it. Application is also required in practising a non-judgemental approach to one's Mindfulness so that instead of criticising oneself for having forgotten one rejoices that one has noticed and is therefore back with Mindfulness. It is one's personal diligence in the practices that reaps benefits in terms of being more mindful, no-one else can do it for one.

Nhat Hanh's practice of meditation includes concentration and insight as well (1992d: 135, note 2) as it is the insight expressed in the sitting practice that informs action taken which Nhat Hanh formulated in his articulation of *meditation in action* whilst in Vietnam (see Chapter 3). There is a danger, however, of seeing sitting meditation as 'just ... sitting and breathing in and out' without recognising the next step of 'observing what's going on in your body and mind' (Nhat Hanh 2009d: 10). Looking deeply is crucial for the sitting meditation to be of value rather than just being a lovely experience of retreating from the world for a while, yet I do not surmise it is always apparent in the practice at Plum Village. It has led to criticisms of Nhat Hanh's practice that one is only required to breathe and smile and that sitting meditation is not taken seriously (SI, Person 15 2009).

However, this fundamental teaching is based on the *Anapanasati Sutta* which Nhat Hanh recommends as crucial to the practice of meditation along with the *Satipatthana Sutta* (Nhat Hanh 1992a: 19). With these *sutra*s it is vital one follows the whole practice rather than just staying with the awareness of breathing which, at times, can seem like all one is being asked to do; 'mindful breathing is the basis of mindfulness practice. When we practice mindful breathing, we bring our mind back to our body and establish our true presence' (Nhat Hanh 2010e: 35). 'Most meditation teachers recommend some samatha at the outset: Westerners in particular have lively minds that need some calm and restfulness' (Shaw 2009: 30), however, in my experience there is so much emphasis on the stopping and calming aspect of meditation, especially with regard to concentrating on the breathing, that it was some time before I realised Nhat Hanh's teaching of meditation also included *vipashyana*. This could be an area that needs examining for Plum Village, to check what is being conveyed to its retreatants.

Two interviewees indicated that in other Buddhist traditions a formal practice of sitting meditation is the main focus, with several hours a day devoted to this practice (SI, Person 15 2009; Person 24 2010), yet the emphasis is different at Plum Village because Nhat Hanh teaches that any practice can be regarded as a meditation if Mindfulness is brought to bear on the activity.

> Walking meditation, sitting meditation, or listening to the bell are all the means to practice in order to reach peace, joy and liberation. But if we are just doing these things and we don't feel happy, it means that all of these things are just

forms and words. They don't benefit us at all and we in turn can't benefit others (Nhat Hanh 2007e: 98).

The employment of Mindfulness in these activities is paramount in ensuring they do not become stale or repetitive and this will be further discussed in later sections.

In introducing this next point it must be noted that much of the interviewee data for this section is based on their experiences and my own field research mainly from the Summer Retreats. Other retreats throughout the year at Plum Village, which tend to be more formal, will have a programme that includes an evening as well as morning sitting meditation. At Plum Village the longest period for a sit is about forty-five minutes followed by reading a *sutra* or chanting and for two interviewees this is not enough; 'I would have preferred if there was more time to practise Mindfulness meditation in a formal way in that we would sit together in the hall and be guided in meditation' (SI, Person 24 2010);

> it bothers me that ... there isn't really much emphasis on formal meditation practice now ... there's actually ... frequently no more than forty minutes a day at sitting meditation and ... I'm sad that they've stopped doing that and I certainly hear a lot of laypeople commenting on that. So I actually wrote to Thay and said I don't think this is a good thing ... I know some of the monastics are worried about that as well ... they've kind of moved towards doing more outside walking and maybe sitting and looking at the view, whatever, but it doesn't have the same quality of concentration ... it doesn't give the same quality of concentration that ... sitting doing *Zazen*[46] can have. So it's become ... more a beginner's practice (SI, Person 17 2010).

Person 25 also noted, in a non-critical way, '... we don't spend a lot of time meditating' (SI, 2009). Whilst these viewpoints represent only 8% of the interviews I consider them to be raising an important

---

[46] *Zazen* is the Zen Buddhist term to describe sitting meditation.

point. Plum Village is known for its 'joy and light-heartedness' (SI, Person 6 2010) and 'light structure' (SI, Person 22 2011; Person 29 2009) yet this could be interpreted as pandering to newcomers to the practice who may find it difficult to sit for long periods. From what Person 17 says it appears Plum Village used to practice more sitting and whilst Nhat Hanh deliberately terms other practices as meditations, in order to emphasise the mindful aspect that can be applied to them, I concur with Person 17's statement that there is a different quality to them. It could be a timetabling issue as the evenings on a Summer Retreat are taken up with presentations that are important in introducing people to the practices, but this could suggest that the Summer Retreat weeks are only for newcomers and not necessary for people used to the practices. Conversely, I recommend that those conversant in this tradition are valuable in supporting newcomers in the practices. It could be that if one has been practising in this tradition for a while it is assumed that one will be responsible for one's own practice and find time to meditate as a personal practice. However, this is not the same as sitting with hundreds of others in a guided meditation. Although Nhat Hanh's gentle approach suits many laypeople whose busy lifestyle cannot accommodate several hours a day of sitting meditation even some first-timers to Plum Village expected a more formal approach with more meditation (SI, Person 6 2010; Person 11 2009). Given that five interviewees including a *Dharmacharya* expressed a notable lack of sitting meditation Plum Village may need to review their timetable to include a second sitting practice each day during the Summer Retreat, as takes place on other retreats throughout the year.

A further point is that 'very little teaching [of sitting meditation] ... actually goes on ... I'm not sure I've ever had any instruction for sitting, or I'm not sure I've ever discussed meditation in a *Dharma* discussion group' (SI, Person 3 2011). Whilst Person 3 found this a welcome change from the 'rigidity' she had experienced in a Soto Zen tradition she did find it 'puzzling to begin with' although she came to appreciate 'it's more about finding out, there are some very loose boundaries and you find out what suits you within that ... I think that's quite unusual really in our society' (SI, Person 3 2011).

As retreatants sometimes come from different Buddhist traditions, as in Person 3's case, or are new to sitting meditation I propose clear directions about posture and the process of meditation need to have more emphasis, otherwise one could be practising all sorts of things, supposing one is following Nhat Hanh's direction without really being sure.

In other Buddhist traditions, for example Tibetan practices, meditation can only be learnt through a close teacher-pupil relationship (Trungpa 1991: 126). The same relationship is not evident at Plum Village although currently everyone has a close affiliation with Nhat Hanh. This, however, is patently not the same as a one-to-one interview with one's teacher on how the practice of meditation is progressing. Meditation is offered through guided meditations and encouragement to rest one's attention on the breath as it enters and leaves the body. This approach encourages one to be responsible for one's own practice rather than relying on the impetus from an outsider. Furthermore, *Theravada* retreats of up to three weeks are completely silent aside from 'private interviews with the retreat leader' (Bluck 2008: 28). A close one-to-one interview is not part of the Plum Village tradition although it could be requested if needed and will be further considered in section 5:7. Another aspect of Plum Village somewhat different to other Buddhist retreats is the application of silence, which will be examined next.

5:2:2 Silence

A major part of the day on a retreat is taken in silence, termed Noble Silence, from 9pm each evening (or the end of evening meditation if there is one) until after breakfast the following day, and at mealtimes. It is not an imposed silence, but one that the community consents to, as described by one of the interviewees,
> it's not an uncomfortable silence, it's silence where everyone else is practising and it's not a silence that can't be broken if necessary if you want to ask something. I think it's very helpful to have that space. There isn't much opportunity for silence really in daily life so it's a gift ... to share it out. I

think that's the benefit. It takes a while to get used to, but once I got used to it I really appreciated it (SI, Person 12 2009).

Katherine's reflection that silence can take some getting used to echoes other interviewees' viewpoints, that '... many adults ... are very scared of silence, are frightened and unable to deal with it' (SI, Person D 2010); the '... vast amounts of silence [can be] ... very nourishing as well as being difficult ... challenging' (SI, Person 13 2010); 'I think it can also be quite oppressive if people are not familiar with it' (SI, Person 17 2010). Whilst there is an understanding from the interviewees that silence nourishes and heals (SI, Person C 2010) there is also recognition that it can lead to '... odd social dynamics [and] ... can create some kind of difficulties' if one hasn't had the chance to speak to one's roommates during the day (SI, Person 20 2010). Likewise, Person 4's experience with her Unit is, 'in the Sangha you don't always get to know people because although you communicate with them in silence, you don't get to find things out about them' (SI, 2010). Whilst this observation specifically relates to the Unit it is also relevant to the retreat experience. Although the main point of a retreat is not to socialise some people can find it difficult spending time living closely with others and not getting to know personal details about their life, home situation, family or work because of the periods of silence.

The purpose of silence on a retreat is to be with oneself and notice the thought patterns that can play without one being aware; 'silence is something that comes from your heart, not from outside. Silence doesn't mean not talking and not doing things; it means that you are not disturbed inside, there is no talking inside' (Nhat Hanh 2009a: 76). Several interviewees appreciated the value of Noble Silence in helping '... us recognise the extent to which we can get sucked out of ourselves, out of our awareness through chatting to people' (SI, Person 22 2011) and giving a valuable opportunity to '... look at your own thoughts and your own emotions, ... because it's so easy to go from thinking about something to speaking and not really have an opportunity to reflect on what thoughts are actually ... in our own

heads' (SI, Person 24 2010). Monk A reflected Nhat Hanh's words in denoting,
> for me it's more in the silence of the mind versus silence of the mouth, of speech. I tend to think a lot, so I appreciate the Noble Silence time in the schedule, that helps remind me that I can stop thinking, at least for this period, or think less so that I can be ... calm, just relax instead of constantly thinking, because ... thinking is also working, working in your head all day. So I think Noble Silence is very good, it's a crucial part of the time (SI, 2010).

Noble Silence can seem, at times, quite the opposite to silence because although it is free from external sounds and noise one becomes more acutely aware of the constant thinking that can take place. Person 16 denoted,
> ... usually the critical mind comes into play immediately, who do I like the look of? Who am I interested in? Who is sharing my opinion? Or whatever, but by having Noble Silence on that retreat I only met these people non-verbally and it actually, it disables the critical mind (SI, 2010).

This indicates the level of distraction that one can use in one's daily life to cover what is taking place in the mind, television or radios being increasingly relevant here (SI, Person 28 2011). Nhat Hanh suggests watching television can be particularly toxic because it is a habit one can easily slip into without being aware of the consequences of sitting for hours ingesting whatever is on the screen (1995: 13-14; 2003a: 80-82; Nhat Hanh & Cheung 2010: 156-159). If used in an unmindful way it can become a cover that one uses to avoid silence. On a retreat one cannot so easily escape silence and therefore whilst appreciating its good qualities it can also be something people find difficult to cope with as discussed above. Person 3 further emphasised this point by indicating,
> the first time I ever went on retreat [in a different Buddhist tradition] ... and we had some silence overnight, and I hated it, I just thought this was such an imposition and I railed against it ... and I felt told what to do, ... but ... I matured, luckily, and ... I began to appreciate ... that silence is

needed in order to digest the richness that you experience during the day (SI, 2011).

Therefore whilst accepting Noble Silence can present difficulties retreatants are prepared to work with this, acknowledging it as another practice. The Plum Village community are aware of this difficulty for some people and offer periods of silence without imposing it throughout the whole day. For Person 10 it has enabled her to '... become a lot quieter person, and I come from a culture, ... from a Jewish background, where people talk a lot and certainly in the States, if you had a group of people together, it would be considered impolite to be silent, and people would feel obliged to fill the space' (SI, 2010). This suggests one reason retreatants could be initially uncomfortable with the silence, as it is unusual for daily life and not part of one's cultural norm.

The periods of silence are intended to provide space for one to notice thought patterns that can appear to be constant. Person D felt that compared to *vipashyana* retreats, which are silent the whole time, Plum Village has both positive and negative elements to its silence. Although having only periods of silence means the retreat is accessible for young children, there is an aspect to a *vipashyana* retreat of having to stay with the 'garbage' that is coming up, 'whereas in Plum Village you can move away from it because you start to get engaged in a conversation' (SI, 2011). Even here, Person D has experienced being able to distract oneself by falling into a habit energy of chat even if it is a better quality of conversation than one may partake in at home. This demonstrates one cannot assume that the practice is easy just because one is with the *Sangha*, yet it becomes easier because of the communal energy. Furthermore, it is important to realise that in Plum Village,
> you [are] still allowed to look at people, or smile at people ... I didn't have to ignore people to be silent with them. And it feels very nice when your friend looks at you, smiles and then you both carry on with eating or walking or doing what you're doing (SI, Sue 2010).

The silence is not for retreating into oneself or one's thoughts, but another means of recognising the interbeing aspect of humanity that goes beyond casual conversation and niceties.

With the space provided on a retreat, both physically and mentally, one can notice the habit energies that one forms in order to create a separate existence. It is the mental space that is important because this can get overlooked in one's day-to-day living and silence can give '… me ownership of my own thoughts' (SI, Person 27 2010), allowing one to '… be aware of what's going on … in our minds' (SI, Monk B 2010). Therefore silence can also be a '… gentle space that we inhabit, and … a supportive practice' (SI, Person 6 2010).

The aim of the Plum Village retreat programme is to help individuals recognise that in silence one can become aware of the interconnectedness of all beings and appreciates their similarities; that knowing the shallow details of someone's life can highlight differences between people rather than bringing them closer together. Although Person 4 expressed earlier some difficulty with not getting to know people because of the silence (SI, 2010) I propose there can alternatively be benefits to this in that one becomes less involved with the usual mental activities of one's daily life and can be more open to experience interbeing. Nonetheless, friendships are formed on retreats and these can survive going back to one's everyday life and having to communicate by email or phone rather than face to face. The friendships formed here are informed by the harmony discussed earlier in this chapter and the understanding of interbeing where one can appreciate unity rather than diversity. Another practice that can be equally transformational is walking meditation, the mindful practice with which Nhat Hanh is perhaps most renowned which I will now examine.

5:2:3 Walking meditation

There are two forms of walking meditation practised at Plum Village, both of which are silent. The first, *Kinh Hanh*, is a very slow processional walk practised indoors after sitting meditation around the cushions in the meditation hall. The second form is usually performed outdoors and whilst being gentle is not as slow as *Kinh Hanh*.[47] On an outdoor walking meditation Nhat Hanh often stops half way and sits to enjoy the scenery and the company. It is this second practice that I will concentrate on here. Walking meditation is 'walking not in order to arrive, just for walking, to be in the present moment, and to enjoy each step' (Nhat Hanh 2004a: 123). It is another means of being present whilst performing an activity rather than in order to achieve something. Nhat Hanh uses this way of walking wherever he is going (2002a: 4) and thoroughly recommends it; 'we walk slowly, massaging the Earth and planting seeds of joy and happiness with each step, and following the breathing ... we arrive with each step' (Nhat Hanh 1992e: 43). Whether one is only taking a few steps or walking to catch a plane or bus, walking with awareness can be practised.

It is palpable in the way Nhat Hanh enters the *Dharma* hall and progresses across the room to begin a *Dharma* talk. He is completely present with each step and exudes peacefulness and presence as he walks,
> you could see that he really embodied the teaching that he talks about so much in his books and his videos which is to be mindful and to walk in a mindful way. So he walked ... slowly up to the front and began with some silence and ... it's not so much ... the content of what he was saying but the way he was walking ... that really had an effect on me (SI, Person 24 2010).

---

[47] In *Kinh Hanh* one takes one footstep per in-breath and one footstep per out-breath. The outdoor walking meditation is paced to incorporate approximately three steps per in-breath and three or four steps per out-breath.

From my field research walking meditation can be a powerful practice especially if the slowness of it is something one is unused to. As with the silence it provides space in the mind to notice what is taking place. One can recognise how often one takes a walk being so busy in the mind that nothing is noticed about where one is walking or what one is walking on or through. Person 22's experience of walking meditation was transformational,

> I also learned walking meditation is really amazing practice in its own right, it's not a kind of funny spin-off from sitting meditation. We did lots of walking meditation and I grew to really love that ... and also at times some of us from my home [Family] group went off and did some walking meditation ourselves and I was ... very touched by that. I think they were some of the moments when I was most affected by the retreat and I could feel some of the transformation taking place within me. For example ... I had an experience of ... getting a sense of what it was like to be in the world if you were not as ... able-bodied as most people. I think there were one or two people who had some disabilities on the walking meditation and I could feel a deep sense of compassion for them and I could feel my slightly constrained heart was opening a bit, that's both a little bit painful and very kind of beautiful and good (SI, 2011).

Practices such as walking meditation can evoke a powerful reminder of the depth of Mindfulness one experienced on retreat as discussed by two interviewees, who found their practice of walking meditation at home enhanced by the visualization of practising with Nhat Hanh and the monastics (SI, Person 28 2011; Person 24 2010), reflecting the aspect of *remembering* from Nhat Hanh's exposition of Mindfulness (subsection 2:1:5).

Although walking meditation is another chance to practice Mindfulness, it is also one of the few opportunities to be physically close to Nhat Hanh as he leads the walking meditations. He often invites children to hold his hand and walk with him and tangibly demonstrates the enjoyment of being with each step, transforming 'our walking path into a field for meditation' so that each step is taken in full awareness (Nhat Hanh 2009d: 13). Practising an activity that one regularly performs many times a day with Mindfulness allows one to appreciate and notice each moment rather than rushing to get somewhere. Nhat Hanh suggests, 'we walk all the time, but usually it's more like running. Our hurried steps print anxiety and sorrow on the earth. If we can take one step in peace, we can take two, three, four and then five steps for the peace and happiness of humankind and the Earth' (2009d: 13). Slowing down the speed with which one walks is a literal as well as a physical reminder to take one's time. The *gatha*[48] accompanying walking meditation denotes the times one walks without Mindfulness.

The mind can go in a thousand directions,
but on this beautiful path, I walk in peace.
With each step a gentle wind blows,
with each step a flower blooms[49] (Nhat Hanh 2006b: 55).

A further practice related to walking is exercise and this is greatly encouraged to balance the stillness of sitting meditation. Nhat Hanh and the monastics have devised a series of ten Mindful Movements (Nhat Hanh 2008d) based on Qi Gong exercises which are recommended after one has been sitting for some time and take place after the sitting meditation period. Alternatively one can choose Qi Gong, yoga or other exercises that will be offered by the monastics. This demonstrates the holistic nature of a retreat where every aspect of body and mind is taken into consideration and nurtured. A further occasion for reflecting on this is mindful eating.

---

[48] 'Gathas are short verses that we can recite during our daily activities to help us return to the present moment and dwell in mindfulness ... [they] are an essential part of Zen Buddhist tradition' (Nhat Hanh 2006b: 1).
[49] This final line alludes to a legend relating that when the Buddha was born he immediately took seven steps and in each footstep a lotus blossom sprung up (Nhat Hanh 1996: 55).

5:2:4 Eating meditation

Mindful eating gives a chance to appreciate one's relationship with food and become aware of the possible struggles that one has developed in terms of over-eating (Nhat Hanh & Cheung 2010) or simply being too busy to take the time to sit and enjoy a meal fully. The formal routine for eating mindfully, which includes silently queuing for food and eating in silence for the first twenty minutes of the meal, is intended to give space to appreciate the many elements that come together to provide one's plate of food. It can engender generosity by acknowledging the needs of others when one is serving oneself, ensuring one takes only a sufficiency and there is enough left for those queuing behind. It may also beget gratitude by appreciating what is being offered. Whilst there is a bounteous table of food from which one can choose many different items one can accept others in the world are not so fortunate (Nhat Hanh 2009d: 41). Additionally, having to wait until everyone is served[50] can develop one's patience as well as making sure that everyone in the community is taken care of.

In the practice of eating meditation Nhat Hanh encourages retreatants before eating to closely observe the food on the plate and notice its colours, textures and smells which brings one into contact with the actual food itself (2009d: 42) rather than a perhaps more usual approach of eating without noticing what one is consuming. Here is a chance to hold *an awareness of what the senses are receiving* (subsection 2:1:5). In this mindful state one may connect with where the food has come from and the many people and processes involved in delivering it to the table. The Five Contemplations[51] are recited

---

[50] At Plum Village one normally begins to eat once the table is full, rather than literally waiting for everyone to be served.
[51] 1) This food is a gift of the earth, the sky, numerous living being and much hard, loving work. 2) May we eat with mindfulness and gratitude so as to be worthy to receive this food. 3) May we recognise and transform unwholesome mental formations, especially our greed, and learn to eat with moderation. 4) May we keep our compassion alive by eating in such a way

aloud by one person before everyone begins eating to acknowledge the interbeing nature of the food, sun, soil, seed etc. and one's requirements for it to nourish body and mind.

Eating in silence can allow one to do only one thing at a time, just eat, and to be present with the eating. It also helps one appreciate the food, fully noticing what one is eating, and also when one has had sufficient. Silent eating, with an appreciation of the food, slows down the rate at which one eats allowing one to notice each taste, smell and texture and enjoy each mouthful rather than shovelling forkfuls until the plate is empty. This also means one tends to eat less because one is more aware of the amount being consumed. The silence also allows one to notice the community that one is eating with even without conversing with them; 'we "turn off" the talking sometimes in order to enjoy the food and the presence of one another' (Nhat Hanh 2009d: 43). This encourages the focus to go beyond oneself and one's thoughts and perceptions and be open to those around one. Being in silence is not an encouragement to daydream or to dwell on inner thoughts and feelings, but to be present with the situation and particularly with those one shares the silence with. After a period of silence, mindful conversation is invited which adds to the atmosphere of Mindfulness already created and does not detract from it, as '… talking to each other is a wonderful way to be in touch' (Nhat Hanh 2009d: 43). Person 27 found this a helpful balance and it took away the emphasis of feeling one had to make conversation (SI, 2010).

Person 18 discussed that on an early Plum Village retreat she found it alienating to eat alone and in silence (SI, 2010), but this has been addressed by the Plum Village community and one now eats in Family groups (see subsection 4:4:1) which means that whilst still in

---

that reduces the suffering of living beings, stops contributing to climate change, and heals and preserves our precious planet. 5) We accept this food so that we may nurture our sisterhood and brotherhood, build our Sangha and nourish our ideal of serving living beings (updated 2014).

silence one doesn't feel alone because of familiar faces. Furthermore Person 4 indicated the difficulty of practising this with a young child,

... eating is hard. I'm trying to make an effort to eat mindfully with [name], but it's difficult when all the time you're saying, "stay on your chair, etc", but we light a candle at mealtimes and sing something at either end. I try to do what Thay says about counting the number of chews, and I think if I can do that twice in a meal that's good (SI, 2010).

Person 4's comment emphasises that whilst one may endeavour to follow the Plum Village practices they are guidelines rather than imposed roles and it is for each individual to discover how they can apply these practices at home. As Nhat Hanh denotes, 'the first time you eat in silence, it may seem awkward, but after you get used to it, silent meals can bring a lot of peace, joy, and insight' (2009d: 43).

Here I have considered many aspects that, due to Mindfulness, all contribute to what in normal circumstances one pays little attention to which is the simple process of eating a meal. Most people eat two or three times every day, but how often does one actually notice and appreciate these distinct aspects? From my field research, when people partake of a meal in these circumstances, in the company of a *Sangha*, their experience of the food is greatly enhanced especially the taste of the food. One interviewee described it as being as if there was a magic sauce on the food (IC, Person H 2012). Nhat Hanh suggests that practising with others '... we begin to see our connection with other human beings ... Being with a Sangha can heal ... feelings of isolation and separation' (2009d: 69). Therefore, even a simple practice like eating meditation can engender the transformation of suffering into happiness.

5:2:5 Singing

Singing is an important aspect of expressing the teachings by another means and there are two forms of singing at Plum Village. The first is chanting by the monastics and the second is singing *gathas* relating to Nhat Hanh's teachings. Each meditation session is

In the Tradition of Thich Nhat Hanh

introduced with a chant, such as the Morning Chant (Nhat Hanh 2007b: 25) and each *Dharma* talk commences with one or two chants by the whole monastic community, beginning each retreat with *Namovalokiteshvara* (Nhat Hanh 2007b: 386). However, it is the second aspect I will focus on in this discussion. Often the gathering of people is brought together with songs before commencing the walking meditation. Whilst singing clearly cannot be practised in silence, like the *Dharma* sharing (discussed in subsection 5:4:1), Mindfulness can be applied in a different way by offering deep listening and loving speech so that 'the way we speak and listen can offer others joy, happiness, self-confidence, hope, trust, and enlightenment' (Nhat Hanh 2004a: 133).

The Plum Village Songbook, in which many of Nhat Hanh's teachings and verses have been set to music, sometimes to recognisable tunes, has been recently updated to include the same songs in English, French, and Vietnamese and at EIAB, German and Dutch. By this means everyone can participate and learn a little of each other's language through the medium of song. Several of the songs are *gathas* set to music reflecting the guided meditation practices such as;
Breathing in, breathing out,
breathing in, breathing out.
I am blooming as a flower,
I am fresh as the dew,
I am solid as a mountain,
I am firm as the earth,
I am free.

Songs such as this one are accompanied by gestures which, from my field research, I recognise some people can find childish, but this does mean everyone can join in whether or not one knows the words or language. The songs present a split reaction with people either loving or hating the simplicity of them.
Happiness is here and now,
I have dropped my worries,
nowhere to go, nothing to do,

no longer in a hurry.
Happiness is here and now,
I have dropped my worries,
somewhere to go, something to do,
but I don't need to hurry.

Some people find it difficult to sing words they are not experiencing such as 'I love you so', 'I am free'. In this instance I argue they are designed to 'assume a virtue if you have it not' (Shakespeare 1985: 1056) in that they encourage the feeling to arise by stating it. The songs acknowledge interbeing as a reality rather than theory and can open the heart and it may be for this reason that some people have difficulties with them particularly those who are not used to expressing themselves openly in such simple terms. Whilst none of the interviewees directly discussed the singing it is my experience that the songs can reinforce the mindful practices by the simple words and tunes being easily remembered and often sung. They can be a means of connecting directly through the heart rather than the mind and I propose there are other aspects of the Plum Village programme that also instil an emotional connection which will be discussed next.

5:3 Emotional connections

I suggest there are two aspects of Mindfulness at Plum Village towards which there is a particularly emotional connection, the bell and Nhat Hanh himself. Whilst it may seem obvious that Nhat Hanh is a person towards whom people can feel a very deep connection such as 'I have some sort of karma with Thay and he's been my teacher for many lifetimes' (SI, Person 15 2009), the bell as an inanimate object may not appear to stimulate such emotions. Yet it is recognised as 'the voice of the Buddha' (Nhat Hanh 2007a: 108) and thereby people can have a personal relationship with it. This will be examined first.

5:3:1 The bell

Of the twenty-five interviewees who were asked a specific question about the use of the bell all liked it very much and many experienced an emotional response to it that went beyond functionality. The bell is a *bodhisattva* 'the voice of the Buddha calling us back to ourselves ... It is not a Buddha from the outside. It is our own Buddha calling us' (Nhat Hanh 2007a: 108) meaning that it awakens one to the potential of Buddhahood within oneself. Only one person felt its role was to invoke an automatic response, rather like Pavlov's dogs (SI, Person 18 2010), but for others it is almost a living entity that can stir one out of forgetfulness and into the present moment.
One of the bell *gathas* denotes
Body, speech and mind in perfect oneness -
I send my heart along with the sound of the bell.
May the hearers awaken from forgetfulness
And transcend all anxiety and sorrow (Nhat Hanh 2006b: 45).
This speaks of a relationship between the bell and the hearer as it brings one out of forgetfulness, the opposite of Mindfulness; 'the bell is like a friend calling you back to the present moment ... an invention of practitioners to help us' (Nhat Hanh 2009a: 166-167). In this respect one invites 'the bell to sound - in my country we don't say "strike" or "hit" a bell' (Nhat Hanh 1995: 45). The bell is treated with reverence and respect 'before you invite the bell to sound you bow to the bell as a friend' (Nhat Hanh, *Dharma* talk 2010) in order to remind one of its important role in Mindfulness.

Two interviewees recognised a further relationship between the bell and silence,
> the sound is beautiful, secondly it's a reminder [to be mindful] and thirdly the actual quality of the sound itself 'cause it starts with the noise, but it gradually dissipates into the silence. And silence is such an important practice, a part of Mindfulness, so it embodies it really nicely (SI, Person 24 2010).

Likewise 'the bell reminds us that sound is important, but also silence is important and they ... are interconnected, the one is the other' (SI, Person 22 2011). The bell brings one to quietness both internally and externally as it initiates silence.

It also has a functional aspect of reminding
> there is a programme going on and ... in terms of the community ... trying to practise in harmony it's very helpful because it means there doesn't have to be someone telling other people what's going to happen or telling people to do something because the bell does that (SI, Person 7 2010).

Yet for the majority it is more than a practical instrument. The bell is a physical means of prompting Mindfulness in the daily routine and ensuring there are regular reminders to come back to oneself (see subsection 2:1:5). 'It's the main ... signal that helps us avoid unnecessary talking 'cause the bell can give you instructions once you understand the ... process. So you can let go of some of the wordiness and I think that's very helpful' (SI, Person 14 2010). It is an invitation to stop all activity for a few moments and come back to the breathing whatever has been taking place prior to its sounding. Whenever it is sounded the whole community stops and becomes still, whether this is mid-conversation, mid-work or mid-eating. It can be an awkward practice to undertake at first, especially if one is mid-conversation, yet the support of the community practising together enables one to accept the sound of the bell for what it is and allow it to work. It can be a simple yet powerful reminder of being able to drop whatever is running in the mind at that moment and come back to being.

One interviewee found the bell irritating to have to stop mid-sentence in the middle of something that may be important (SI, Person 25 2009). However, I suggest this is the point of the bell that it interrupts the thoughts and daydreams or whatever may be going on in the mind which one normally considers to be important or useful. This is not to suggest that there should be no thinking or all thinking is bad, yet with this practice one can see with detachment what is really taking place. Thus the bell serves a dual purpose of bringing one back to Mindfulness as well as reminding that something is about to happen. As the voice of the *Buddha* it has an emotive content denoting a relationship that goes beyond functionality.

Nhat Hanh intimates that anything can be a Mindfulness bell in a metaphorical sense, as it awakens one to the present moment; 'a serious illness can be a kind of mindfulness bell that starts our true practice and gives birth to our spiritual life' (Nhat Hanh 2009a: 129). 'Thay talks about using other things as bells, the phone ringing, the traffic light ... there's a sense in which that formal practice generalises into other areas of life where you can be reminded that ... you're not being mindful at the moment and can come back to it' (SI, Person 14 2010). In this respect one interviewee uses her church bells at home as Mindfulness bells; 'I think that's important, it does bring you back if you're starting to drift and if you're not it doesn't matter it helps you settle' (Person 8 2009). One can use different forms as a literal or metaphorical Mindfulness bell; it is quite common now to have a Mindfulness bell as an app on one's computer or phone set to go off randomly as 'a helpful aid to Mindfulness practice' (SI, Person 28 2011). Thus the literal practice of inviting the bell and listening to its sound can also be a figurative form as a means to bringing one back to the present moment, and Nhat Hanh encourages his students to find Mindfulness bells, whether they are a baby crying or a car alarm, '... to remind us to return to our conscious breathing' (2009d: 20). The next aspect of emotional connection I wish to examine is between Nhat Hanh and his students.

5:3:2 Thich Nhat Hanh

There is a deep connection to Nhat Hanh in everything that takes place at Plum Village not in an autocratic or oppressive way, but in that it is his creation and as such it revolves around him. This issue is further discussed in Chapter 7 in considering his continuation. It is common among those practising lay Buddhism in the West to experiment with possibly several groups from differing traditions before settling on the one they feel most comfortable with (Bluck 2006: 33) and 20% of the interviewees indicated they had found their path in Plum Village. Other interviewees used the expression of feeling one had 'come home' on discovering Nhat Hanh's teachings (SI, Person 21 2010; Person D 2011; Person 15 2009). This relates directly to his teaching 'I have arrived, I am home' (Nhat Hanh 2003c: 46) expressing the awakening to the present moment, the essence of Mindfulness.

He is the constant reference point to everything that occurs. The monastics directly quote his words and what he has written. Indeed, the mass of literature he has produced features heavily in the day to day running of the retreat, as another form of his teachings emphasising or reiterating the spoken word. I will discuss the issue of his books later after considering Nhat Hanh himself. As the instigator of Plum Village and initially the only monastic (although some of the original *Tiep Hien* members were with him) Nhat Hanh is the central point around which Plum Village revolves and the reason why thousands of people flock to retreats each year. Each formal meeting or *Dharma* sharing begins with an acknowledgement to *Dear Thay, dear Sangha* before proceeding. This is not to massage his ego but to acknowledge that he is the channel through which the teachings are made accessible to those present.

Four interviewees referred to his charismatic qualities (SI, Person 5 2009; Person 11 2009; Person 20 2010; Person 28 2011), and I will now examine what this means. From my field research I suggest he is regarded as having remarkable teaching abilities and able to hold an audience ranging in age from very young children right through the spectrum. It is perseverance that marks Nhat Hanh out as a remarkable leader; his skills are honed over seventy years of diligent practice of Mindfulness. His conscientious efforts have brought him to the stage of being revered by many people because he makes every aspect of his life a moment of Mindfulness and therefore is able to demonstrate to his students through his actions as well as his teachings. 'A living example often can have a stronger effect than thousands of theoretical teachings and rules' (Chan Khong 2007:

286). This is the aspect of Nhat Hanh's teachings that more than half of those interviewed are attracted to and find appealing. He is completely comfortable in his body and mind (SI, Person 4 2010), and embodies the teaching (SI, Person 6 2010; Person 9 2009) by practising Mindfulness every moment of the day. Six interviewees appreciated his teaching capabilities from their own perspective of being teachers themselves (SI, Person 6 2010; Person 7 2010; Person 10 2010; Person 16 2010; Person 17 2010; Person 24 2010); 'there's no gap between how he is and what he teaches ... there's a complete congruity between those two things' (SI, Person 17 2010).

Furthermore, he appears to speak personally to every one of the hundreds of students listening to a *Dharma* talk (SI, Person 14 2010). Four times a week Nhat Hanh offers a *Dharma* talk and these can last for two hours, where he speaks unscripted and without notes, offering the teaching from the position of residing in the practice; and emanating 'deep compassion and loving kindness' (SI, Person 22 2011). Once a week he offers an open Q&A where anyone can sit next to him and ask a question. When he is asked a question he gives it all of his attention and considers before giving an answer. He does not (in my limited experience) imply it is an unnecessary question although he may suggest it has been answered previously, and yet will still offer an answer. For Nhat Hanh this may be the only way he knows how to reply; yet for the individual asking the question it seems as if nothing matters more to him at that time than giving a full and appropriate answer. In the Q&A he delights in each question and relishes giving as full an answer as possible prompting interviewees to declare, 'it just feels like a huge privilege to be in the presence of such a great teacher' (SI, Person 3 2011); 'the quality of the way he simply describes things is superb, so to hear him talk is very special' (SI, Person 29 2009). At Plum Village there is a palpable air of gentleness, kindness, patience, perseverance and happiness that emanates from him and the other monastics and these are the qualities he wishes for his students to realise. However, gentleness is not to be equated with quietism in the sense of just accepting things without inquiry or consideration, it is Nhat Hanh's way of demonstrating nonviolence in every moment of life.

There could be a danger of admiration for Nhat Hanh turning into idolisation because of his charismatic nature. Although 'he's not teaching a practice that depends on him ... The practice is more important than the personality' (SI, Person 4 2010) people could attribute to him characteristics he does not possess. Nhat Hanh denotes 'people in the Western world suffer a great deal psychologically, and that is why many have become Buddhists, practicing meditation in order to solve psychological problems' (2007a: 49) and in a vulnerable state Nhat Hanh could appear like a redeemer who can answer all their problems. Is there a danger that whilst people are learning how to deal with their own suffering they confuse what he offers as general advice to be personal salvation? He has certainly never played this role or encouraged anyone to assume that position of him. Indeed, he was not a guru in search of disciples and it took him some time to acknowledge that the role of teacher-student was one he should be developing (Nhat Hanh 2003c: 25).

Given his personality and charismatic presence it is easy to be drawn to his charming character and the many qualities he possesses and compare oneself unfavourably to him. This is not due to the teachings per se, but to a perhaps natural reaction of doubt or inferiority that is due to one's personal habit energy. This is, however, recognised and addressed formally at the beginning of each *Dharma* talk with the words

> the Sangha is invited to go back to our breathing, so that the collective energy of Mindfulness can bring us together as an organism, flowing as a river with no more separation. Let the whole Sangha breathe as one body, chant as one body, listen as one body, transcending the frontiers of a delusive self, liberating ourselves from the inferiority complex, the superiority complex and the equality complex (unnamed monk, *Dharma* talks 2010).

The final words here can be perplexing but indicate that all notions should be let go of and also acknowledge the more subtle ideas that one can cling to which seem to be acceptable. Surely it is satisfactory to hold an idea of equality? This may be better than the two previous complexes, yet this is not about making everyone the same but acknowledging that there are differences. 'We suffer when we get caught in the complex of equality' (Trai Nghiem 2011: 27). The practice of Buddhism is to let go of all ideas, not to replace old ones with *better* ones. The *Buddha* used the analogy *the raft is not the shore*[52] to demonstrate how the practice of non-clinging applies to Buddhism itself 'the Buddha's teaching is not something to adhere to or cherish or possess' (Gowans 2003: 60) and this likewise applies to the Buddha himself as it does to Nhat Hanh. As discussed earlier, everything Nhat Hanh performs is a message of Mindfulness for his students. From my field research I propose he does not teach in order for people to like him or want to be with him he teaches in order for people to be free. If people adore Nhat Hanh it is useful only in drawing them closer to the practice so they can take it on board for themselves. He would not in any sense encourage adoration. Further issues relating to Nhat Hanh concern his calligraphy and his books and I shall address the issue of calligraphy first.

Whilst any iconography is deliberately simplistic and minimal in appearance much more in evidence is Nhat Hanh's calligraphy. Every room in Plum Village has several pieces, either formally framed or stuck to windows, and each serves as a reminder of why one is there. Mindfulness is the practice and the *gathas* are beautifully rendered and adorn the walls in several languages recognisable as Nhat Hanh's distinctive handwriting. He produces a prolific amount of calligraphy, small and large pieces, which are sold through the bookshop (for a minimum of £40) and have a further purpose of raising funds for the Vietnamese charities[53] which Plum Village supports. The calligraphies are designed to be another type of Mindfulness bell, yet is there a danger of his calligraphy becoming idolised, becoming necessary pieces of adornment for people to take

---

[52] MN 22.13

[53] Sr Chan Khong is instrumental in raising funds for charities that are operating in Vietnam providing much needed funds for hungry children in particular.

home? As with his books I find the potential cupidity for such pieces at odds with the path he presents. Even here one has to be aware of mindful consumption. Nhat Hanh has written over a hundred books and the bookshop at Plum Village sells them in many different languages. He himself refers to particular books during his *Dharma* talks and the bookshop is open immediately the talk ends. On sale are also DVDs of previous *Dharma* talks, chanting, songs, t-shirts and other clothing.

One could also question whether the purchase of books is feeding Westerners' acquisitive and materialistic nature and playing to the need to have something concrete for the money being spent rather than asking for *dana* (donations). Is it the case that in acquiring a handful of books to take home one's conscience is somehow soothed; one can spend freely in the knowledge that the profits are being put to good use? Or does this promote greed because one can take a piece of Nhat Hanh home in his written words? A further matter of concern is that the bookshops sell virtually nothing but Nhat Hanh's books or the occasional book by a member of the community, yet is only just starting to include books on the wider realm of Buddhism from other authors. Although the library at Plum Village has a wide-ranging source of books incorporating many different traditions and religions this is not reflected in the bookshop, which is the focus of attention on retreats. Whilst teaching inclusivity through interbeing the almost exclusive promotion of his books in the bookshop is at odds here. The promotion of other Mindfulness teachers –Buddhist or not – and poetry would not be harmful to the clear message that emanates from Plum Village. It can also seem at odds with the ethos of a retreat for Nhat Hanh to be promoting his own books.

However, there are several genuine reasons for the bookshop that are not associated with materialistic acquiring. All the profits go to Vietnam to support charities in that country and Nhat Hanh and the monastics have no qualms about promoting sales that will benefit Vietnam. Furthermore, this is where his teachings exist and the books are written in an open and accessible way; accurately reflecting Nhat Hanh's own words. He is assuring his continuation through his books by fully applying his writing talent and making his teachings available to as wide an audience as possible not just those who are fortunate enough to attend a retreat. Indeed, it is usually the group of monastics who edit his books that make the decision about publishing a new one, not Nhat Hanh himself.

For many of the people who attend retreats, whether those new to Buddhism or more practised, his books are often their first introduction to his teachings and the reason they investigate further. They can also provide a useful introduction to friends and family at home as people often share books with others. Likewise, the calligraphies have the dual purpose of being a reminder of the practice once one is back home as well as sending necessary funds to the charities in Vietnam. Both the books and calligraphies are a connection to Nhat Hanh as well as a means of making sense of his teachings and implementing them into one's daily life. They can be seen as another form of Mindfulness bell. As discussed in subsection 2:1:5 having reminders of the practice back home is a helpful aspect of Mindfulness. The next aspect of the discussion focuses on the means of creating an intimate atmosphere on a retreat, something that is valuable among hundreds of people.

5:4 A familial atmosphere

A familial atmosphere is engendered at Plum Village by the care taken to ensure an intimate situation, and secondly by implementing practices that deal with conflict resolution. Here I review the Family group, examine Beginning Anew as a process of conflict resolution and discuss the ecumenical aspect of Plum Village.

5:4:1 Family *Dharma* sharing group

This subsection discusses not only the social formation of a Family Group, but also the meaning of *family* in the wider context as it applies to Plum Village. It is instituted through the familial terms of brother and sister in the way monastics speak to one another and their lay visitors; it is represented by the role of father and mother that have been taken up by Nhat Hanh and Sr Chan Khong and it is demonstrated through the acceptance and encouragement of children with family-friendly retreats.

Nhat Hanh has deliberately implemented the family model at Plum Village by using the familial terms of uncle and aunt etc. to address one another and thereby reaffirm relationships between people; employing the natural rapport that exists in family situations to include and nourish everyone (Nhat Hanh 1992e: 106-7). Familial relations are adopted of elder and younger brother and sister, referring not to age but to experience of practice, and emphasises a natural atmosphere that has no sexual overtones. This is not a group of disparate individuals who happen to be in the same location, but a community living and working together creating a family situation in order to demonstrate to retreatants that harmony and conflict resolution within a family is possible. This is further addressed in subsection 5:4:2. The sense of Plum Village as a family is also accentuated by the role of Sr Chan Khong alongside Nhat Hanh. She has worked closely with him since 1959 and is the force behind many of the projects set up by Plum Village supporting charities in Vietnam. They are perceived as the mother and father of the community (IC, Person F 2011) roles that have arisen organically rather than intentionally. Sr Chan Khong offers personal consultations to individuals during a retreat taking care of the emotional realm while Nhat Hanh nurtures the reasoning side through his teachings. Together, they provide the holistic care that a mother and father offer to their family and it will be interesting to see whether these roles are continued with different monastics once they have passed on.

Furthermore, in this family-oriented setting children are welcome and accepted as part of the retreat. They are not considered to be a nuisance, instead they are acknowledged as the future generation with 'a unique role in awakening the community [because they] ... are looked upon as persons who already know something about being truly mindful' (Sawatsky 2009: 229 &188). This makes their inclusion on the retreat a necessity for the continuation of Plum Village. From the age of six they are offered a specific programme which involves them attending the *Dharma* talk for a short while at the beginning during which time the teachings are specifically aimed at them. Afterwards they follow their own programme. Likewise, teenagers and young adults (Wake Up movement) have separate programmes that run parallel to the adults, sometimes merging. These separate programmes indicate the investment Nhat Hanh perceives in encouraging youngsters to be part of a retreat. These are the ones to take forward the teachings and continue them in the future.

Although parents with children under the age of six are encouraged to bring their offspring, they remain in the care of the parents, there is no programme offered for them. While this caused difficulty for one interviewee I suggest this is an apposite approach as the monastics and laypeople who care for the older children are volunteers, but for younger children this would be inappropriate and qualified nursery nurses would be required. Plum Village cannot cater to everyone's needs and it is perhaps a small price to pay that parents adjust their participation on retreats until their children are six or older, or work closely with other parents to balance the children's needs with attending the *Dharma* talks.

More than one third of the interviewees perceived the acceptance of children as one of the unique aspects and a positive part of the retreat experience. Nhat Hanh is encouraging towards them, having them close by when he leads a walking meditation. The open and relaxed atmosphere of a retreat allows for the inclusion of children to be an easy decision and parents are grateful that the option of the children's programme allows them to partake in the retreat themselves (SI, Person 23 2011). All retreatants are likewise taken care of through the organisation of Family groups.

On a retreat that may involve more than nine hundred people across four hamlets Family groups are arranged of about twenty people with whom one will spend much time. The Family is usually accommodated together, has the same job and sits together each afternoon for a *Dharma* sharing.[54] This is the nub of the retreat for many people, facilitated either by two or three monastics or a senior (in terms of experience in the practice, not age) layperson. The Family group provides a small unit of people one can associate with and turn to for help, advice or community, offering a sense of belonging amid the hundreds of other retreatants. 'The heart of the practice is the *Dharma* sharing ... and certainly we created a space whereby people could share very deeply, both personally and from the heart, their difficulties and troubles, their life and their practice and that creates very strong bonds' (SI, Person 22 2011).

Although nominated leaders lead the *Dharma* sharing sessions their role is facilitator, not one who has all the knowledge and provides the answers. A person can present a question to the Family within the sanctity of the *Dharma* sharing and may or may not receive an answer. The answer could come from anyone within the Family not just the facilitator. The *Dharma* sharing operates on the assumption either that the knowledge is present within the group, or that the questioner may discover the answer for himself or herself in time. This type of sharing is not for those who want to be told what to do, or be presented with a specific plan to which they adhere. The Plum Village Model (see section 5:6) in this situation provides opportunities for one to discover for oneself on the basis that what works for one person may not be right for another and also that what may be appropriate for one situation may not be useful in another.

---

[54] The *Dharma* sharing 'is an opportunity to benefit from each other's insights and experience of the practice ... a special time for us to share our ... joys ... difficulties, and our questions relating to the practice of mindfulness' (Nhat Hanh 2009d: 106).

One interviewee, who has practised with several other traditions and for a while became a nun in Thailand, suggests the concept of *Dharma* sharing is unique to Plum Village, 'I haven't come across [it] in the same way in any other tradition' (SI, Person D 2011).

The crux of a *Dharma* sharing is deep speaking and listening so that both the person speaking and those listening are enabled to hear what is coming from the heart. This is facilitated in a formal way in that the person wishing to speak bows to the group to indicate this. Whilst they are speaking no one can interrupt them. Once they have finished they bow again and it is recommended that one takes a minimum of three breaths before the next person speaks. Indeed, if one wishes to respond to something another has said one is counselled to wait until someone else has spoken rather than immediately replying with what may be an automatic response. Although this method of sharing is rather formal I suggest it is necessary as it sets out a clear format that is apparent to everyone and easy to follow. It assists the practice of deep listening through Mindfulness by hearing what is actually being said without having to think of a response.

This method of facilitation rather than autocratic leadership is practised by Nhat Hanh and emulated by the monastics and lay teachers. It is an indication of the subtlety in different approach between East and West (see Chapter 1) which employs a non-discursive rather than assertive methodology (Krus & Blackman 1980: 951). Nhat Hanh synthesises the best of both worlds by accepting democracy from a Western ideology and combining it with the Eastern approach of negotiation rather than a didactic approach; 'I have learnt over the past thirty years not to use my authority as a teacher to resolve conflicts. We have to use awakened understanding and love' (Nhat Hanh 2003c: 28). In his tradition the senior abbot made the decisions which everyone was expected to abide by (Nhat Hanh 2003e: 72), but Nhat Hanh realised this approach is not the most useful in dealing with many people, especially in recommending an approach where one's own experience is utilised rather than relying on knowledge passed down by elders. Therefore, 'at Plum Village we combine the principles of seniority and democracy so that everyone in the community has the right to offer their experience and ideas' (Nhat Hanh 2003e: 72).

As stated earlier, the basis for this working is deep speaking and listening. The faculty of deep listening, whether it is to oneself or another, alongside confidentiality allows people to address what may have been a burden in their heart for a long time. It also allows one to hear another's point of view without the criticism or commenting that may normally take place especially if this is an opposing point of view. This practice is employed equally on Summer retreats as well as specific retreats, such as for Palestinians and Israelis (Nhat Hanh 2004a: 133-136).

Through the confidentiality of the *Dharma* sharing healing within oneself can begin to take place by allowing one to see more clearly perceptions one is holding onto. The process of reconciliation can also begin, even with a person who is not present, just by examining the stance one is holding onto that may get in the way of hearing what the other person is actually saying. This is not to assume that one side is wrong and the other right, indeed, these dualistic ways of thinking are not appropriate in this setting where interbeing is the basis as discussed previously. If one person takes up the position of being right it automatically assumes the other is wrong and this inevitably creates conflict whether on a small or large scale. In a conflict situation Nhat Hanh proposes recognising both parties suffer and thereby one can begin to '... look at the other person with the eyes of compassion ... and communication is possible' (2004a: 49). Despite the aim towards a harmonious community conflicts inevitably arise and a process of Beginning Anew has been developed to address this.

5:4:2 Beginning Anew ceremony

Beginning Anew has been instigated at Plum Village as a means of attempting to restore relations when communication breaks down. This is the community's approach to problems that arise among people living so closely together. These are not to be shied away from, but addressed openly from the viewpoint that there may be a wrong perspective being held which leads to misunderstanding. In situations such as these it is crucial that matters are addressed openly. One interviewee lived at Plum Village as a layperson for four years and recognises 'it wasn't always easy ... living in a community of people, all dynamics, but being with people trying to really practise ... made it easier, certainly a rich experience' (SI, Person 21 2010). Beginning Anew is a weekly practice at Plum Village because 'the health and happiness of the whole community depends on the harmony, peace, and joy that exist between everyone' (Nhat Hanh 2009d: 72).

Similar to *Dharma* sharing, the formality of the practice is that everyone sits in a circle with a vase of flowers in the centre. Calling it a ceremony signifies the importance with which the community regards it. When someone wishes to speak they bow and then collects the vase and hold onto it while they are speaking; during this period no one can interrupt them. 'The ceremony has three parts: flower watering, expressing regrets and expressing hurts and difficulties. This practice can prevent feelings of hurt from building up over the weeks and helps make the situation safe for everyone in the community' (Nhat Hanh 2004a: 141). It begins by expressing the positive attributes of the others present and may be directed at one person or several people, continues with apologising for one's unskilful behaviour that may have hurt others and concludes by voicing situations when one has been hurt by another's words or actions. The essence of these three aspects '... is to restore love and understanding between members of the community ... Loving speech is crucial. We want to heal the community, not harm it. We speak frankly but we do not want to be destructive' (Nhat Hanh 2010e: 170).

By employing all three aspects the process reaches a conclusion in which any aspect of hurt or difficulty has been addressed. In the *Dharma* sharing that takes place between Family groups it may be that only the flower watering aspect is needed because in a week there may have not been any problems created, but within the long-term community the further two aspects are essential in clearing the air and not allowing problems to linger. As with other aspects of the programme this ceremony is dealt with in a gentle yet open way that allows all present to feel any difficulties have been addressed and nothing is being held on to. Person 22 recognised within the monastics a sense of joyfulness despite it not all being 'sweetness and light, as in any community, you know the first rule is there will be conflict and how to handle that but I thought the way they lived and the way they demonstrated the practice was very inspiring, very good to be around, very open-hearted' (SI, 2011).

Beginning Anew is the means of addressing conflict in the community but, as has been demonstrated in earlier sections, the whole ethos of Mindfulness that pervades Plum Village is aiming in the direction of a harmonious community. It can also be practised in a less formal way between two individuals and is jokingly recognised that if someone invites another for a cup of tea this is in fact leading to Beginning Anew (IC, Monk E 2012). Each retreat includes a presentation about Beginning Anew before a chance to practise within the Family group. This introduction is to demonstrate the possibility of employing the practice at home with family members or work colleagues, emphasising the aspect of *engaging with the world* (subsection 2:1:5).

As these two subsections have demonstrated the implementation of the Family group as well as the practice of Beginning Anew are the key means of introducing the possibility of a harmonious community to retreatants. Harmony and reconciliation are not synonyms for trying to avoid conflict or suppress it; the aim is to firstly accept it then look deeply at how it can be transformed into peaceful coexistence and Beginning Anew plays a crucial role in conflict resolution. It is a testament to the efforts and hard work by all who practise at Plum Village guided by Nhat Hanh as the paradigm that this has succeeded for thirty-two years. The next aspect of Plum Village I shall consider is a metaphorical sense.

5:5 Plum Village as a metaphor

> If you come to Plum Village for one day, you have an idea about Plum Village, but the idea isn't really Plum Village. You might say, "I've been to Plum Village," but in fact you've only really been to your idea of Plum Village. Your idea might be slightly better than that of someone who has never been there, but it's still only an idea. It's not the true Plum Village. Your concept or perception of reality is not reality. When you are caught in your perceptions and ideas, you lose reality (Nhat Hanh 1999d: 55).

What is Plum Village? As Nhat Hanh suggests here, and Shakespeare recognised (1985: 912), the name can create many ideas attached to it[55] which tell one little or nothing about the form. Plum Village is a place where people practise Pure Land Buddhism without it being named as such. People may not even be aware that this is what they are practising (Laity 2003: 9). What does it mean to be a Pure Land? It can be, as discussed in Chapter 3 regarding the lay practitioners in Vietnam, a sense of a future perfection where everything is lovely, peaceful and happy and there are no defilements, wars or poverty; some may liken it to heaven. Yet Nhat Hanh teaches the Pure Land is to be found 'now or never' (2003b: 11). It is the present moment when one awakens to the being-ness of now, not a future idea that one is striving towards.

'What is the Pure Land if it is not a place where conditions for the spiritual practice are ideal so we can quickly realize the Buddha nature?' (Laity 2003: 8). In terms of Plum Village ideal means a place of practice where everyone else is also practising which makes one's own endeavours all the easier. Its primary function for a layperson is a place for people to retire from the world in order to refresh oneself to return back into society. This may only be a brief

---

[55] "What's in a name? That which we call a rose
By any other name would smell as sweet." Romeo and Juliet (II, ii, 1-2).

respite, one week, but if one takes the opportunities of practising mindfully it is enough to return refreshed and reinvigorated. Its atmosphere is conducive for practice and self-discovery which one cannot hope to emulate at home except perhaps through the Unit meetings. Pure in this setting means not being polluted by afflictions (Nhat Hanh 2003b: 64) or suffering that one is normally attached to at home. It is not a place of no-suffering but it is a place where there is more than suffering, where one can be detached from and appreciate suffering without being hurt by the second arrow[56] of attachment to the suffering (Nhat Hanh 1992c: 433).

Plum Village can also be what Knott terms 'an imagined space, alive in the minds and hearts of devotees, poets, artists' (2005b: 13). As well as a geographical location it becomes an idealistic metaphor for those who have yet to visit and a bell of Mindfulness for those who have been. It can serve as a powerful reminder when practising at home; it can take one back to a vivid memory of a walking meditation with Nhat Hanh or some other poignant practice (SI, Person 16 2010; Person 24 2010; Person 28 2011); 'when you walk you can still be in Plum Village ... you can ... recreate that for yourself' (SI, Person 6 2010). This aspect of metaphor was recognised by one interviewee who echoes Knott in discussing where Plum Village is; 'it is all the things that happen because it's there' (Person 2 2010). In this respect Plum Village signifies an ideal that people use to motivate themselves in the practices at home.

The discrete practices at Plum Village are characteristic of any religious community, and are not unique to Plum Village, yet I submit the combination of them along with a light approach to the teachings, that offers guidance rather than rules, produce an exceptional atmosphere which engenders and encourages individual practice. It is a living practice that is ready to be modified or changed if proved to be unsuccessful or not useful and has been adapting to meet the needs of retreatants over its thirty years. From its

---

[56] Samyutta-nikaya, xxxvi.6 (the Sallatha Sutta).

beginnings as a mainly Vietnamese community to one incorporating Westerners from many different countries, it is constantly reappraising what it offers in order to be of most benefit to those who practise there as well as the wider community. I have been endeavouring through this chapter to formulate a Plum Village Model, which encapsulates all the disparate aspects of practice that coalesce in one identifiable package. This is now described in my diagram below and given the title *meditation in action*.

5:6 *Meditation in action:* the Plum Village model

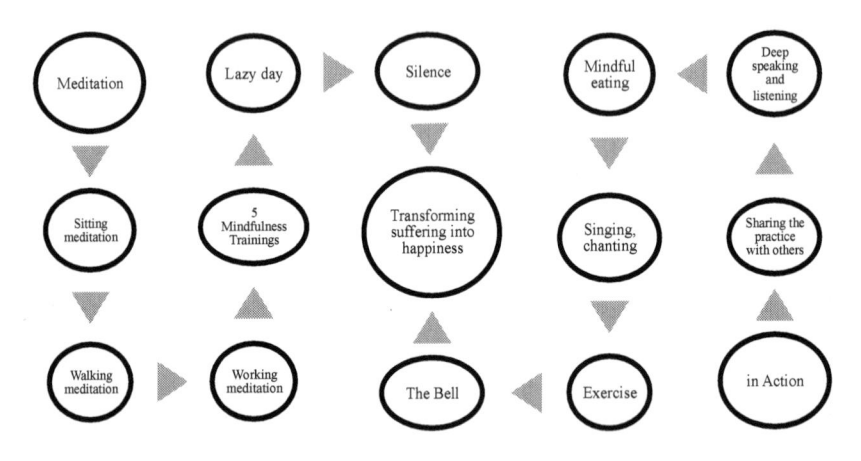

[Diagram showing interconnected circles with arrows: Meditation → Lazy day → Silence → Mindful eating ← Deep speaking and listening; Sitting meditation, 5 Mindfulness Trainings, Transforming suffering into happiness, Singing chanting, Sharing the practice with others; Walking meditation → Working meditation, The Bell ← Exercise, in Action]

Figure 3

This diagram expresses both aspects of meditation and action that are vital in comprising the Plum Village Model. This model can be transplanted into many new situations not just other monastic centres but can be used in brief on a DoM or a Unit evening (see Chapter 7) which integrates all the aspects because they are interrelated and because Mindfulness is integral to each and every aspect.

'Sharing the practice with others' incorporates a *Dharma* talk from Nhat Hanh as well as any individual being with others in a mindful way. The arrows express interbeing reiterating that all these aspects are interlinked and not discrete. The diagram expresses movement not as a progression from one step to the next but a fluidity that centres on 'transforming suffering into happiness', both for oneself and others. This is not a selfish practice that concentrates only on one's personal happiness, the intention is that, due to interbeing, the wish for happiness is a global concern; 'happiness is not an individual matter' (Nhat Hanh 2003d: 84). The aim of the practice is to give up ideas and notions that one can hold onto dearly. By applying Mindfulness to one's ideas one can gain insight into whether they are useful and true or not. One's idea of happiness can be the most difficult notion to give up 'so if you are free from your notion of happiness, happiness may come right away to you' (Nhat Hanh, Q&A 2012). This discussion on happiness and suffering continues in Chapter 6.

This diagram indicates that each section is not more important than another, each is vital to the completion of the whole. Although they can exist as separate entities it is the whole combined that achieves more than the sum of its parts as each has an effect on the other. This is a model where the view and understanding is from the perspective of the whole not the individual. In starting with this as a premise everything that becomes part of the Plum Village daily or weekly programme is designed to affirm this aspect of interbeing.

The 'lazy day' may appear to be an anomaly, yet it too is fundamental as it counteracts the usual busyness of life and the idea that can urge many people into a stressful, achievement-driven way of living. It is not a selfish time in which one forgets the practices, but a chance to reflect on them and begin to see how they can be implemented into one's daily life. It serves as a reminder that this diagram expresses *being peace* as the more important facet rather than *doing peace*. As in walking meditation, where one walks 'not in order to arrive, just for walking' (Nhat Hanh 2006b: 55), the lazy day is a day where nothing is scheduled in order to 'just let the day unfold naturally, timelessly [and] ... has been prescribed for us to train ourselves not to be afraid of doing nothing' (Nhat Hanh 2009d: 103). It can be more difficult than one imagines. One interviewee was frightened by the concept of doing nothing as she regularly worked a ninety-hour week and rarely stopped even to eat, so the prospect of doing nothing for a whole day was almost incomprehensible (IC, Person G 2011). Although this may sound extreme, the overuse of TV, videos and music that currently accompany many situations as background noise indicates that this is not such an uncommon experience. This therefore, makes the lazy day all the more imperative in resisting the habit energy that suggests one should always be doing something (Nhat Hanh 2009d: 104).

5:7 Reflections on the retreat experience

In this section I begin by examining a critique of Nhat Hanh's work before reflecting on the retreat experience and in particular aspects that were highlighted from the interviews undertaken and from my field research.

5:7:1 A critique of Thich Nhat Hanh

The previous sections have considered the elements that contribute to a centre for the practice of Mindfulness combining teachings that Nhat Hanh learnt as a novice monk in Vietnam, practices that he further developed through earlier mindful communities he originated and new developments in order to meet the needs of Westerners he is now teaching. I have demonstrated that there are aspects transplanted from Vietnam as well as ones that have since been developed in the West. Cuong Tu Nguyen & A.T. Barber, however, suggest

> Thich Nhat Hanh, though he was never known as a Ch'an [Zen] master in Vietnam, has become a famous master in the West. He oversees several retreat centers in America and Europe where his Western and Vietnamese disciples engage in a "New Age"-style Zen and rituals created by him that do not have any affinity with or foundation in traditional Vietnamese practices (1998: 131).

As has been discussed in Chapter 3, Nhat Hanh was well-known in Vietnam and taught extensively in the Van Hanh University although he had no chance to practise formally as a *Dharmacharya* as he ordained only days before leaving Vietnam in 1966. I would challenge the term 'New Age' and whether that is appropriate to describe Plum Village. If it means alternative approaches to traditional Western culture then this could reflect Plum Village to some degree, however, it appears this term is used in a demeaning way to suggest something insubstantial, a new movement that has no foundation or basis. If this is what is meant then I do not consider it can be applied to Plum Village. The suffix '-style Zen' also suggests there is something disingenuous about what Plum Village is offering. Finally, I do not agree with the statement that his teachings have no foundation in traditional Vietnamese practices unless they are referring wholly to the practices that Nhat Hanh wished to reinvigorate when he was in Vietnam. I propose that Nhat Hanh's continued connection to Vietnam has been adequately established throughout this chapter.

Melvin McLeod could be referring to this comment by Nguyen & Barber in discussing that at one time Nhat Hanh's 'versatility and engagement with the world was seen as a disadvantage' when he first began teaching in the West as he was accused of watering down Buddhist teachings, appearing to adopt Western techniques and offer teachings without substance, which ignores the fact that they are founded in an ancient Vietnamese tradition (2009: ix-x). Whilst Nhat Hanh's teachings cannot appeal to everyone they have an openness and create a 'sanctuary' that allows those who wish to attend a retreat to 'heal at a visceral level' (SI, Person D 2011). Certainly those interviewed were complimentary about Plum Village, describing it as a place of 'healing' (SI, Person C 2010) and 'positive energy' (SI, Person 28 2011), with a 'buoyant, relaxed, familial atmosphere' (SI, Person 6 2010), full of 'spaciousness' that allowed one to experience solitude even among hundreds of people (SI, Person 14 2010). This, however, is clearly not the whole story and in the next section I will examine some of the aspects that I deem are not quite so lovely.

5:7:2 Issues arising from a retreat

The purpose of the retreat is to help us untie the knots inside. There are two kinds of knots. One knot is our notions and ideas. Everyone has notions and ideas and we are attached to them, we are not free, so we have no chance to touch the truth in life. The second knot is our afflictions like fear, anger, discrimination, despair and arrogance. All these things should be removed in order for us to be free. The things you do on a retreat, like walking, sitting, breathing, smiling, and listening to a Dharma talk, should have the same function of helping you undo these two kinds of knots (Nhat Hanh 2009a: 80).

I suggest the space and silence offered on a retreat gives the chance to see the knots that one has created and begin to unravel them, but it is not always a comfortable experience. As interviewees indicated one does not attend a retreat just to have a lovely time; that is a bonus that may or may not be an outcome. Being on a retreat, as seven of the interviewees expressed (Person 2 2010; Person 7 2010; Person 17 2010; Person 12 2009; Person 22 2011; Person 25 2009; Person 28 2011), can be challenging, unsettling, daunting and scary when one's dearly held perceptions are shaken or revealed as being insubstantial. As indicated from interviewees the point of a retreat is not to shy away from the issues that come up, but to use the emotional support of the other practitioners, especially the Family members, to help one address these issues; how much one can do that is up to the individual. There is recognition that meeting and addressing one's difficulties is part of the retreat experience; 'it's really helped me to grow, and at times it's been very supportive of me and my family and difficulties' (SI, Person 10 2010). Furthermore, Person 22 indicated being out of one's comfort zone was difficult at times '... because all that's familiar is no longer there' yet he also considered it right to be challenged sufficiently (SI, 2011) in order to be able to meet the storms of life, that one can prepare for by practising in the safe and secure environment of the retreat (Nhat Hanh, Q&A 2009).

Issues that interviewees raised in terms of areas of difficulty they encountered only serve to demonstrate that a retreat cannot encompass all variances; it can only stay true to its stated purpose. The question is whether a retreat at Plum Village accurately reflects Nhat Hanh's teachings. I have described in detail above all the particular aspects pertaining to a retreat and clearly there is a lot of thought put into what does and does not take place. As evidenced from the field research some people discussed there not being enough sitting meditation or too much Noble Silence, but these minor issues could reflect the preconceived ideas one has based on former experience. Compared to a *vipashyana* retreat there is less sitting meditation and less silence, but that will offer a different outcome to a Plum Village retreat. As Person 2 recognised things can be *right* or *wrong* from one's own perspective at different times (SI, 2010), yet it is not that these should be changed. One's perspective can change over time and what one is glad of at one time can be annoying or frustrating on the next retreat.

Some interviewees reported a feeling of loneliness, especially due to the silence, which could be an alienating experience (SI, Person 18 2010; Person 13 2010). Another felt it was challenging to be there alone amidst people who clearly knew each other and could be exclusive or unaware of new people (SI, Person 20 2010). Whilst this is understandable, these episodes can be learning experiences that one appreciates from the other side of having prevailed. One realises they are not personal, but universal traits that everyone can experience to some degree at some point. As denoted earlier in this chapter, Person 2 recognises 'I know that I may not have a very easy time and I may have a lot to work with but actually I always come back inspired' (SI, 2010). The ability to reflect on what one is experiencing rather than be overwhelmed by it allows the possibility of growth from each occurrence,

> it needs a sufficient degree of discomfort of some description to be as powerful as it is. If it was a perfect retreat centre and everybody who went there was perfect nobody would do any growing and it would actually be a complete waste of time (SI, Person 17 2010).

Recognising that Plum Village does not set itself up as a perfect model I submit there is one weak aspect in particular that could be refined which is the pupil-teacher relationship discussed in subsection 5:2:1. Nhat Hanh does not partake in private interviews only the weekly public Q&A. Does Plum Village therefore need to develop a different pupil-teacher connection that gives each retreatant direct access to a *Dharmacharya* given that 'the whole tradition of Zen is based on transmission from teacher to student' (SI, Person 7 2010)?

I came across a variety of examples of one-to-one interviews on retreat; at Plum Village Sr Chan Khong offers private interviews of fifteen minutes to the whole community which means it is not always possible to see her given the hundreds of people present. At Nottingham private interviews were offered more widely and this could be with any monastic or lay Order member. In theory one can request an interview with the person facilitating the Family group, but it is left to the retreatant to initiate. Whilst the *Dharma* sharing is designed to be an opportunity when problems can be aired and hopefully discussed it is rather public and one may prefer a private consultation which there may not be time for. My observation here is that when something emotional comes up on retreat it is unclear what the means are of speaking to someone about it, which could mean people miss the opportunity to address their individual concerns. Whilst it is not possible to have one-to-one consultations with Nhat Hanh it could be made more apparent that those facilitating the Family group or other monastics are available for personal interviews if required.

There are two further points raised by interviewees that warrant additional consideration, both relating to what Nhat Hanh says. The first is that he often repeats what has been said previously and Person 1 was disappointed particularly by the Q&A (2009) which he felt he could have scripted himself 'and usually people are asking him to go a little beyond what he's already said and written and he just went right back to the text' (SI, 2009). However, others considered it to be a pedagogic tool implementing repetition in order for the teachings to sink in because 'when you hear it at a different time you take something different from it and it's relevant to yourself in a different way at that particular time so I've always gained something from retreats with Thay' (SI, Person 18 2010). I conclude by this repetition that Nhat Hanh's message is consistent and there is often so much knowledge transmitted in a *Dharma* talk it would be impossible to cognise it all first time around. Also, one's state of mind can differ from one time to the next and one can hear things in a different way second time around.

The second aspect of disagreement with what Nhat Hanh said came from Person 28 who was concerned that,
> sometimes Thay teaches on areas which I feel are outside his expertise, e.g. advocating the Ayurvedic practice of "oil-pushing" as a means of promoting physical health, or advising on the treatment of severe mental illness. I feel uncomfortable when this happens. However, this serves as a reminder that nobody has all the answers and that ultimately one has to think for oneself (SI, 2011).

The process of rationalisation that Person 28 demonstrates here is exactly what Nhat Hanh advocates. One should not take his words as absolutes, but examine what is being said in the light of one's own experience and discover for oneself what is appropriate. This can also be said of the whole Plum Village experience in that whilst the programme offers many and varied opportunities to practise Mindfulness one has to take from this what is most beneficial for oneself and not just practise without awareness.

5:8 Conclusion

Throughout this chapter I have argued that the various elements of the Plum Village daily programme demonstrate the application and evolution of Nhat Hanh's teachings outside of Vietnam. Any activity can be a meditation if Mindfulness is applied to it and the programme's elements are called meditations in order to emphasise this. At various points throughout the chapter I have related back to the diagram in subsection 2:1:5 indicating Nhat Hanh's exposition of Mindfulness and how these specific elements can be recognised in the daily programme. Silence is a contributing factor to these elements as it is in silence that one becomes aware of what is going on in the mind. Silence enhances the practices and provides mental space. The mindful practices aim at one becoming more aware of what is taking place internally, seeing the desires and volitions that initiate one's actions.

There are many opportunities to practice deep listening and loving speech which contribute to a harmonious society. Plum Village aims towards harmony and reconciliation in all matters, however small, and this can be achieved by the application of Mindfulness throughout the day as well as an effective means of conflict resolution through the practice of Beginning Anew when difficulties occur. This is highlighted by the different cultures that have come together at Plum Village, yet in spite of the differing worldviews they demonstrate a harmonious relationship and an effective ecumenical society.

Whilst there are several distinctive aspects of the Plum Village programme I hesitate to call them unique, although the ease with which children are incorporated into the daily programme of a retreat and the efforts to produce a truly fourfold community that does not demonstrate the superiority of the monastics over the laity can be considered rare. Furthermore, the inclusivity of anyone wishing to follow a mindful path regardless of whether they are Buddhist or not is commendable. However, uniqueness is not something Plum Village is striving for. I suggest the principal aim is to demonstrate that practising Mindfulness can be joyful and rewarding as well as transforming suffering.

In detailing each element that comprises the Plum Village Model I endeavour to give a flavour of the experience of Nhat Hanh's teachings in praxis bearing in mind that the understanding of being on a retreat in the company of like-minded people cannot be imagined or surmised, only experienced. For example, eating together in silence without any distractions is perhaps the most alien practice for many people and it is for this reason I propose it is the most powerful. It can highlight the way one usually eats at home especially the distraction techniques such as watching television or even conversation that can come between noticing what one is digesting. The essence of Plum Village is to live and demonstrate the teachings on Mindfulness from the *Satipatthana Sutta* in such a way that retreatants feel they can likewise implement these practices into their life once back home. I suggest there is a great deal of awareness of the difficulties this can pose even when one has both the desire and motivational energy on returning from a retreat. It is for this reason that, whilst the practices are demonstrated as being a reasonable change to effect in one's life, there is no compunction or expectation. They are offered freely without any suggestion that this method is the only true way to practise and others are incorrect because 'such a statement is not in accord with the spirit of Buddhism' (Nhat Hanh 2003b: 35). Nhat Hanh has chosen a particular way of life that deeply embeds Mindfulness demonstrating, for those who wish to hear, a way of living which is less harmful to other beings and more conducive of an interbeing lifestyle.

The purpose of a Plum Village retreat is to indicate how to be mindful in all situations of one's daily life and how to bring Mindfulness out of the meditation hall. I suggest it does that successfully. In basing the teachings of Plum Village in the *Satipatthana Sutta* and other early Buddhist texts Nhat Hanh is re-interpreting an ancient tradition to make it more relevant to current society in the full knowledge that his students will re-interpret it again in a few decades. The continued emphasis on Mindfulness indicates that the practices are not to be used mechanically, but consciously with awareness of what one is doing. Through these practices one can address the rampant individualism in Western society in the twenty-first century by offering a paradigm of community.

Community building is the most important action of our century ... Individualism is predominating, families are breaking down, and society has become deeply divided as a result. For the twenty-first century to be a century of spirituality, we must be guided by the spirit of togetherness (Nhat Hanh 2009c: 90).

The 'spirit of togetherness' tangibly permeates everything that takes place at Plum Village. This is a necessary aspect of community living without ignoring the individuals who make up the community. Plum Village demonstrates the delicate balancing act required in supporting both the community and the individuals comprising it. In this respect interbeing is vital to be understood and practised both within the retreat setting and back home. Whilst it may at times feel as if one is being asked to drop heartfelt thoughts or feelings relating to oneself as an individual I suggest more often one is glad to let go of burdensome ideas in favour of interbeing as a more natural way of being.

As denoted in subsection 5:3:2 the atmosphere at Plum Village is permeated with gentleness and kindness reflecting Nhat Hanh's nature which emanates from him to everyone who attends a retreat. I propose that his role at Plum Village has become one of being a living example of Mindfulness and through this his relationship with his students appears to be carefully managed so that one can feel close to Nhat Hanh without that relationship getting in the way of the practices. Although this is a Buddhist monastery its foundation of practice is the MTs which, whilst being initially enunciated by the *Buddha*, are ethical trainings that anyone with a moral outlook would wish to deeply consider and reflect upon in order to see how they could be implemented into one's life. The next chapter further investigates Nhat Hanh's interpretation of Mindfulness through these ethical documents which underpin the mindful practices undertaken at Plum Village.

6. 'The Miracle of Mindfulness'[57]: Transforming Suffering into Happiness

My hope is that these Mindfulness Trainings can represent a Buddhist contribution to a global ethic, a way for the human species to sustain itself in these dangerous and difficult times. After almost seventy years of practice, I have found these Mindfulness Trainings can help relieve suffering and produce happiness by helping us generate the energies of mindfulness, concentration and insight. The practice of these three energies can open the door to liberate people from the prison of suffering (Nhat Hanh 2014: 10).

Introduction

This quotation demonstrates the belief that Thich Nhat Hanh has in these ethical teachings, as a means of relieving suffering and producing happiness through Mindfulness. In the previous chapter I demonstrated how Nhat Hanh implements Mindfulness into all aspects of daily life with the aim of transforming suffering into happiness and here I discuss the prominence given to the MTs, introducing an ethical aspect to the practice. The 5MTs can be a bridge between a retreat at Plum Village and practising at home, ideally with a Unit. They are a specific set of guidelines that reinforce the teachings learnt at Plum Village, indicating a direction to move in. As will be discovered throughout the chapter, the MTs

---

[57] Nhat Hanh 2008e.

are not absolutes '... but a path to walk on' (Nhat Hanh 2014: 36). As with many of Nhat Hanh's teachings the simplicity of the words belies a depth that needs to be plumbed in order to fully understand them.

In this chapter I discuss the research question as to how Nhat Hanh's pedagogy has developed by establishing that it continues the practices begun in Vietnam offering a consistently nonviolent, compassionate and ethical approach to life with Mindfulness as its foundation. The key argument for this chapter is that Mindfulness continues to be a crucial aspect of his teachings with the MTs at the crux. Out of these emerge the qualities of compassion and focussing on the positive, wholesome aspects of life. These qualities are investigated in the second half of the chapter through Nhat Hanh's poem *Call Me by My True Names*, which I suggest is the epitome of his prominence of compassion, interbeing and ethics, and the question 'what's not wrong?' (Nhat Hanh 1995: 77) before concluding with a consideration of how his teachings are expanding beyond the Buddhist world in which they originated. These two sections further emphasise the aspect of transforming suffering into happiness.

6:1 The Mindfulness trainings

I begin with an examination of the 5MTs, a document Nhat Hanh developed to closely reflect the ethical teachings the *Buddha* imparted to the lay practitioners. The 14MTs are an expanded form of the 5 and therefore the discussion relating to the 14 compares the original document from 1964 with an updated version in 2012. The 5 and 14MTs are Nhat Hanh's seminal teaching on Mindfulness which lies 'at the heart of the Buddha's teaching' (Nhat Hanh 1999d: 64). In the *Anguttara Nikaya* (AN 8:54; IV 281-85 & 8:49;IV 269-71) they are listed as the attributes of a person '... accomplished in moral discipline' and are given to laity to abstain '... from the destruction of life, from stealing, from sexual misconduct, from false speech, and from wines, liquors, and intoxicants, the basis for negligence' (Bodhi

2005: 126 & 130). 'The Buddha offered five mindfulness trainings ... as a practice to ... live a wholesome and peaceful life' (1992e: 81) and the 5MTs are Nhat Hanh's interpretation of these Five Precepts. These are '...voluntarily undertaken moral commitments that go back to the beginnings of Buddhism' (Harris 2010: 64). As with the *Theravadin* texts discussed previously (*Satipatthana Sutta* and *Anapanasati Sutta*) Nhat Hanh has also incorporated these Five Precepts into his pedagogy as a concrete means of offering the teaching to laity.

Whilst they were originally expressed negatively as an abstention, each has a positive counterpart or virtue; 1) love, 2) generosity, 3) contentment, 4) truthfulness, 5) mindfulness and awareness (Triratna; Mitchell 2002: 54-55; Harris 2010: 65). It will be seen that Nhat Hanh has included each positive aspect in his interpretation. He had originally used the word precept as the *Buddha* did; however, 'Western friends' advised him that this had a negative effect, akin to *thou shalt not* of the Christian commandments, evoking 'in them strong feelings of good and evil; that if they "break" the precepts, they feel great shame' (Nhat Hanh 1992e: 81-82). The '... five precepts (*panca-sila*; more accurately translated as "the five virtues") ... are often referred to as training precepts (*sikkhapada*)' (Fronsdal 2002: 291) and it is this term training that Nhat Hanh has now adopted. The MTs demonstrate that being open to others' insights is a key feature of Nhat Hanh's teaching and, as in this example, he is willing to learn from his students as well as teach them,

> Zen is radically different from the generally-held view that religion is adherence to a set of beliefs and truths. Although, at first, the Zen attitude towards life and the world may appear to be extremely liberal, in reality, it is a way of life acquired through the rigorous practice of mindfulness. This practice takes one beyond any dogmatism about the understanding of reality (Fernando 2007: 18).

The non-dogmatism and non-adherence to views that Fernando discusses here permeates the MTs by requiring the practitioner to look deeply at each situation for himself or herself. As Fernando denotes, the 5 and 14MTs are guidelines rather than rules, they cannot be practised perfectly and are like the North Star by indicating a direction to take (Nhat Hanh 2008f: 53). They are '… called trainings because they are something to practice each day, not something we're expected to do perfectly all the time. They are there to remind us of our aspiration and our commitment' (Nhat Hanh 2014: 23). Furthermore they are experiential rather than intellectual (Henry 2008: 207) which is entirely compatible with Nhat Hanh's teachings. One can theorise about each point but it is the practical application of each MT that is relevant, as one only finds out through observation and experience how to apply them to one's daily life.

They are 'derived from rational principles intended to promote human well-being' (Keown 2003: 223) and can be people's first introduction to the practice of Mindfulness. The 14MTs can be seen as a second step of practice as trainings for Order members that includes both monastics and laity. The Two Promises[58] is another simpler version that children can receive in a ceremony reflecting the care taken by the community to include everyone at all levels. The 5 and 14MTs, are offered on a retreat through a formal ceremony in which the recipient commits to a regular recitation, study and practice. The emphasis placed on their regular recitation and examination (Nhat Hanh 2000a: 11) indicates the significance of these ethical values for the Plum Village community. Whilst Person 3 suggests shared values are what makes *Sangha* (SI, 2011) there is no implication that one has to hold these values to be part of the CoI yet they form a significant aspect of the practice. These are not intended to be set in stone so that one either follows them rigidly or fails. They are recommendations suggesting how one can live ethically and harmoniously with people, animals, plants and minerals and '… should be understood as deep aspirations, which help

---

[58] 'I vow to develop understanding, in order to live peacefully with people, animals, plants, and minerals. I vow to develop my compassion, in order to protect the lives of people, animals, plants, and minerals' (Nhat Hanh 2007b: 94).

participants to grow in mindfulness' (Henry 2008: 206). One should not feel guilty if an MT is broken as they are '... guidelines for ethical living ... At the same time, taking the precepts is itself intended to be a source of inspiration which will in turn strengthen a person's practice and intensify her commitment' (Brazier 2003: 216-217). The continued recitation can assist with this and can be seen as a positive means of bringing them to the front of one's mind in order to be constantly reminded (SI, Person D 2011).

There is also an element of seriousness in the formal ceremony with the statement 'that the transmission is dependent on regular ... study and recitation of the Mindfulness Trainings and that if you fail to recite them within three months they become null and void' (SI, Person 14 2010). This does not evoke the same sense of experimentation that 'guidelines' conveys but indicates the necessity of their practice over theorising. Nhat Hanh offers a practice that allows the individual to discover and realise for themselves rather than being told what to do or how to behave. For the sake of clarity I refer to the individual 5MTs as trainings in order to distinguish them from the 14MTs to be discussed later. They

> express Nhat Hanh's innovative style and close attention to the experiential approach, in which the mind and the world are inseparable. The trainings are not prescriptive, emphasising the notion that by following them (and they are presented in great detail) one creates less suffering for oneself and for those one is in contact with ... The Mindfulness Trainings prompt serious consideration for everyday issues of concern including: the environment, sexual health, wellbeing, consumption and oppression (Henry 2008: 231).

This ethical function of Mindfulness as 'being part and parcel of the attempt to eliminate the unwholesome and establish the wholesome' (Bodhi 2011: 28) is emphasised throughout the MTs as an integral aspect to Nhat Hanh's elucidation of Mindfulness as discussed in

Chapter 2. I begin with an examination of the 5MTs as revised by Nhat Hanh and the Plum Village community in 2009.

6:1:1 An assessment of the 5 Mindfulness trainings

The 5MTs are the basis of Manifesto 2000 a document produced by UNESCO and a group of Nobel Peace Prize Laureates, plus Nhat Hanh, indicating a path of peace and reconciliation for the world (UNESCO). It can be seen that certain phrases particularly 'share my time and material resources' have been directly lifted from the 5MTs. Nhat Hanh stresses signing the Manifesto is not enough 'it must be the practice of our ... everyday life' (Nhat Hanh 2012c). Manifesto 2000 indicates the way in which the 5MTs are a viable means of integrating ethical teachings into secular life and an aim that Nhat Hanh has expressed.

The introductory paragraph to the 5MTs lays out the principles of interbeing and global ethics behind them.
Sisters and brothers in the community, this is the moment when we enjoy reciting the Five Mindfulness Trainings together. The Five Mindfulness Trainings represent the Buddhist vision for a global spirituality and ethic. They are a concrete expression of the Buddha's teachings on the Four Noble Truths and the Noble Eightfold Path, the path of right understanding and true love, leading to healing, transformation, and happiness for ourselves and for the world. To practice the Five Mindfulness Trainings is to cultivate the insight of interbeing, or Right View, which can remove all discrimination, intolerance, anger, fear, and despair. If we live according to the Five Mindfulness Trainings, we are already on the path of a bodhisattva. Knowing we are on that path, we are not lost in confusion about our life in the present or in fears about the future.

As is demonstrated here and throughout each training Nhat Hanh has expanded upon each aspect from the original Precepts. This paragraph signifies their purpose is '... to train oneself to develop the kind of behaviour that does not cause suffering' (Henry 2008: 206).

The last sentence indicates the perception of certainty that comes from having a path to follow and therefore 'we are not lost in confusion about our life in the present or fears about the future'. This is not to suggest that one has achieved *nirvana* or liberation, but that one has a firm foundation from which to base one's actions.

1) The first training, based in the Buddhist term *Ahimsa*, is Reverence for Life.
Aware of the suffering caused by the destruction of life, I am committed to cultivating the insight of interbeing and compassion and learning ways to protect the lives of people, animals, plants, and minerals. I am determined not to kill, not to let others kill, and not to support any act of killing in the world, in my thinking, or in my way of life. Seeing that harmful actions arise from anger, fear, greed, and intolerance, which in turn come from dualistic and discriminative thinking, I will cultivate openness, non-discrimination, and non-attachment to views in order to transform violence, fanaticism, and dogmatism in myself and in the world.

This training recognises that the relationship between all living beings, without distinction, is so close that to harm any living creature inevitably harms oneself (Saddhatissa 1987: 74). Through the recognition of interbeing 'one avoids killing because all living beings feel pain and desire happiness as much as oneself' (Harris 2010: 125). There is no understanding here of an anthropocentric viewpoint (as discussed in section 1:3), all sentient beings, including animals, plants and minerals are accorded equal status. There does, however, also have to be an understanding that

> ... no one, not even a buddha, can hope to live in the world and cause absolutely no harm to any living being ... that this is so is an aspect of the deepest level of the first noble truth: the world, samsāra, is by its very nature an imperfect place, a place where suffering is always lurking in one form or another. The question of acting ethically becomes one of where to draw the line (Gethin 1998: 172).

This further emphasises the practice of moving in the direction of nonviolence in the same way as using the North Star as a guide '... it is impossible to arrive at the North Star. Our effort is only to proceed in that direction' (Nhat Hanh 2007c: 12). In this way one can develop a '... stability of mind and an awareness of suffering, which cultivates compassion to protect people, animals, plants and minerals' (Henry 2008: 206), again bringing out the interbeing aspect of each training.

2) The second training is True Happiness.
Aware of the suffering caused by exploitation, social injustice, stealing, and oppression, I am committed to practicing generosity in my thinking, speaking, and acting. I am determined not to steal and not to possess anything that should belong to others; and I will share my time, energy, and material resources with those who are in need. I will practice looking deeply to see that the happiness and suffering of others are not separate from my own happiness and suffering; that true happiness is not possible without understanding and compassion; and that running after wealth, fame, power and sensual pleasures can bring much suffering and despair. I am aware that happiness depends on my mental attitude and not on external conditions, and that I can live happily in the present moment simply by remembering that I already have more than enough conditions to be happy. I am committed to practicing Right Livelihood so that I can help reduce the suffering of living beings on Earth and reverse the process of global warming.

This training expands the notion of not stealing to 'generosity in my thinking, speaking, and acting ... and [sharing] my time, energy, and material resources with those who are in need'. Nhat Hanh indicates three types of giving in Buddhism; material resources, to help people help themselves, and non-fear (2007c: 21). This teaching aims to show that it is important to recognise the fullness of generosity and that is not just about having material resources to give. Being able to offer someone time, attention, deep listening and energy are equally valid. The training further emphasises interbeing through the expression 'the happiness and suffering of others are not separate from my own happiness and suffering'. The MTs are continually bringing one back to the recognition that one is not a separate individual but part of a much larger organism and that the behaviour of each has an effect on the others; 'we are each one cell in the Buddha body' (Nhat Hanh Vimeo 2012). Nhat Hanh suggests writing down '... some conditions of happiness that are available to you right now' in order to recognise and benefit from them and to '... arrange your life to make these conditions for happiness available' (2008h: 59).

3) The third training is True Love.
Aware of the suffering caused by sexual misconduct, I am committed to cultivating responsibility and learning ways to protect the safety and integrity of individuals, couples, families, and society. Knowing that sexual desire is not love, and that sexual activity motivated by craving always harms myself as well as others, I am determined not to engage in sexual relations without true love and a deep, long-term commitment made known to my family and friends. I will do everything in my power to protect children from sexual abuse and to prevent couples and families from being broken by sexual misconduct. Seeing that body and mind are one, I am committed to learning appropriate ways to take care of my sexual energy and cultivating loving kindness, compassion, joy and inclusiveness – which are the four basic elements of true love – for my greater happiness and the greater happiness of others. Practicing true love, we know that we will continue beautifully into the future.

This reflects the large numbers of people Nhat Hanh has met who have suffered from sexual abuse (Chan Khong 2007: 234) yet it also calls for all to behave responsibly with one's sexual energy. Although Nhat Hanh's view is a traditional one based on an understanding where husband and wife treat each other like honoured guests (Nhat Hanh 2007c: 27) I suggest it is important to encourage sexual restraint particularly among young people who may not be aware of the emotional damage they are potentially doing to themselves by partaking in casual sex on a regular basis. Relationships based on a 'long-term commitment' can indicate forethought in this respect, although the term 'long-term commitment' is somewhat vague. It is based in the understanding that sexual urges are the strongest instinct and more difficult for humans to control than animals, as they are continual for humans but seasonal for animals (Saddhatissa 1987: 88).

4) The fourth training is Loving Speech and Deep Listening.
Aware of the suffering caused by unmindful speech and the inability to listen to others, I am committed to cultivating loving speech and compassionate listening in order to relieve suffering and to promote reconciliation and peace in myself and among other people, ethnic and religious groups, and nations. Knowing that words can create happiness or suffering, I am committed to speaking truthfully using words that inspire confidence, joy, and hope. When anger is manifesting in me, I am determined not to speak. I will practice mindful breathing and walking in order to recognize and to look deeply into my anger. I know that the roots of anger can be found in my wrong perceptions and lack of understanding of the suffering in myself and in the other person. I will speak and listen in a way that can help myself and the other person to transform suffering and see the way out of difficult situations. I am determined not to spread news that I do not know to be certain and not to utter words that can cause division or discord. I will practice Right Diligence to nourish my capacity for understanding, love, joy, and inclusiveness, and gradually transform anger, violence, and fear that lie deep in my consciousness.

This training invites 'loving speech and compassionate listening' in order to redress the suffering caused by 'unmindful speech and the inability to listen to others'. Nhat Hanh uses the question 'are you sure?' (1999d: 60; 2011: 62) in his teachings reminding that misperceptions can easily arise if one holds onto views as changeless. This training indicates '... words can create happiness or suffering' and much damage can be caused by words, whether deliberately or accidentally; yet this also suggests that words used effectively can nourish and heal and that one should not avoid situations where truthful speech is required.

Anger is one of the Five Hindrances described in the *Satipatthana Sutta* and is the focus of many of Nhat Hanh's teachings as he indicates '... when you are angry, you are not lucid enough for your action to make sense' (Nhat Hanh & Berrigan 2001: 84). This is the reason for refraining from speech when anger is present. Whilst I appreciate that speaking in anger can provoke words that one may later regret discord or anger, however, can be seen as an element that motivates change. To actively retreat from a situation of discord could be understood as meaning that one should suppress all speech that comes from anger. Instead what is being recommended here is that one puts distance between an angry dispute in order to let things calm down and the situation can be addressed from a calm state of being. There is no suggestion that one buries anger or discourages it from being addressed. By looking deeply at anger and what has caused one to feel angry '... we see that the person we call our enemy is also suffering. As soon as we see that, we have the capacity of accepting and having compassion for him' (Nhat Hanh 1993a: 76). This training demonstrates a skilful means of moving beyond anger in a way that does not leave a residue for either side, similar to the Beginning Anew practice discussed in Chapter 5.

5) The fifth training is Nourishment and Healing.
Aware of the suffering caused by unmindful consumption, I am committed to cultivating good health, both physical and mental, for myself, my family, and my society by practicing mindful eating, drinking, and consuming. I will practice looking deeply into how I consume the Four Kinds of Nutriments, namely edible foods, sense impressions, volition, and consciousness. I am determined not to gamble, or to use alcohol, drugs, or any other products which contain toxins, such as certain websites, electronic games, TV programs, films, magazines, books, and conversations. I will practice coming back to the present moment to be in touch with the refreshing, healing and nourishing elements in me and around me, not letting regrets and sorrow drag me back into the past nor letting anxieties, fear, or craving pull me out of the present moment. I am determined not to try to cover up loneliness, anxiety, or other suffering by losing myself in consumption. I will contemplate

interbeing and consume in a way that preserves peace, joy, and well-being in my body and consciousness, and in the collective body and consciousness of my family, my society and the Earth.
Revised 2009 (Plum Village5).

Whilst this specific training can be challenging as alcohol in particular is prevalent in society, 'it is not the taking of alcohol or other drugs as such that is problematic, but the state of mind that it generally induces: a lack of mental clarity with an increased tendency to break the other precepts' (Gethin 1998: 170-171). Mental clarity is an important aspect of Mindfulness and those undertaking a commitment to the MTs may wish to re-examine their consumption in all areas, food being another relevant area as indicated by Nhat Hanh & Cheung's book *Savor* (2010).

In the *Anguttara Nikaya* (AN 8:39, IV 245-47) the *Buddha* expounds that by giving up and abstaining from '... the destruction of life ... taking what is not given ... sexual misconduct ... false speech ... wines, liquors, and intoxicants [the disciple] ... gives to immeasurable beings freedom from fear, hostility and oppression' (Bodhi 2005: 173). Likewise Nhat Hanh is also offering 'freedom from fear' in his expanded elucidation of these MTs as indicated by one interviewee, '... I'm so grateful, I feel like Thay has given me fearlessness' (SI, Person 15 2009). Whilst retaining the essence of the trainings he has contemporised them to be entirely relevant to today's society. The fifth training in particular demonstrates aspects of possible addiction or intoxication that are available today, such as websites, TV programmes and films, that had no relevance in the *Buddha's* lifetime. Yet the addition of these features is intended to give a clearer understanding of their specific meaning and the path one can take towards a more ethical lifestyle. As can be seen, each of the trainings are written in a way that addresses the Four Noble Truths by acknowledging there is suffering present in the human experience but offering the means to move beyond it.

All the aspects of Nhat Hanh's exposition of Mindfulness (subsection 2:1:5) can be recognised within the 5MTs. One is called on to have an *awareness of what the senses are receiving* particularly in the 5th training by having a wide picture of what one is consuming. Each training begins with *recognising wholesome from unwholesome* through being aware of what causes suffering and endeavouring to stop practising it. By recognising the wholesome one can develop *insight* on a more mindful way of moving forward. This can be achieved by coming back again and again (i.e. *remembering*) to the present moment (*simple moment-by-moment awareness*) from which one can *engage with the world* by acknowledging '... the happiness and suffering of others are not separate from my own happiness and suffering' (2nd training).

The interviewees spoke positively about the MTs (eleven specifically mentioned the 5 or 14MTs) suggesting they are viewed in the experimental way Nhat Hanh proposed. Three interviewees acknowledged they were values already practised in one's daily life and not something new to adopt; 'they dovetailed perfectly with what I was trying to practise anyway as a Quaker' (Person 8 2009); 'in my own mind I had gone with ... those things beforehand' (SI, Person 10 2010); 'I feel like I'd already been practising them quite assiduously' (SI, Person 22 2011). Whilst there is a sense of feeling one's way with both the 5 and 14MTs and discovering step-by-step what they can mean in practice Brazier indicates, '... if they are to be meaningful the words must echo something already heart-felt' (2003: 216) and this is the sense in which they are offered to the community. They are not new teachings; they express a specific intention to look deeply into the way one lives one's life. Whilst they are deemed to be helpful in one's life and '... taking the precepts is itself intended to be a source of inspiration which will in turn strengthen a person's practice and intensify her commitment' (Brazier 2003: 216-217) equally, there are 'really fantastic practitioners' who have not taken the 5MTs ceremony (SI, Person 7 2010). This further underlines the non-dogmatic way in which one approaches them and whilst one may adopt the ethical principles personally there is no requirement to publically declare this.

Despite the reservations of one interviewee that one had to follow the 5MTs 'properly' she found the evening presentation on the 5MTs at Plum Village helpful to 'deepen my understanding ... and let myself off the hook' (SI, Person 29 2009). Again, this emphasises that there is nothing dogmatic about these statements and there is no requirement to adhere to them fully. Instead interviewees conclude that 'they've helped me enormously with my life, transforming my suffering' (SI, Person 9 2009); 'I felt that the Mindfulness trainings protected me and protected my life' (SI, Person D 2011); 'they are ethical guidelines for how I can skilfully navigate myself through this world' (SI, Person 15 2009). These responses signify the value interviewees place in the 5MTs. The fifth training can be the most problematic as for some people completely giving up alcohol presents a difficulty and can deter them from taking the 5MTs ceremony (SI, Person 18 2010). Person 18 further discussed only initially taking four of the 5MTs because she did not agree with giving up alcohol yet at a later date, having reflected, she 'saw it would be a good idea to move in that direction' and took all five (SI, 2010). Nhat Hanh proposes if you practise one training deeply all five will be observed (2007c: 20-21), due to their interbeing nature each one is taken care of in the others.

Nhat Hanh indicates there is not one particular way in which they are to be employed; 'what is the best way to practice the mindfulness trainings? I do not know. I am still learning, along with you. I appreciate the phrase that is used ... to "learn ways". We don't know everything. But we can minimize our ignorance' (2007c: 3). The emphasis here is on applying the MTs in ways appropriate to one's personal life rather than trying to emulate an idea of how they should be followed. One can find each time they are recited that a different aspect or sentence stands out as relevant depending on one's current mind-set. In a recent publication that thoroughly examines the 5MTs and the ethics related to them Nhat Hanh introduces the preface from the *Dharmaguptaka* School[59],

---

[59] One of the original early Buddhist schools that had a lot of influence in China and therefore Vietnam (China Buddhism Encyclopedia).

the mindfulness trainings are like the ocean. One lifetime alone is not enough to study and to practice them. They are like precious treasures. We never grow tired in their pursuit. It is because we want to protect our sacred inheritance of the true teachings that we have gathered today to hear the recitation of the mindfulness trainings (2014: 191).

They are trainings that can be revisited often to gain a deeper understanding.

Through examining the detail of the 5MTs I have indicated their practical and experiential side and emphasised they are guidelines and not rules to be strictly adhered to. They are offered for each individual to practise from one's own current understanding and lifestyle rather than set up unrealistic aims. Therefore, if one has difficulty with any particular aspect, as discussed above in relation to alcohol, one does not have to blindly accept this as an imperative but investigate for oneself what it means. With each MT there is an appreciation of the tension between having an aim of creating less suffering and the reality of achieving this aim, as indicated in the language that begins with an awareness of suffering and proposes 'cultivating ... learning ways ... I will practice'. The use of language is further investigated in the next subsection. Thus the emphasis is on recognising what one already does to reduce suffering as well as moving further towards happiness by amending one's behaviour. These are not impositions which in themselves can set up a state of dissatisfaction as they may appear to be unachievable. The awareness of these ethics and the intention to practise them indicates *being peace in order to do peace* as one moves towards transforming suffering into happiness, both for oneself and for others; they cannot be practised perfectly (Nhat Hanh 2008f: 53).

The 14MTs are an expanded version of the 5 and the discussion relating to the 14 need not replicate the analysis that has been delivered above. Therefore, in the following subsection I will compare the original version of the 14MTs created in Vietnam with a recent update from April 2012, highlighting the changes that Nhat

Hanh and the Plum Village community have deemed necessary to make. He recommends they need revising and updating approximately every twenty years (*Dharma* Talk 2009) in order to ensure they are entirely relevant to current society, giving a further indication of the openness with which one approaches these MTs.

6:1:2 Comparison of the original and revised versions of the 14 Mindfulness trainings [60]

The importance of this document is that it was originally formulated in 1964 in the midst of the Vietnam/American War in order to assist the *Tiep Hien* members to not become overwhelmed by the suffering and horrors they experienced during the War. The Order or 'core community' (Nhat Hanh 2000a: 10) is particularly for those who have chosen Nhat Hanh's teachings as their path and have embarked on a deep study and practical examination of the 14MTs. This is not to suggest the MTs are limited to Order members. As with the 5MTs they are conceived not only as an internal document, but to be of use to anyone wishing to practise an ethical lifestyle and are intended to be reflected upon regularly in order to understand what each one is saying and how they are relevant to one's own life.

Whilst the original version of the trainings teaches through succinct aphorisms such as 'do not accumulate wealth while millions are hungry' (5th MT) the revised version spells out in a paragraph or two more universal ways of behaving. The amendments from the original precepts where all apart from number thirteen begin with 'do not' to inclusive declarations that one can take into one's practice, 'aware of' or 'aware that', move from a negative to a positive affirmation and are more encouraging.

The original speaks of 'you' whereas the revision uses 'we' signifying a more intimate understanding from a communal perspective. The use of 'we' is deliberately inclusive as it sets up a group that includes the reader (Helmbrecht 2002: 31) yet is it also

---

[60] See Appendix 3 for the full version of each document.

excluding anyone? If one disagrees with any part of what is being stated does that exclude one? It creates a sense of community, which I surmise is intended, yet does this indicate those who are in the community and those who are not? It specifies the intended use for the MTs is to be recited as a community or Unit which makes them sound odd if read alone. Furthermore, does the use of 'we' imply general agreement which could make one feel in the wrong if that is not the case? Clearly 'we' is meant to be inclusive rather than exclusive indicating interconnectedness and is aimed at 'those who attempt to live up to the spirit of the Order' as well as the core community (Nhat Hanh 2000a: 10), yet there are some difficulties presented by using language in this way including a presumption that one has to be part of this community to practice these MTs. Nhat Hanh often reiterates, as he himself found, this type of mindful practice is easier within a *Sangha* or community (Nhat Hanh 2002a: 58) and it is perhaps from this intention that the term *we* is used.

In the revised version each begins with 'aware' emphasising that awareness, or Mindfulness, is the starting point from which the practice emanates. The openness and non-attachment of the 1st MT is reflected in this language as the use of 'aware' rather than 'knowing' infers a possibility of change instead of permanence. Moreover, each MT expresses determination and commitment to fulfill these trainings without making unrealistic assertions. The use of language such as 'learn', 'do our best', 'practice' and 'try' also accentuates an intention without a connotation of a particular outcome. The phraseology such as 'determined to' and 'committed to' suggests an appreciation of endeavour whilst being sensitive that one learns on the path of practice and adjustments may be needed to one's viewpoint or beliefs. Calling them trainings rather than rules leaves room for mistakes and failure without judgement. The quality of non-judgement is further accentuated by the lack of binary opposites and the emphasis on interbeing.

Is it necessary to have both sets of trainings, given that Nhat Hanh wants to eradicate the differences between the practices of monastics and laity? Whilst this is possible within the monastic setting of a fourfold *Sangha*, there are differences between practising in a monastery full-time and practising as a layperson with many other requirements on one's time. The 5 and 14MTs are both based on teachings from the *Buddha* and I would suggest they are both necessary as they appeal to different stages of understanding. The 5MTs are usually the first contact one has with these ethical teachings and once one has practised them for some time one could move on to the 14. Having said that, it is possible to begin with the 14MTs but again I propose this could be difficult without the support of a *Sangha* of some form.

Having examined the ethical qualities of the MTs it is apparent that compassion is a necessary characteristic in undertaking them. This is explored in the next section through one of Nhat Hanh's poems.

6:2 Please call me by my true names

As has been discussed earlier in this chapter, Nhat Hanh's teaching on Mindfulness incorporates an 'ethic of non-dualism' (Fasching & Dechant 2001: 159) and deep understanding of compassion centred in the phrase *my happiness lies in the happiness of others*. All the MTs are expressions of the Buddhist concept of compassion and the question arises how does one develop compassion? The answer is given in the 4th MT 'be with those who suffer'. Nhat Hanh advocates 'we need to stay in touch with suffering only to the extent that we will not forget, so that compassion will flow within us and be a source of energy for our actions' (2007c: 9). One should practise being with those who suffer without taking on their suffering like the analogy of a doctor who can identify an illness and cure a patient without having to directly experience the illness themselves (Nhat Hanh 2007f: 6). Again this reflects Nhat Hanh's teachings that whilst acknowledging the presence of suffering one does not stay there but opens up one's view to the prospect that there is more than suffering and it is possible to appreciate happiness and other positive qualities whilst still being aware of suffering. One does not negate suffering as a part of human existence nor does one wallow in it. The relationship

In the Tradition of Thich Nhat Hanh

between suffering and happiness is further explored in the following section.

Compassion is 'an orientation of the mind that recognises pain and the universality of pain in human experience and the capacity to meet that pain with kindness, empathy, equanimity and patience' (Feldman & Kuyken 2011: 145). It can further be described as 'the ability to stand in another's shoes' and is tested to the limit (Harris 2010: 125) in Nhat Hanh's poem *Please Call me by my True Names*.

Don't say that I'll depart tomorrow -
even today I am still arriving.

Look deeply: every second I am arriving
to be a bud on a Spring branch,
to be a tiny bird, with still-fragile wings,
learning to sing in my new nest,
to be a caterpillar in the heart of a flower,
to be a jewel hiding itself in a stone.

I still arrive, in order to laugh and to cry,
to fear and to hope.
The rhythm of my heart is the birth and death
of all that are alive.

I am the mayfly metamorphosing
on the surface of the river.
And I am the bird
that swoops down to swallow the mayfly.

I am the frog swimming happily
in the clear water of a pond.
And I am also the grass-snake
that silently feeds itself on the frog.

I am the child in Uganda, all skin and bones,
my legs as thin as bamboo sticks.

In the Tradition of Thich Nhat Hanh

And I am the arms merchant,
selling deadly weapons to Uganda.

I am the twelve-year-old girl,
refugee on a small boat,
who throws herself into the ocean
after being raped by a sea pirate,
and I am the pirate,
my heart not yet capable
of seeing and loving.

I am a member of the politburo,
with plenty of power in my hands.
And I am the man who has to pay
his "debt of blood" to my people,
dying slowly in a forced-labor camp.

My joy is like Spring, so warm
it makes flowers bloom all over the Earth.
My pain is like a river of tears,
so vast it fills the four oceans.

Please call me by my true names,
so I can hear all my cries and laughter at once,
so I can see that my joy and pain are one.

Please call me by my true names,
so I can wake up,
and the door of my heart
could be left open,
the door of compassion. (Nhat Hanh 1999a: 72-73).

The poem begins with an expression of interconnectedness with natural forms and does not distinguish between a bird, mayfly, frog, snake or myself. This viewpoint suggests one would not exploit nature, but would treat it in a nonviolent way as one's self (Clough 2005: 124). Later in the poem Nhat Hanh denotes developing one's compassion to the extent that one can appreciate the circumstances that arise to create a pirate, a rapist, or an arms dealer rather than emitting repulsion or disgust. From an individualistic stance it seems an almost impossible task to stand in the shoes of another, yet from the viewpoint of interbeing one can appreciate the necessity of seeing how another's viewpoint can arise. This non-dogmatism and openness is emphasised throughout the MTs. The poem does not judge or condemn the rapist. Nhat Hanh

> ... cannot separate himself from either the good or evil ... in the world, whether in the world of nature or of human society ... Nhat Hanh expresses the omnipartiality of enlightenment, refusing to judge others – an enlightenment that carries him beyond dualistic judgements of good and evil (Fasching & Dechant 2001: 158.)

Nhat Hanh indicates that given the same conditions he might have become the same as the pirate (2007a: 62) thereby converting his anger or sense of injustice into compassion. He calls upon one to recognise the rapist suffers too. Sawatsky comments 'for some people this language may seem too airy, romantic or even naive' (2009: 178) yet the concept of non-judging pervades Nhat Hanh's pedagogy and is necessary in order to begin the process of understanding and compassion that Mindfulness denotes. One is being called upon to drop one's preconceived notions and practise the teachings from the *Satipatthana Sutta*, ' ... with clear understanding, mindful, having abandoned every craving and every distaste for this life' (Nhat Hanh 2006c: 15). Nhat Hanh equates compassion with happiness and the lack of it with suffering (2003a: 46), as discussed in the following section.

6:3 Thich Nhat Hanh's teaching on suffering and happiness

> Every day we touch what is wrong, and, as a result, we are becoming less and less healthy. That is why we have to learn to practice touching what is not wrong - inside us and around us. When we get in touch with our eyes, our heart, our liver, our breathing, and our non-toothache and really enjoy them, we see that the conditions for peace and happiness are already present (Nhat Hanh 1992e: 7-8).

Here Nhat Hanh indicates Mindfulness is an activity that encourages well-being by focussing on the positive rather than negative aspects of life. That is 'intentionally redirecting the focus of attention to aspects of experience less likely to support the arising and continuation of configurations that cause suffering' (Teasdale & Chaskalson 2011: 104). Focussing on happiness and 'what's not wrong' instead of things that are *wrong* can bring the being to a positive state of mind and focus instead on what is possible (Maex 2011: 170). When the focus moves away from dwelling on suffering one can begin to notice and appreciate aspects of life that promote happiness.

As discussed in the previous chapter an aim of Plum Village is to transform suffering into happiness through Mindfulness. What does Nhat Hanh mean by happiness? It is not the removal or the opposite of suffering; 'happiness and suffering inter-are. It is like left and right. To think that the right can exist without the left is absurd' (Nhat Hanh 2004a: 65) which demonstrates his view of the interconnectedness of both happiness and suffering further expounded in his teaching 'no mud, no lotus' (2003a: 201). 'From the mud we can create the beautiful, fragrant lotuses of understanding and compassion' (Nhat Hanh 2003a: 202). Nhat Hanh equates happiness with understanding and compassion and demonstrates that even in the most difficult personal circumstances compassion is possible; 'I have lived through a lot of suffering myself, and I can tell you that compassion can free you from the most difficult situations' (Nhat Hanh 2002a: 32). As discussed in Chapter 3, by displaying compassion in Vietnam Nhat Hanh was able to walk a neutral path that did not take sides in the conflict and because of its detached position he was able to propose a nonviolent path that offered happiness to the greatest number of people.

He further elucidates 'I do not want to go to a place where there is no suffering, because I know that in such a place I have no means to learn and to cultivate my understanding and love' (2003b: 56). Nhat Hanh's teachings are founded in the principle *my happiness lies in the happiness of others* which indicates it is only by nurturing and expanding one's compassion, understanding and love that happiness becomes available. 'When we practice mindfulness, we are in contact with life, and we can offer our love and compassion to lessen the suffering and bring about joy and happiness' (Nhat Hanh 1999d: 81). He does not see a difference between individual suffering and the suffering of *others* therefore any work done to reduce suffering will benefit more than the individual.

Moreover, 'happiness is possible only when you stop running and cherish the present moment and who you are' (Nhat Hanh 2009a: 17). Happiness is not to be attained in the future, but is only available through Mindfulness of the present moment. The 2nd training, as discussed above, determines Nhat Hanh's interpretation of happiness which 'depends primarily on our mental attitude and not on external conditions'. Consequently he construes happiness to be contentment and an acceptance of things the way they are as desire for things to be different can lead to a lot of suffering. Also it is looking within oneself for the source of happiness rather than assuming it can be procured externally through acquiring material goods or from other people.

Furthermore, what does Nhat Hanh mean by suffering? Although some scholars suggest the original word *dukkha* cannot satisfactorily be translated into English because it has several connotations such as impermanence and unsatisfactoriness (Keown 2003: 81), Nhat Hanh uses the term 'suffering' which he indicates was the means by which the *Buddha* liberated himself; 'without suffering, you cannot grow. Without suffering, you cannot get the peace and joy you deserve' (1999d: 3-5). He further indicates there is more to life than suffering and whilst some 'students of Buddhism' suggest all life is suffering, Nhat Hanh argues it is one's attachment that causes suffering not the thing itself (1999d: 19-23). This is reiterated in the phrase 'pain is inevitable, but suffering is optional. You may choose not to suffer even when the pain is there' (Plum Village Online Monastery 2011) as demonstrated in the analogy of *the second arrow* (Nhat Hanh 1992c: 433).

The second arrow is a description of attachment without Mindfulness. There is an experience of suffering in terms of unpleasant feelings or physical pain (the first arrow) which is one kind of suffering, but added to this can be the emotional feelings 'by the way we relate to them' as if one has been hit in the same spot by a second arrow (Teasdale & Chaskalson 2011: 91). It is this second layer of judgement superimposed on the first that magnifies 'the actuality of pain and distress' (Feldman & Kuyken 2011: 145). By awakening oneself to the possibility one does not have to be hit by the second arrow that causes much more suffering than the first, happiness is possible. 'Mindfulness tells us that there is a distinction between simply hearing [a] sound and the story that we build around it' (Salzberg 2011: 179). This indicates the suffering of the second arrow is in the mental formations that are watered by associating with the pain. Instead one is simply required to observe what takes place in body, mind and feelings with gentle interest accepting '... things as they are' (Nhat Hanh 2009a: 23) and allowing change to happen naturally. This allows for a detachment from the thoughts or feelings which one can observe without the usual connotations that they are personal, that they belong to *me*. With Mindfulness one can be detached from and appreciate pain without being hurt by the second arrow of attachment to the suffering. Here Nhat Hanh denotes a difference between pain felt as part of the human experience and suffering which is a mental formation added on top.

The third of the Four Noble Truths denotes there is a cessation of suffering which Nhat Hanh terms 'well-being' juxtaposed with the 'ill-being' that is often called suffering (Nhat Hanh 2012c). In the 14MTs each one examines suffering in a specific instance and then offers the means of transforming it into happiness through Mindfulness and in this respect they concentrate much more on 'the wondrous, refreshing, and healing elements that are inside and around us' (7th MT) than on suffering. Nhat Hanh's pedagogy intends to show that by concentrating on the joys and delights found in the present moment it is possible to move beyond suffering. This is demonstrated throughout Plum Village which 'is a place of flexibility, suffering and joy, but the emphasis is on joy' (Sawatsky 2009: 185).

Nhat Hanh proposes Mindfulness can be an antidote to alcohol, drugs and unrestrained consumerism all of which can be sought as a means of achieving inner peace and whilst the effect may be achieved temporarily it does not last. 'Consuming itself can become a kind of addiction, because we feel so lonely ... when we watch TV, read magazines or books, or pick up the telephone, we only make our condition worse if our consuming is not mindful' (Nhat Hanh 1992e: 92-3). Consumption of this kind can be toxic and unfortunately one is not aware of its effects when lost in forgetfulness. 'To live mindfully means to stop ingesting these kinds of poisons. Instead, choose to be in touch with what is wonderful, refreshing, and healing within yourself and around you' (Nhat Hanh 2002a: 18).

Forgetfulness, the opposite of Mindfulness, produces a lot of unhappiness, dissatisfaction and dis-ease. A Zen story aptly describes this condition. A man sits on a horse which is galloping very quickly. A passer-by enquires to the rider where he is going and the rider replies, "I don't know, ask the horse" (Nhat Hanh 2007a: 65). Caught in usual habit energies where one takes one's thoughts to be true and is guided by them is analogous with the rider being led by the horse. Mindfulness, however, when practised regularly allows the rider to be in control and to choose which thoughts or feelings require attention and which can be allowed to pass by. This method can offer 'renewed strength and vitality' (Singh 2003: 4) as well as a reduction in stress, anxiety and the eruption of emotions such as anger and fear. Independent happiness which 'arises from within a mind that has been trained and has attained some degree of inner peace' (Payutto 2002: 92) does not depend on external or material phenomena in order to be achieved and is therefore within the power of each individual to experience, as it is not conditioned by situation or status.

As discussed earlier, Mindfulness means one can develop 'an awareness of how one can live responsibly, responding to the needs of others' (Mitchell 2002: 57) because of the awareness that suffering arises not only within oneself, but within others also. With the awareness and wisdom which Mindfulness cultivates one can be open not only to the needs of others but also to how one can help them in response. The cultivation of Mindfulness can enrich one's life imbuing it with happiness and a sense of meaning (Paramananda 1999: 34) and it can do the same for others as well by providing balance and stability (Boyatzis & McKee 2005: 115). Throughout the MTs Nhat Hanh develops this aspect of ethical responsibility, which is nurtured through being concerned for the welfare of others.

In this section I have demonstrated Nhat Hanh's teaching on the interrelationship of suffering and happiness, succinctly depicted in the phrase *no mud, no lotus* (2003a: 201). This teaching further expands the pedagogy of the MTs by indicating the self-responsibility that one has for one's own happiness. The Four Noble Truths are subtly woven into each of the MTs, beginning by acknowledging an awareness of suffering, yet also the path leading to the end of suffering which for Nhat Hanh is embedded in Mindfulness. In the next section I explore how this teaching is permeating out into the world.

6:4 The expansion of Mindfulness from Thich Nhat Hanh's teaching

Previously I have established the emphasis Nhat Hanh places on Mindfulness as the crux of his pedagogy. In this chapter I have concentrated on the MTs as the means by which he imparts Mindfulness to the community and demonstrated in the previous chapter how every activity at Plum Village aims towards this key Buddhist teaching as its foundation. The significance that Nhat Hanh accords to Mindfulness goes beyond other Buddhist practices. For example, Gunaratana (2002) writes predominantly about Mindfulness within meditation and less on its effects in one's daily life whereas for Nhat Hanh the practices of Mindfulness throughout the day are important, not just what takes place in sitting meditation. Furthermore, Shaw denotes the more usual practice of Mindfulness within sitting meditation, 'an important distinction must be made between the kind of sustained sitting practice that needs regular sessions and the full attention of the practitioner, and things that can be done as part of a daily routine ... so as to develop more fully mindfulness and concentration' (2009: 263). Conversely, I propose that Nhat Hanh's teachings are in order to infuse all aspects of one's life with Mindfulness rather than restricting it to periods of sitting meditation. He places equal worth on the daily practice of Mindfulness and the formal sitting practice, as can be seen in the discussion above, and it could be that the weight he consigns to it is having an effect worldwide as the following example shows.

There is no conclusive proof that Nhat Hanh's emphasis on Mindfulness has directly affected its prolific growth in mental health and clinical settings, yet one conversation with a monastic indicated his belief that this is the case, it is permeating out into society through osmosis due to Nhat Hanh's influence (IC, Monk C 2011). This is substantiated by the fact that Kabat-Zinn attended a retreat with Nhat Hanh in 1987 (Nhat Hanh 1993a: 87) having instigated a Mindful-based Stress Reduction (MBSR) programme at the Center for Mindfulness in the University of Massachusetts Medical

School[61]. The programme successfully aims to institute a lifestyle change by gradually establishing meditation practices that are to be used on a daily basis. More recently both MBSR and MBCT (cognitive therapy) have become recognised practice programmes worldwide and in 2011 the journal *Contemporary Buddhism* dedicated an entire volume to Mindfulness practitioners from both Buddhist and secular backgrounds. This exponential growth in MBSR and MBCT courses, Mindfulness in schools programmes, mindful retreats and workshops demonstrate that Nhat Hanh's teachings are employable in secular society beyond the realms of Buddhism which, no doubt, Nhat Hanh would approve of. It is my understanding that this rapid expansion of interest in Mindfulness is due to the emphasis Nhat Hanh has given it.

6:5 Conclusion

In this chapter I have examined the ethics of Mindfulness through the 5 and 14MTs, as a means of disseminating Mindfulness into society and further demonstrating the applicability of Mindfulness to all aspects of daily life. I have established that both the 5 and 14MTs reveal Mindfulness is a step-by-step process and demonstrated these are not rigid prescriptions that one has to strictly adhere to, but proposals through which one looks deeply into each situation. One takes an ethical stance by examining one's perceptions, beliefs and understanding in order to be more mindful rather than adopting a blanket formula to apply to any and all situations. The MTs may be deliberately vague in places in order for one to responsibly decide for oneself what appropriate action to take. This ensures one is not creating more suffering, both for oneself and others, but actively doing what one can to appease it. I do not suggest Nhat Hanh is being ambivalent, instead he is requiring his students to find for themselves a way of living nonviolently and compassionately with

---

[61] The clinic offers an eight-week programme that introduces Mindfulness and meditation practices to people who may never have come across these before, as a means for reducing stress in their lives and aiding chronic illnesses often related to lifestyle (Kabat-Zinn 1997: 117-127).

recognition that they are one cell in an interconnected body and the interviewees who discussed the MTs concur with this viewpoint.

The balance between theory and practice signifies the MTs are to be studied and analysed only as a forerunner to being put into practice in order to really discover their meaning. They are intended to be an ethical path by which one may choose to lives one's life, not a theoretical document. Throughout, the MTs address suffering in its widest sense so as to indicate there is no area that Mindfulness cannot be applied to and this is aptly demonstrated by the consideration given to consumption in the fifth training. Here, it indicates one looks at everything one consumes using all the senses. Nhat Hanh's prominence in applying the MTs is in transforming suffering into happiness not negating that suffering exists, but demonstrating that there is more to life than suffering. If one gets caught in the idea of suffering one cannot see beyond it to the simple joys and beauties the world has to offer. According to the MTs, holding onto dualistic perceptions or viewpoints through which a lack of communication and misunderstandings develop creates suffering and selfish behaviour is paramount. The solution Nhat Hanh suggests is interbeing which promotes qualities such as compassion, generosity and caring for the welfare of others as well as nurturing wholesome seeds such as joy, peace, love, understanding and healing.

The consistently nonviolent, compassionate and ethical approach that Nhat Hanh promotes is not vastly different to the moral or common sense teaching that one may find in any religious institution or school. Yet the non-dogmatic approach that Fernando highlights in subsection 6:1:1 demonstrates that the application of Mindfulness through the MTs is not concerned with adhering to a set of beliefs or truths but examining one's life with an open-minded and ethical understanding that reveals the realm of 'things as they are' (Nhat Hanh 2010b: 23), discussed in Chapter 2.

In the second half of the chapter I have examined the aspects of suffering and happiness as elucidated by Nhat Hanh as well as compassion, demonstrated by the poem *Call Me by My True Names*. This pertinent and profound poem brings to life the aspect of interbeing by showing how conditions can arise to create a pirate, a rapist or an arms dealer and that one needs to develop an appropriate response of compassion and understanding rather than judgement. Understanding and compassion are further expanded upon in section 6:3 considering Nhat Hanh's teaching on suffering and happiness. These inter-be with one another and cannot be unpicked, as depicted in the analogy 'no mud, no lotus'. Here the lotus cannot exist without the mud from which it grows. Likewise happiness is born out of suffering and cannot exist without it. In transforming suffering into happiness one is not looking to reach a utopian state of no suffering, instead one can appreciate the learning that can come from being with one's suffering and acceptance of things the way they are.

Finally I propose my own understanding that the proliferation of Mindfulness teachings in many spheres such as MBSR and MBCT courses, NHS, schools and a recent All Party Parliamentary Group in the Government (Oxfordmindfulness) is due to Nhat Hanh's concentration on and advocacy of Mindfulness as '... an important agent for our transformation and healing' (1992e: 27). I suggest his view of Mindfulness as an essential teaching has been demonstrated throughout the chapter and is apparent from the prolific amount Nhat Hanh has to say on the subject in both his *Dharma* talks and books.

Through the necessary transplantation process that Nhat Hanh underwent due to his exile, his teachings have evolved to concentrate on Mindfulness. This does not mean he no longer expounds Engaged Buddhism, but in meeting Westerners he realised a different approach was necessary. As discussed in the previous chapter he had to adapt his teachings to meet these diverse needs, responding with a teaching that addressed the individual whilst recognising that said individual is part of a greater whole. Therefore, whilst the practice and application of Mindfulness has not altered from the one he was introduced to at the age of sixteen he has fine-tuned his teachings to respond particularly to the Western society in which he is now living. Like the *Buddha* Nhat Hanh teaches to a particular audience, sometimes in response to specific questions, addressing a precise form of suffering. His transplantation from Vietnam to France, and from an Eastern to a Western culture has engineered how his practice and his teaching have been reshaped over the past few decades and this theme is discussed in the next chapter.

7. The Transplantation of Thich Nhat Hanh's Teachings into the West

Buddhism is not one. The teaching of Buddhism is many. When Buddhism enters one country, that country always acquires a new form of Buddhism (Nhat Hanh 2007a: 84).

Introduction

As Thich Nhat Hanh recognises here one cannot expect the Buddhism that he practised in Vietnam to be replicated in the West due to differing circumstances and worldviews that it meets. In this chapter I examine the transplantation process and what has happened in Nhat Hanh's situation by considering the '…complex relationship between tradition and interpretation' (Pye 1969: 236) and how Nhat Hanh has worked with this tension in his teaching and his way of life. I have adopted Knott's categories for transplantation as the framework for this chapter,

> … for understanding what happens to a religious group and its tradition when it moves to a new geographical and social location. When such a change in circumstances occurs a number of factors contribute to producing new patterns of religious behaviour, organisation, experience and self-understanding (1986:10).

Knott initially proposed five aspects for consideration; home traditions, host traditions, nature of migration process, nature of migrant group and nature of host response (1986:10-13). In 1991 she added a further seven points; language, transmission, identity of the individual, identity of the group, leadership, universalization and the impact of Western ideas (1991: 100-106). I will select the relevant sections for discussion, as some of Knott's points are more pertinent to Nhat Hanh's particular situation than others. Of paramount importance, I suggest, are the home traditions and these will be expanded upon in section 7:1.

In Chapter 4 I presented a Plum Village Model which not only encapsulates the details of Plum Village but also demonstrates that this can be transplanted into other settings. Thus, transplantation in Nhat Hanh's case is not just from Vietnam to France, but further extends to other monasteries that have been founded since 1982. If Plum Village is the hub then these monasteries are satellites which are connected to the hub but not entirely the same as it. This creates a tension between autonomy and contingence which will be addressed in this chapter as one of the aspects of transplantation. As religions have spread in the world they have 'adapted to local circumstances and incorporated local religious beliefs and practices' (Winzeler 2008: 255). There has been a degree of localisation for the Plum Village monasteries whilst seeking to retain the tradition as a practice with strong links to Vietnamese Buddhism, its teachers and ancestors. This will be further examined in section 7:2. There are currently (as of 2014) seven worldwide monasteries[62] that have formed from the hub of Plum Village, three in the USA, and one each in Germany, Australia, Hong Kong and Thailand.[63] Most of the satellite monasteries have arisen out of a desire from the lay

---

[62] *Bat Nha* in Vietnam manifested as another satellite from 2005 to 2009 and although it has since closed down is discussed in Appendix 4 as it reflects Vietnam's current attitude towards Nhat Hanh which has not materially altered from the 1960s.

[63] Deer Park Monastery, California; Magnolia Grove Monastery, Mississippi; Blue Cliff Monastery, NY state; EIAB Germany; Entering The Stream Monastery, Victoria, Australia; Asian Institute of Applied Buddhism (AIAB) Hong Kong and Thai Plum Village, Thailand.

community for monastic support closer to home than Plum Village (this especially applies to those in America). However, the EIAB was Nhat Hanh's idea, which he put into operation with the support of other monastics, choosing its site centrally within Europe. Australia is a new manifestation and there is little information about it as yet on the Internet and no link from the Plum Village website. Blue Cliff in New York State and EIAB in Germany provide the focus of observation as monasteries I have conducted field research in.

Plum Village has created a model of harmony, which has arisen from adapting to its new situation as a centre of many cultures, and this exceptional circumstance is transplanted into further communities blending with other cultures. Although there are many facets in each that are recognisable from the Plum Village Model there are also individual qualities that naturally occur as each develops. The success, or otherwise, of this transplantation will be considered in this chapter.

The purpose of this chapter is to investigate the transplantation and retransplantation of Nhat Hanh's teachings and whether there is a continuation of the pedagogy beyond Plum Village. I shall address the following questions; has the retransplantation process produced any material differences between Plum Village and the other monasteries? How is the continuity that exists between the hub of Plum Village and its satellites demonstrated? Is autonomy recognisable in the satellite monasteries worldwide? How does the lay community interact with these monastic ventures? The key argument for this chapter is that the Plum Village community has successfully negotiated the transplantation process and I will demonstrate how it confirms Knott's theory relating to transplantation.

As indicated in the quotation at the beginning of the chapter Nhat Hanh is aware that a new form of Buddhism will be created in any new cultural and social situation. Through meeting and working with different cultural expectations and norms he has developed a teaching that does not deny the history or traditions on either side, but seeks to blend these together.

7:1 Home traditions

The 'home traditions' Knott identifies mean that Nhat Hanh did not arrive in France empty-handed; he brought religious and cultural traditions with him; 'it is these, in interaction with the new environment, which produce consequent religious changes' (Knott 1986: 10). I begin by reflecting on the home traditions that have been a considerable influence on Nhat Hanh's teaching and practice, whilst the 'consequent changes' in fact fall into the next section.

It is important for Nhat Hanh to retain Vietnamese traditions for the continuation of the culture even though he is no longer in Vietnam. Although Plum Village is open to visitors from any country, and the monastics come from a wide array of different countries, they are a predominantly Vietnamese community following the tradition of Vietnamese Buddhism (Plum Village3). The food and the ceremonies undertaken come from Nhat Hanh's traditional culture. Initially the Summer Retreats focussed on realising his ideal to maintain the home traditions. The same desire was felt by the diaspora attending Plum Village in the early years which became a home from home for them and linked the children with their Vietnamese ancestors; classes in the mother tongue were offered to the children every afternoon (SI, Person B 2010) thus allowing for continuity. This point incorporates two later aspects of Knott's, language and transmission, and how, or whether they further the '... retention of religion and culture' (Knott 1991: 100). To ensure this retention is taking place all monastics have daily lessons in Vietnamese as well as reinforcing traditions by '... the repetition of rituals' (Knott 1991: 101) such as *Tet*[64], the main celebration of the year. Whilst the numbers of Vietnamese monastics may be in the

---

[64] *Tet* is the celebration of the Vietnamese New Year and takes place in January or February.

minority at the satellite monasteries they are substantial enough to preserve the traditions of Vietnam that Nhat Hanh wishes to uphold and revitalise. Furthermore, numbers have recently increased, as Vietnamese monastics via Thailand[65] are relocating to monasteries in America as well as Plum Village. Indeed, all monastics perpetuate the Vietnamese traditions through the food and culture, not just those who originate from Vietnam. Moreover, supporting charitable aid to Vietnam is an ongoing process through fund-raising and profits from the sales of Nhat Hanh's books (Sr Chan Khong comment after *Dharma* talk 2010).

Maintaining the home traditions has been vital for Nhat Hanh and the Vietnamese diaspora who formed the majority of the original community. However, the community quickly became multi-cultural. Twelve years ago Nhat Hanh stated 'our Sangha is made of twenty or more nations and cultures' (2003c: 26). Currently (2014) the international Sangha directory of the Mindfulness Bell lists thirty-five countries (Mindfulness Bell/International). For many of these people the Vietnamese traditions that Nhat Hanh follows are not their own home traditions. Therefore Nhat Hanh made the following appeal on a UK retreat in 2010, as he recognises his aspirations for Vietnam are not yet fulfilled,

> the work is not entirely done, we are half way on realisation, so it is my desire, my aspiration that my friends, you are here, you continue the work. We need several decades more in order to completely renew the teaching and the practice of Buddhism, to offer them to the younger generation (Nhat Hanh Q&A 2010).

Thus, an aim of the monasteries is to continue to revitalise Buddhism in Vietnam in order to complete the job Nhat Hanh started. However, this does not seem to be taking place in the lay community.

---

[65] See Appendix 4 on *Bat Nha*.

From my field research I conclude in the UK Units[66] there is no discernible Vietnamese influence as is palpable at Plum Village. I propose this is one area connoting a difference between the monasteries and Units and an aspect of adaptation of the transplantation process. Given the small Vietnamese population in the UK it is understandable that whilst I have come across the occasional Vietnamese person practising with UK Units they are in the minority, 'overwhelmingly, the C of I are ethnically white (94%), Western converts (69%), middle aged, well educated and largely middle class' (Henry 2008: 233). However, this does lead one to wonder whether the charitable support for Vietnam that is active in Plum Village will diminish once Nhat Hanh has passed on. Nhat Hanh's focus of attention is aimed firmly towards the continued suffering in Vietnam, yet this could present problems for future generations who no longer have the understanding that he has due to his proximity to the suffering caused by war. This adaptation of the transplantation process indicates the interaction Knott discusses that will formulate how the Plum Village Model moves forward.

Whilst efforts towards maintaining the home traditions are currently strong will they diminish once Nhat Hanh is no longer living? Nhat Hanh's connection to his antecedents and forefathers and therefore his country is not just a Buddhist perception, it is also cultural. He is closely empathetic to his country of birth, his ancestors and teachers and the interdependence on their input into him as a person. Yet there could come a time when the concerns for Vietnam are not the priority that they are for Nhat Hanh and the links may be severed. As each monastery develops in its new context, especially in a European

---

[66] Although Nhat Hanh refers to any group practising Mindfulness as a *Sangha*, for the purposes of clarity, I will refer to the monasteries as *Sanghas* and use the term *Unit* in examining the role of *Sangha* in the lay communities. The distinction is made between monastic communities living together on a full-time basis and lay groups which meet regularly (weekly, fortnightly or monthly). Some interviewees refer to their Unit as *Sangha* and in these instances *Sangha* will be retained.

setting, the priorities may focus on the needs of that country rather than one in Southeast Asia.

Will the monasteries' focus of charitable attention then concentrate on their host nations? Alden suggests Nhat Hanh is promoting a spirituality '... which appears to be free from worries about French state and its politics' (2006: 144). Given the discussions in Chapter 3 it is not surprising that Nhat Hanh does not engage in French politics yet is it the case that as efforts are concentrated towards Vietnam and the home traditions the French suffering is being overlooked? Could there be an over-emphasis on Vietnam, where in fact he has little influence, which detracts from the pressing needs of Europe? Does there now need to be a greater balance between the home traditions and host traditions? This is not an either/or situation. Concentrating on the charities in Vietnam does not necessarily mean the host countries are ignored. Yet, one could enquire why Nhat Hanh has apparently not done more to alleviate suffering in France where he has been living for over thirty years and yet insists on focussing on Vietnam. Whilst the discussion so far has indicated a confirmation of Knott's theory relating to home traditions I propose these questions demonstrate the changing form of Nhat Hanh's Buddhism as it moves into its fourth decade at Plum Village. It seems Plum Village and the satellites are retraditionalizing (Knott 1986: 13) as they begin to engage with their host communities, by which I mean they are finding their own ways of practising the Plum Village Model that does not replicate entirely what Nhat Hanh has begun.

Although there are no obvious social programmes coming from each monastery, as discussed in Chapter 6, with the proliferation of Mindfulness into many secular aspects monastics are gradually taking the teachings into schools, prisons and the like. As further discussed in section 7:2, the satellite monasteries are engaging with their local communities by offering workshops or DoMs when invited. They work with retreatants to bring Mindfulness out of the monastery and into the local community, reflecting Nhat Hanh's early work of Engaged Buddhism in Vietnam (see Chapter 3). Whilst there are no discernible programmes or projects being set up that are identifiable as Engaged, the monastics are offering Mindfulness to a secular audience with a slow-growth approach that ensures the practitioners have a firm foundation of Mindfulness themselves before connecting with others to pass it on. This approach answers the question from Chapter 3 about whether engagement has to be visible to be effective. It is happening in a step-by-step way, adopting a long-term approach, yet at the moment it is still nascent and in formation.

The '... consequent religious changes' (Knott 1986: 10) are discussed in the next section examining how Nhat Hanh has connected with Western retreatants and created a form of teaching that '... is not a Vietnamese temple set on European land' (Nhat Hanh 2003c: 21) but also incorporates Western traditions. Plum Village has been the means for Nhat Hanh to implement his vision of a community dedicated to reinvigorating the practise of Buddhism that has been a part of his country for many hundreds of years, as well as a community that upholds Vietnamese traditions and cultural aspects, ensuring they are not lost. This has only been possible once he left Vietnam as the government and the Buddhist elders were not prepared to accept Nhat Hanh's adaptations (as discussed in Chapter 3). Next I examine the process of relocating into a mainly Christian country.

7:2 Relocating into a Christian country

This section combines the second and fifth of Knott's aspects, that of host traditions and host response, i.e. the various ways in which the migrant community come into contact with the established traditions of the host community and whether they meet any attitudes of racism or issues '... concerning assimilation and integration' (Knott 1986: 11-12). This section also examines the '... consequent religious changes' (Knott 1986: 10) as mentioned above. Here I consider the particular aspects of relocating into a mainly Christian country and the ease or otherwise with which this has been accomplished. It would appear France was an easy country to gain access to because of its former colonisation of Vietnam and therefore a Vietnamese community was already established. It was also preferable to America as a base because Nhat Hanh's experience was, 'in France it's more relaxed ... in the United States it's like [a] craving, very hungry animal'; Nhat Hanh was offered so many invitations to speak in America that he would have had no time for his own practice (SI, Chan Khong 2011).

7:2:1 Host traditions

Examples of the Plum Village community working with host traditions are firstly that both Christmas and Easter are celebrated at the monasteries, alongside *Tet*, the Vietnamese New Year (mentioned earlier); secondly Nhat Hanh does not ask people to drop their original traditions in favour of becoming Buddhist, but re-examine them from a Buddhist perspective (Nhat Hanh 2007c: 105) and many Christians find these two traditions complementary; finally, in incorporating Western religious ideas into his teaching he compares *nirvana* to the Kingdom of God, thereby seeking to speak in terms that are comprehensible to his audience. Kay refers to this as a trans-cultural process (2004: 13-14), i.e. transplanting Buddhism into a country with a Christian heritage relies on working with its inherent values, as well as providing another option if said values are being rejected by the individual. Buddhism presents something different, and can respond to the current needs of some people in a way that Christianity can be found wanting (Knott 2005: 55). Buddhism offers a non-theistic approach that gives responsibility for one's actions back to the individual as opposed to being deferred to God. It also offers a psychological approach that unites mind and body and investigates the effect the mind has upon the body. However, this universality does not negate the fact that this is a Buddhist monastery, and stories of the *Buddha*'s teachings, meditation practices and philosophical concepts relating to Plum Village are passed on by '... imitation and gradual absorption through participation' (Knott 1991: 101). As discussed in Chapter 5 the practice is experiential and at Plum Village one is expected to take part in the meditations and ceremonies on offer. Nonetheless, lay retreatants are not expected to be Buddhist or convert to Buddhism as will be further discussed in section 7:3.

Do the two communities (i.e. Asian, mainly Vietnamese and Western) work harmoniously together? There is a recognised tension between cultural differences (Nhat Hanh 2003c: 26) yet because of the foundation of interbeing this is not an insurmountable difficulty, but one of the many ways in which the practice is to be applied. Nhat Hanh addresses the issue of host versus home traditions by denoting,
> sharing the practice, we have to learn to understand the culture and the environment of the West. We have to present our own jewels in the way that is appropriate to the Western way of thinking. If we don't understand anything about the language or the behavior of the Western people, how can we offer anything? (2003c: 26).

This was something he recognised as a young monk in Vietnam and was one of the points of disagreement with the Buddhist hierarchy. Understanding another's perspective as the basis for working together is something that Nhat Hanh brings into his teachings. From working on a basis of understanding rather than imposing a Vietnamese approach the international community comes together and is able to move beyond the differences.

7:2:2 Host response

Next I examine a couple of examples of working with the local community that have been experienced by the monastics, addressing the aspect of host response and what difficulties, if any, there have been in establishing Plum Village and the satellite monasteries. Although there was initially some tension from neighbours close to Plum Village, and reluctance to sell them land, this was quickly dissipated by the openness of the monastics and their invitation to welcome the neighbourhood to open days, in order to be transparent about what was taking place there. Any funds raised from the open days, in which traditional Vietnamese food is offered, goes to a local 15th century church (IC, Nun A 2009). I am not aware of any other instances of racism or prejudice towards the monastics in their endeavours to establish Plum Village. Furthermore, at Blue Cliff they have not yet installed a big temple bell '... which is usually invited early in the morning and late in the evening ... The reason being, our neighbours prefer us not to make too much noise in the early morning, so that's a reason why we haven't got a big bell' (SI, Monk A 2010). This demonstrates their preparedness to be considerate towards the neighbours rather than imposing a practice which may be usual for a monastery but unusual for New York state.

The adaptation of the Plum Village model to progress the transplantation process involves the relationship each satellite monastery builds with the local, and nationwide, lay community as it is only through their continued support that the monasteries can exist and continue to flourish. If everyone chose to go to Plum Village because of Nhat Hanh the other monasteries would be unsustainable. The reason for their existence, however, is twofold. One is the request of the local lay community to have more immediate access to the teachings, especially for those outside Europe, where Plum Village is not an easily accessible option. Combined with this is the easier means of the teachings permeating into society through local centres.

What is the role of the lay community within these satellite monasteries? In many respects it is quite a traditional, mutual role. The lay community provide for the material needs of the monastery and the monastics respond by offering teachings; 'the monastic community (Sangha) in its classic form, emphasizing monastic and lay interdependence, was the longstanding ideal of Buddhist organization' (Cantwell & Kawanami 2002: 45). The satellite monasteries could not exist without the continued support of the local laity. Nhat Hanh emphasises a fourfold community comprising monks, nuns, laymen and laywomen and he suggests if the monasteries are thus composed 'the laypeople living there [will] be a bridge between the monastic community and the laypeople in society' (Nhat Hanh 2003c: 29). A further positive aspect of the satellite monasteries is that the lay community comes to rely less on Nhat Hanh as the only teacher by interacting with other monastic teachers, which is further discussed in section 7:4 on the question of leadership. Yet another reason is to keep the monastics in touch with the wider world, an aspect Nhat Hanh considered was not happening in Vietnam when he became a novice.

How does each monastery balance its existence within society and yet live apart from it? Each of the monasteries holds weekly and sometimes twice-weekly DoMs to which anyone is invited for free although a donation towards the cost of lunch is requested. This is an important means for the local community to have a connection with the monastery, to remove the sense of mystery and otherness and to forge harmonious relations. For those new to the practice it is a feasible way of getting a taste of the Mindfulness practices without having to commit to a week's retreat. And for those more experienced in Nhat Hanh's teachings the DoMs provide frequent contact with the wider monastic *Sangha* and direct contact with the teachings.

These monasteries and retreat centres are not isolated or cut off from the society into which they have placed themselves and care has been taken in each circumstance to choose an appropriate site bearing in mind nearby neighbours and local community, as well as accessibility. They actively seek to understand and work with the host response by assimilating and integrating with (Knott 1986: 12) the local community rather than being separate from it. The purpose of each monastery is to work for the enlightenment of all beings not just those that step within its boundaries. As well as local neighbourliness Nhat Hanh and other monastics make visits to prisons and detention centres to teach Mindfulness to the inmates and reaching out to those who want to access the teachings but cannot attend a retreat (Nhat Hanh 2002a; NBCUniversal 2011). The monastics need to be aware of the influences that are playing out in society in order to be of most use to visiting retreatants. Although they are detached from the world in order to benefit from a full-time practice of meditation and Mindfulness they are not detached from its influences or the suffering that people in society are experiencing. One monk at Plum Village undertook an experiment to investigate the effects of war video games by spending several hours each day himself playing the type of games currently popular with young people and monitoring his own reactions. Due to practising within the monastic setting he was able to see clearly the negative aspect of aggression that he felt within himself and how it affected his relationship with others, even those he lives closely with and regards as brothers (IC, Monk D 2011). In this intelligent way the monastics are able to understand and respond to the stimuli that are affecting people in daily living and which they may feel they have no control over. The resistance that the monastics build up in practising Mindfulness is palpable when one comes into contact with them and is transferable to laypeople who wish to operate in a more mindful way in their daily lives.

These are but a few examples of the monasteries seeking to integrate themselves with both the host traditions and response as opposed to being cut off from them. It would be nonsensical to practice interbeing inside the monastic walls and not expect to integrate with one's neighbours outside of them. As discussed in Chapter 3 the monasteries are viewed as garden nurseries in which the 'seedlings' are nurtured until strong enough to be planted in society; 'our training and our practice in the monastery are a preparation to go into the world' (Nhat Hanh 2010c: 7). The monastics are taught in order to be able to go out into diverse circumstances and lead retreats within lay society as will be further discussed in section 7:4.

A further adaptation of working with the host traditions and response in a co-operative relationship between monastics and laity is through offering *Dharma* talks and retreats in locations beyond the monasteries. Nhat Hanh tours the world on a regular basis offering retreats to thousands of people. He employs the *Buddha*'s exhortation (see Chapter 3) to 'go forward for the benefit of many people … out of compassion for the world, for the good, welfare, and happiness of gods and humans' (Kloppenborg 1973: 43). Nhat Hanh imitates the *Buddha's* modus operandi by travelling to teach for the greater part of the year before returning to Plum Village for a three-month Winter retreat. In Nhat Hanh's case his travelling is extended worldwide. The monastics likewise go out from their monasteries and return home for the Winter retreat which is their main teaching period. The monasteries allow them to be detached from society whilst maintaining a close connection with it in order to further understand the suffering in the world; i.e. being free from its influences which can cause great unhappiness. Here, the reciprocity of the monastics and laity is a vital means of disseminating Nhat Hanh's teachings to society in general as well as ensuring the monastics are kept in touch with the suffering in the world.

The raison d'etre for the monasteries is to counter and transform 'the individualism, isolation, and greed fostered in modern Western societies' yet being enough removed so as to not succumb to individual and societal practices (Hunt-Perry & Fine 2000: 54). They are addressing individualism and its by-products from a standpoint that is detached from society rather than embroiled in it. The monasteries support the lay community and wider society by demonstrating a mindful way of living. They have taken a decisive stance of being apart from society, yet are engaging with it through the lay community. The main reason for being apart from society is in order to be able to practise Mindfulness on a full-time basis without the distractions of family or having to earn a living, and yet they are not entirely cut off from society because of the strong interaction with the lay community. There are mutual benefits between the monastic and lay communities.

In this section I have discussed some of the aspects relating to introducing the Plum Village Model into Western countries and how they thereby engage with the host traditions and response. Unlike the animosity that Buddhism received from Christianity in Vietnam (see Chapter 3) from my field research there have been few difficulties in this transplantation process. Perhaps this could be, particularly for Plum Village, because of the nature of the migrant group. I briefly address the next two aspects (of migration process and migrant group) here as they do not require a separate section.

When Nhat Hanh left Vietnam he believed it would be only for a few months, and was expecting to return shortly. He had to adjust to the idea of exile once he was abroad, and the possibility that he may never return to Vietnam again. It would appear it was not Nhat Hanh's intention to stay abroad, although by settling in France he must have been reconciled to the idea it would be some time before he returned to Vietnam. He came to France as an individual, yet others came as Boat People at the end of the Vietnam/American War deciding to leave once the War had ended and political instability gave them no choice. Others, such as Sr Chan Khong, voluntarily came to join him. They came looking for his teaching. Both Kollontai and Van der Veer denote the possibility of migrant communities becoming more conservative (Van der Veer 2002: 101) or '... traditional and perhaps fundamentalist' (Kollontai 2007: 65). Is this the case with Nhat Hanh? I suggest not because he has established a practice of not adopting ideologies, dogmatism or fanaticism and non-attachment to views (2nd MT). He has adopted a middle path that retains both the host traditions of the new country into which he has located as well as the home traditions, culture and religion of Vietnam as he has been practising for seventy plus years. Nhat Hanh is not seeking, as Knott argues, to '... standardize [his] beliefs and practices' yet is creating a contemporary form of his religious tradition (1986: 13). This involves both the monastic and lay communities. In the next section I consider two aspects in Knott's theory of the identity of the individual and of the group (1991: 102-103), which I discuss as one aspect because, due to interbeing, the identity of the individual and the group are interrelated. As part of this discussion I consider Nhat Hanh's interpretation of *Sangha*.

7:3 Identity of the individual

The identity of the individual has been dealt with in section 1:3 relating to interbeing and section 4:3 on the individual's role within the *Sangha*. However, Nhat Hanh's emphasis on *Sangha* on the issue of identity of the religious community and its believer during and after the transplantation process is relevant to this aspect of Knott's framework, which discusses how the individual self-describes and what is the individual's role within the community? (1991: 102). In this section I address these questions as two subsections.

7:3:1 How does the individual self-describe?

In considering the identity of the individual the interviewees emphatically concurred that the Plum Village Model is not only for Buddhists and many retreatants do not label themselves Buddhist as Person 25 denotes, '... I don't know that I consider myself one at all' (SI, 2009). Nhat Hanh and his simplistic yet effective teachings attract people, not necessarily the Buddhist aspect although that has an effect on all that takes place, '... it's a very coherent philosophy that one does not have to choose to identify with in order to gain something out of it' (SI, Person 1 2009). The interviewees recognise the openness of the teachings and the practices, '... anyone can come here, but obviously it's a practice centre in this tradition of Buddhism ... but mindfulness isn't a Buddhist thing, mindfulness is a human thing' (SI, Person 15 2009). Expanding this point, there is an appreciation that the teachings (particularly the MTs) are not exclusive to Buddhism, the ethical content (as discussed in Chapter 5) is also available in the host traditions and one does not have to be a Buddhist or become one to undertake them, '... most people I've met here seem to belong to or are affiliated with other religions or none' (SI, Person 11 2009). Indeed, as mentioned above, Nhat Hanh encourages people to reconsider their own religion and discover the jewels there rather than converting to something new (Nhat Hanh 2007c: 105; 2009a: 86-88). Person 29 reiterates this point, '... he's very very clear about ... "don't give up your beliefs, we don't need more Buddhists" ... but we need more people to be engaged with the mindfulness' (SI, 2009). Mindfulness is the key aspect of the practice and is what draws individuals to monasteries and Units, to become part of a *Sangha*, as discussed in the next section.

Nhat Hanh is quoted as saying he is 'a Buddhist free from Buddhism' (SI, Person 15 2009) which is reiterated in the 1st MT; one does not hold onto any ideology not even Buddhism (Nhat Hanh 2000a: 17). Perhaps it is this quality of freedom from dogma and the practical application, as the *Kalama sutta* suggests (see Chapter 1), of knowing for oneself through experience that has such an appeal to non-Buddhists. The Plum Village website states 'the Buddhism that we offer to the world is not a religion, but an art of living, with methods to transform and heal' (Plum Village2) and two interviewees confirm this statement '... I wouldn't be here ... if the religion were to be forced upon me' (SI, Person 26 2009); ' ... a way of life, as a practice, is I think how they would describe it not as a religion' (SI, Person 1 2009). People are searching for ways of transforming and healing their everyday lives and many find answers in Nhat Hanh's teachings. 'I think that it can give you important tools that we all need and things that are missing in our culture, western culture' (SI, Person 25 2009). The missing aspects that Person 25 raises echo Knott's point in section 7:2:1 that people can find answers in Buddhist practices they did not find in Christianity (2005: 55). Furthermore, Person 25 discussed that the practices of Mindfulness have helped her to improve her relationship with her husband by them making time to sit down and truly listen to each other (SI, Person 25 2009). The individual does not need to describe himself or herself as Buddhist in order to practise Mindfulness but may instead indicate they follow Nhat Hanh's teachings. In the next subsection I examine the individual's role within the community (*Sangha*).

7:3:2 What is the individual's role within the *Sangha*?

As discussed previously (sections 1:3 and 4:3) Nhat Hanh's original interpretation of *Sangha* encompasses the role of the individual as the concept of interbeing denotes a collective rather than an individual worldview. He defines *Sangha*-building as 'the most important action of our century' (2006a: 294) indicating the prominence he places upon its role within the community of practice. By this he is suggesting that forms of *Sangha* or community are vital to combat growing individualism. From Nhat Hanh's point of view, with a philosophy on integration rather than differentiation and interbeing as the foundation of thinking, the individual is taken care of within the *Sangha*, but the first consideration is always the *Sangha* not the other way round. In returning to Knott's theory concerning the allegiance to a group and in relation to belief and practice this emphasis on *Sangha* as foremost instead of the individual relates closely to the aspect of communal decision-making and '... learning to look with the eyes of interbeing and to see ourselves and others as cells in one Sangha body ... to realize collective awakening' (10th MT). The allegiance to the group, whether this is Plum Village, another satellite monastery or the local lay Unit, is strong and reinforces the practice of working towards collective insight (8th MT).

Nhat Hanh indicates,
in my tradition we learn that as individuals we cannot do much. That is why taking refuge in the Sangha, taking refuge in the community, is a very strong and important practice ... Without being in a Sangha, without being supported by a group of friends who are motivated by the same ideal and practice, we cannot go far (Nhat Hanh & Lawlor 2002: 21).

The emphasis on the necessity of a *Sangha* is further accentuated by Nhat Hanh's unique interpretation of *Maitreya* and I shall examine this concept next.

Maitreya is usually recognised '... as the future Buddha currently residing in the Tusita heaven who will follow on from Sakyamuni[67] Buddha' (Keown 2003: 170). In *Mahayana* Buddhism it is acknowledged that there have been many *Buddhas* and *bodhisattvas*, and *Maitreya* is a generic name for the next *Buddha* 'the Buddha of love' (Nhat Hanh 2007c: 17; Gombrich 1998: 377). 'Maitreya literally means benevolent, and he will come ... as an incarnation of great benevolence, just as Sakyamuni Buddha did' (Yamaguchi 1956: 181). At a time when the practice of Buddhism has diminished

---

[67] Sakyamuni Buddha is the title of the *Buddha* '... found particularly in Mahayana sources where it distinguishes him from the numerous other Buddhas mentioned in the sutras' (Keown 2003: 245).

'because the world is caught up in cycles of destruction and renewal' (Bell 1991: 120) *Maitreya* will manifest as a cosmic saviour in order to 'establish a utopian state of justice, peace, and truth' (Sponberg 1988: 7). Note that both Yamaguchi and Sponberg refer to an individual. However, Nhat Hanh's interpretation of *Maitreya* is that 'the next Buddha may be a Sangha, a community of people who share the same values, and not just an individual person, because love is to be practiced collectively' (Nhat Hanh 1999c: 69). This appears to be a personally held but often-used elucidation (Nhat Hanh 2008b: 111; 2011: 18),

> a Sangha that practices loving kindness and compassion is the Buddha that we need for the twenty-first century ... We have the power to bring ... *Maitreya* Buddha into existence just by sitting together and practicing deeply. So the next Buddha may not take the form of an individual. In the twenty-first century the Sangha may be the body of the Buddha (Nhat Hanh & Lawlor 2002: 17).

Nhat Hanh's emphasis on *Maitreya* as a *Sangha* further confirms the allegiance of the individual to the group in Knott's theory and indicates an adaptation of the transplantation process in which the *Sangha* becomes more and more important compared to other Buddhist traditions. It supplants an alternative view, such as on *vipashyana* retreats, of the practitioner liaising with a teacher but not communicating or reflecting upon their own practice with anyone else.

In the Samyutta Nikaya XLV.2 Ananda suggests to the *Buddha* that *Sangha*,

> "admirable friendship, admirable companionship, admirable camaraderie" is half of the holy life, but the *Buddha* responds it "is actually the whole of the holy life. When a monk has admirable people as friends, companions & comrades, he can be expected to develop & pursue the noble eightfold path" (cited in Maex 2011: 174).

Person 17 suggests this is the ethos of the Plum Village tradition and even if people don't live up to it *Sangha* is the emphasis (SI, 2011).

How can *Maitreya* become a reality? This is achieved through the praxis of theory by turning Nhat Hanh's words into practical application through collective energy. In order to emphasise the collective energy Nhat Hanh also uses the analogy of a river to indicate *Sangha*;

> if we try to go to the ocean as a single drop of water, we will evaporate before we even arrive. But if we go as a river, if we go as a community, we are sure to arrive at the ocean. With a community to walk with us, support us, and always remind us of the blue sky, we'll never lose our faith (2006a: 294).

The proposal to join together as a river instead of struggling as a droplet of water addresses the rampant individualism he met in coming to the West. The European environment is different from Vietnam, and for the Plum Village community to adapt successfully in its transplantation process it addresses suffering in its Western context which is generally psychological rather than physical. Therefore many of the practices are aimed at healing broken relationships as well as providing a harmonious foundation from which to move forward which is supported by the *Sangha*, whether monastic, lay or a combination of the two. *Sangha* therefore becomes the vehicle for moving the transplantation process forward as individuals closely relate to their Unit (see more discussion on the Units in section 7:6) in a way that Person 2 indicates; whereas '... Plum Village is a rejuvenator, but realistically once a year is about as much as it's going to happen' the local Unit's weekly meeting provides valuable friendship and community (SI 2010). In this respect the Plum Village Model has adapted considerably from the practices Nhat Hanh grew up with in Vietnam that focussed on monastic practices and did not consider meditation important for the laity (see Chapter 3).

In the next section the question of leadership is addressed specifically through Knott's points relating to future leaders and how decisions will be made.

7:4 Leadership

The aspects of leadership as Knott defines them relate to where the teachers (*Dharmacharyas*) come from i.e. do they have to also be Vietnamese, how will future decisions be made and who will make them? These questions will be addressed through examining the two satellite monasteries visited as part of my field research, Blue Cliff and EIAB, as well as worldwide retreats.

In relation to Plum Village leadership currently focuses on Nhat Hanh as its inaugurator although there are many other *Dharmacharyas* who can also take the lead and this is happening more frequently as small groups of monastics run retreats in other countries without the presence of Nhat Hanh. From my field research at Blue Cliff and EIAB these monasteries adhere closely to the Plum Village Model with the same careful attention to Mindfulness. Continuity is assured because the majority of monastics have been trained in Plum Village initially before moving to a satellite and they do not necessarily stay long in each place, but move around as the need requires or they particularly request. The fluid interchange of monastics from one monastery to another assures stability in the teaching. DVDs of Nhat Hanh's *Dharma* talks are also a regular feature of the satellite monasteries maintaining close links with the teaching. The Q&A session at Blue Cliff, which at Plum Village would have been led by Nhat Hanh, was delivered by a panel of monastics and lay Order members, however, the content and quality of the teaching was in no sense lacking because of this, demonstrating the *Dharmacharyas* are already active.

A further indication of this came in 2009. 'One Buddha is not Enough' was the title of a retreat held in Colorado, August 2009 as part of Nhat Hanh's American tour. Its prophetic name led to a unique retreat out of which a book of the same name has been published (2010d) recording the *Dharma* talks given there as well as reflections of many retreatants. It was unique because Nhat Hanh, who had been ill on the previous retreat, was in hospital for its duration and not able to lead the retreat. Nearly one thousand people attended and each had to personally address why they had come, whether it was for the practice of Mindfulness or to see Nhat Hanh. Eight people went home, but for those that stayed it turned into a remarkable demonstration that Nhat Hanh's teachings are not reliant on him, but upon the practitioners themselves; 'by staying together as a Sangha, we broke through the habitual patterns of avoiding and running away from pain. Transformation and healing took place in every person' (Nhat Hanh 2010d: xiv). The sixty monks and nuns, who thought they were there to support Nhat Hanh by facilitating Family groups, became the teachers themselves. Although no successors to Nhat Hanh have been publicly named the implications from this retreat are that many monastics can teach in a way consistent with Nhat Hanh's pedagogy. It is also a visible demonstration that Nhat Hanh's teachings are assented to and practised both by the monastic and lay communities, accepting his pedagogy and that of the *Buddha*'s that, for the teachings to be of use, one has to become one's own teacher and seek one's own liberation with diligence[68] (Armstrong 2000: 171). This is especially relevant in not relying on Nhat Hanh as the teacher but discovering for oneself the path of practice.

This is what the monastics are trained for and it is not only in this extreme situation that monastics are asked to lead retreats, it is happening consistently now. In one example, the UK saw a greater presence of monastics throughout 2011 with several visits taking place including a two-week Wake Up tour visiting five Universities throughout the UK and culminating with a two-day retreat in Kent in March, a Wave and Water seaside retreat in April, a Monastics Spring Retreat in Scotland in May, a family-friendly retreat at the New Barn centre in Dorset in May, a health retreat in West Sussex in June and a combined CoI/Quaker retreat at Woodbroke Centre in Birmingham in September. Furthermore, EIAB utilises lay *Dharmacharyas* to lead many of its courses, as discussed below. The above examples indicate the 'future' *Dharmacharyas* are already

---

[68] DN 16; A 4: 76.

present and teaching in a way consistent with Nhat Hanh's pedagogy.

The question of what will happen once Nhat Hanh is no longer living is answered in that there are many monastics already in the role of *Dharmacharya* despite the fact that Nhat Hanh continues to be the focal point from which the teachings emanate. Indeed, it is not clear why these people are not encouraged to offer more teachings on retreats where Nhat Hanh is present as well. Perhaps he is not yet ready to go into retirement.

When asked about the continuation of Plum Village after Nhat Hanh has passed on, interviewees note there is no one person in particular who stands out as the successor, but more likely is a group of monastics to take forward Nhat Hanh's pedagogy. This suggests his interpretation of *Maitreya* has been taken on board by the community and is seen as the way for Plum Village and the CoI to continue. The following quotation from one interview summarises the opinions of half the interviewees (eighteen out of thirty-six).

> There's no replacement like him but I think later on maybe one person will be really good about teaching about the breathing, maybe another will be good at Touching the Earth, the other will be good at Buddhist ecology, the other is about building the monastery, or the other will be good at making music out of his poems, so each person will be helpful, under his guidance about how to go as a river, and I think like that in the long run they could carry on and from there they will grow into a new generation of maybe Thich Nhat Hanh (SI, Monk B 2010).

The consensus seems to be Nhat Hanh will be a hard act to follow and therefore it will need many people to continue the roles he currently undertakes. This, however, reiterates the discussion in subsection 7:3:2 on the importance of *Sangha* for taking the adaptation process forward. Indeed, the editing committee who prepare Nhat Hanh's new books for publication (discussed in Chapters 5 and 6) already demonstrates this.

In relation to the question as to what will happen to the Plum Village Community once Nhat Hanh has passed on this could be a difficult shift for the community to undertake having been used to what Kay describes as 'the compelling and unifying authority of its charismatic founder' (2004: 217). Although Kay is referring to a specific death of a leader in the Order of Buddhist Contemplatives (2004: 217) the comparison to Nhat Hanh is relevant. Yet the indications are that many *Dharmacharyas* are available to continue the teaching and that they are from many different cultures, not just Vietnamese.

In addressing Knott's question as to who will make decisions and how they are made Monk A - a senior *Dharmacharya* at Blue Cliff – expounded, the monks and the nuns have separate councils, 'we have a Bhikshu [monks'] council, and Bhikshuni [nuns'] council and also a Dharma teacher council, which is combined nuns and monks, and so these councils make decisions' (SI, 2010). Involvement from Plum Village in general, or more specifically Nhat Hanh, will only be offered when requested although Blue Cliff is relatively new and may feel it needs guidance as it grows 'but he [Nhat Hanh] likes to let us be autonomous, it's one way to grow' (SI, Monk A 2010).

The issue of adaptation relates to the question of autonomy versus dependence on the Plum Village model. A notable difference for Blue Cliff from Plum Village is that Noble Silence[69] extends from 10pm in the evening until after lunch the following day taking in the whole morning. Within this period there is an hour's working meditation, which may include some talk as necessary, and a *Dharma* talk. The effect of this is that there is little time for chat or idle gossip as the focus is wholly on the purpose of retaining Mindfulness throughout the day in each separate activity. I consider this enhanced the atmosphere of Mindfulness rather than imposing silence upon it. At Plum Village they have not felt it necessary to extend Noble Silence, but this indicates the autonomy of each satellite monastery who, not feeling obliged to copy Plum Village, adjust the programme for their own needs. The overall autonomy of

---

[69] See Chapter 5.

Blue Cliff may not be obvious at first sight as it appears to be a copy of Plum Village, but a mindful community has to be aware of the differing circumstances in which it is operating and there is no compunction that new monasteries replicate what takes place at Plum Village.

A further indication of autonomy comes from EIAB which is engaging with a wider audience than those interested in following Nhat Hanh's teachings with a continuous programme of short courses offering different ways of practising Mindfulness. I attended a health retreat designed to 'help you recover your inner capacity of self-healing to bring joy and wellbeing' (EIAB/health retreat). The courses are aimed at a practical application of the Buddhist teachings to one's daily life, again reiterating that these teachings are praxis, they are not theoretical. A cursory glance at the list of courses offered (EIAB/events) indicates a wide variety in which Mindfulness is specifically applied in divergent situations such as forgiveness, teaching, communication, ill health and psychotherapy to name but a few. In the years since I attended the number and assortment of courses has considerably expanded.

The aspiration of the Institute is to offer long courses equivalent to university modules (IC, Nun B 2010) continuing the work Nhat Hanh began in Saigon with Van Hanh University. It promotes integrating the Buddhist teachings of Mindfulness in a way that is approachable not only to those with a specific interest in Buddhism but to anyone. With this in mind lay *Dharmacharyas* run some of the courses as well as monastics. The health retreat included people who knew little or nothing about Nhat Hanh and were not there because of him, but because of the particular course on offer. This is another adaptation for the institutes in passing the teachings on to a wider community. The monastics' own practices are exactly the same, but Mindfulness is being disseminated to a wider audience without an emphasis on Buddhist practice.

In 2011 a second institute was inaugurated in Hong Kong, the Asian Institute for Applied Buddhism (AIAB). As has been discussed in

Chapter 4 the term Applied Buddhism is now being used to denote a difference in approach to the other monasteries. A further divergence is the use of the term institute which implies a specifically educational establishment as discussed previously. It signifies a more formal approach than that of village. Although the teachings are no different to the Plum Village Model the courses are oriented towards giving a precise focus to the practice. As well as the ones mentioned earlier, courses in 2012 include Yoga and Buddhism, Happily doing business together, a Christian-Buddhist Dialogue and Sound-Colour-Silence (EIAB/events). The institutes aim to demonstrate there is no area that the teaching of Mindfulness cannot penetrate.

EIAB manifests the continuation of the need that Nhat Hanh perceived and briefly implemented in Vietnam which was offering specific short courses with a practical focus. These institutes sit alongside the other satellite monasteries perhaps indicating that there is the need for both types of establishment; those that offer general retreats and those for people wanting a precise focus. Whilst the institutes seek to emulate Van Hanh University in Saigon, the satellite monasteries are more akin to the freedom to practise that was present at *Phuong Boi*.

The above discussion indicates the adaptation process that is taking place as the Plum Village Model evolves and expands over the decades as the '... reinterpretation of traditional beliefs and practices are without end' (Knott 1986: 13), thereby confirming Knott's theory. In each specific setting the satellites and the lay Units are creating their own form of the Plum Village Model as '... they are involved in the making of their religious traditions in its contemporary form' (Knott, 1986: 13). Although Nhat Hanh is currently perceived as the main teacher I have demonstrated that many other monastics and lay teachers are also fulfilling the leadership role.

7:5 The impact of Western religious ideas

In this section I examine the impact that Western religious ideas have on the incoming migrant community. Although this has already been investigated to some extent through the host traditions (section 7:2) there are specific aspects that Knott denotes (1991: 104) (secularisation and ecumenism) which are particularly relevant to the Plum Village Model.

Secularisation is not a fear for Nhat Hanh but something to be embraced, as has been demonstrated in the discussion on the 5MTs in Chapter 6. This is indicated by the inauguration of Institutes of Applied Buddhism and Nhat Hanh's recommendation that '... lately we don't want to use the word Buddhism because the word Buddhism may be an obstacle, so we try to use the word Global Ethics or Applied Ethics' (Q&A 2010). Here he demonstrates a lack of dogmatism in not being attached to the term Buddhism as it can put people off the practices. Instead he has accepted that secularisation is a prevalent force and is meeting this challenge. Furthermore, the issue of ecumenism has been addressed in section 7:3 discussing how the individuals identify themselves and do not feel the need to label themselves as Buddhist in order to follow Nhat Hanh's teachings.

However, although one can see how the term Buddhism could put people off because of its religious connotations there could be similar problems with ethics in terms of people's understanding of it. Nhat Hanh is using this new term to appeal to a wider audience, but is he then discarding the Buddhist roots in which they lie? And is it being deceitful to cover up the Buddhist foundations in which they are based? I find this new phrasing problematic in the sense that it suggests Nhat Hanh has to hide his Buddhist roots. What he offers is different to the secular Mindfulness of MBSR and MBCT courses and should be celebrated as such. Although the term Applied Ethics signifies a declaration that the teachings are applicable for anyone wishing to pursue an ethical path and live a life of happiness that is unconditional, it seems rather short-sighted to discard the Buddhist term at this juncture, given that Nhat Hanh's teachings are deeply embedded in Buddhist teachings and even his particular practices go back forty-two generations.

The question of the impact Western religious ideas have had upon the Plum Village community is also addressed by Kay, has Nhat Hanh's form of Buddhism been '... transformed by the forces of Westernisation and modernisation' (Kay 2004: 14)? Has its early encounter with Christianity in Vietnam influenced what Nhat Hanh teaches in the West? Kay indicates transplantation can be affected by '... the impact of Western cultural, political and ideological forces in Asian countries – particularly in the South and Far east – since the late eighteenth century' (Kay 2004: 13). As discussed in Chapter 3 the French had a powerful influence on Vietnam for a time yet due to this intervention Nhat Hanh as a young monk was impelled to investigate the philosophy and literature of the West, convinced it would have a positive effect on what the Buddhist institute was already teaching. I suggest Nhat Hanh's personal study of Christianity has helped him to understand better the country he is now living and practising in as well as the people he is teaching.

Did Nhat Hanh begin the adaptation process of Buddhism before coming to the West? Events suggest not, as Nhat Hanh indicates that Plum Village was a response to students asking for teachings, rather than a desire on his part to set up a monastery or lay retreat centre (2003c: 25). However, he had begun reforming the practices of Buddhism that he learnt as a novice in Vietnam, (see Chapter 3). As discussed previously this has been fine-tuned during thirty-two years at Plum Village and is still being adapted to meet society's current needs, as the recent interest in Mindfulness in education demonstrates.

Nhat Hanh now indicates a natural maturation process that has taken place; 'not only the monks and nuns and lay practitioners have grown up, but also our methods of practice, our experiences, and the lessons from our own practices have matured like the cedars' (2003c: 20). Furthermore, it is only through coming to the West that he has been able to realise many of the practices he attempted to implement in Vietnam, as denoted in section 7:1 in discussing the home traditions,

> I became a monk in Vietnam. I grew up in Vietnam. I learned and practiced Buddhism in Vietnam. Before coming to the West I taught several generations of Buddhist students in Vietnam. But I can say that I realized the path in the West ... I began to have many deep insights, flowers and fruits of the practice (Nhat Hanh 2003c: 22).

Nhat Hanh goes on to indicate one insight is 'dwelling happily in the present moment' which has become a foundational aspect of his teaching in recent years. The dual purpose of Plum Village has continued to be observed for three decades providing for the needs of both the diaspora Vietnamese community and Westerners. For Nhat Hanh, both are equally important and they validate the fusion of two disparate communities working together to promote unity through diversity. In order to bring diverse communities together there has to be a substantial paradigm of communal living, which others can then emulate. One interviewee denoted,

> I think Plum Village is a slightly bizarre place anyway in that there's all these sort of left of centre Western people and on the other side these probably right of centre Vietnamese people who are very traditional, you know, from traditional monastic backgrounds ... all sort of trying to come together in one place and it works, but I suspect that's a lot to do with Thich Nhat Hanh's strong leadership (SI, Person 20 2010).

This comment highlights the diversity of cultures that come together at Plum Village and yet, because of Mindfulness, can live and work together amicably despite inevitable clashes. I propose the impact that Western religious ideas can have upon the Plum Village Model is lessened by the openness of Nhat Hanh's teachings and the non-attachment to views. As discussed in subsections 7:2:1 and 7:3:1 Nhat Hanh recognises the 'jewels' that are available from all religious traditions and presenting Buddhist ones to a Western audience requires a willingness to find appropriate ways (2003c: 26). Furthermore he does not require Westerners to convert to Buddhism but to find out how Mindfulness works in application for each individual.

Thus far in this chapter I have examined the effect of transplantation upon the Plum Village community using Knott's theory as a framework for exploring the various issues it has met. It has expanded considerably over three decades, opening satellite monasteries in five different countries and developing a lay community worldwide through Units. To some extent the retransplantation process has been examined through Blue Cliff and EIAB, however, I propose there are further questions relating to this, which Knott discusses in terms of the reinterpretation and retraditionalization of traditional beliefs as the youngsters or those new to the tradition make their own contemporary forms (1986: 13). These could affect the continued growth of the worldwide community, and will now be addressed.

7:6 The retransplantation process

The forms of religious traditions that Knott discusses can be multifarious according to factors relating to the group and the new location and these forms are '... not stable ... they change over time' as the contemporary forms of their traditions, beliefs and practices are still in flux (Knott 1986: 12-13). This is demonstrated in the Plum Village community not only with the emergence of satellite monasteries as discussed previously but also by the steady growth of a worldwide lay community, something which Nhat Hanh has encouraged. There are, however, questions relating to this growth in terms of the autonomy of the lay community, whether or how it sustains the Plum Village Model, how the community grows and whether a satellite monastery is an appropriate next step for the UK. These issues all reflect what Pye denotes as the '...complex relationship between tradition and interpretation' (1969: 236).

As indicated at the beginning of this chapter the transplantation of Nhat Hanh's expression of Buddhism has not only happened once, from Vietnam to France, but has also involved retransplanting the Plum Village Model into America, Germany, Asia and Australia as well as throughout the world as lay Units. In the previous sections I have discussed some of the issues that relate to Blue Cliff and EIAB. The lay community represents a further juncture in the transplantation process underpinned by Nhat Hanh's belief that *Maitreya*, the *Buddha*-to-be, will be a *Sangha* not an individual (1999c: 69) as discussed in section 7:3:2. I propose his emphasis on the need for people to form Units within their own communities comes from this declaration. Although not the same as the full-time monasteries, the lay Units are another means of Nhat Hanh's teaching permeating out into society. Furthermore, Nhat Hanh was the only monastic at Plum Village when it began. At this stage it was not certain a monastery was the way forward and he has always encouraged the lay practitioners as he began to develop the practice whilst still in Vietnam with *Phuong Boi*. Therefore a substantial lay community is a natural progression of Nhat Hanh's teachings. The lay Units practising under the umbrella of the Community of Interbeing (CoI) UK will now be examined in order to give some indication as to how they are forming and developing as part of the Plum Village community.

7:6:1 The Community of Interbeing units

The CoI UK is the national organisation which operates autonomously at a local level, and is represented by a group of trustees nationally, through which people have contact with Nhat Hanh's teachings and usually find a Unit to practise with. There are exceptions to this as can be seen on the groups' distribution page from the website (Interbeing/groups) where southern England is well populated with Units whereas these become sparse in the north. Units include the *Deep Listening Sangha*, a telephone community for people who cannot attend a local Unit, and the *Wake Up* movement as well as regular (weekly, fortnightly or monthly) Units lasting approximately two hours. *Wake Up* is one of Nhat Hanh's worldwide initiatives, a Unit specifically for young people (approximately aged eighteen to thirty-five) which offers its own retreats as well as separate programmes within an adult retreat. The Wake Up Units organise free "flash mob" meditations as well as the more usual Unit evenings. These tend to be concentrated in London where the main *Wake Up* Unit is based and are often run as separate events to the CoI Units. Furthermore, *Wake Up* organise their own retreats and whilst these are to be encouraged they do not necessarily promote working together with Units containing people of more mature years. Each Unit is autonomous and democratically makes its own decisions about the programme of the evening or DoM[70] following guidance originating from Plum Village. Whilst autonomy is essential within the local Units there is likewise recognition that 'we are part of the Order, we're not just going off on our own direction' (SI, Person 14 2010). How is this tension between autonomy and dependence addressed? The fact that people are looking primarily for a sense of community suggests they want certain guidelines yet they also want freedom to operate as they see fit rather than a rigid structure that must be strictly adhered to. The shared practice and teachings are what brings the monasteries together and this is likewise apparent within the CoI Units.

The practice that takes place within a Unit comprises many of the elements from the Plum Village Model discussed in Chapter 5. However, with regard to evening meetings of approximately two hours the content can be summarised as a communal practice of meditation, some connection to Nhat Hanh's teachings, Mindfulness and a chance to speak about either one's personal practice or something that has arisen from the evening itself. Each Unit is part of a larger UK organisation that it can refer to for advice if required. Whilst there are means of support and guidance available from both the six lay *Dharmacharyas* and other Order members this has to be requested otherwise the Units run themselves. There are both strengths and weaknesses in this process. The strength comes from each Unit developing an individual responsibility for its own

---

[70] Appendix 5 indicates possible programmes for both a Unit evening and a DoM. Appendix 6 details statistics of the four Units I accessed for the research.

personal practice and expansion, however, the weakness is that a Unit could develop under the umbrella of the CoI, advertise itself on the website and operate without any form of checking or clearance needed from the national *Sangha* as to what is actually being practised. As discussed above the form that each satellite monastery takes is determined by a balance of the Plum Village Model within its host context, creating a form of practice appropriate to each particular setting and the same applies to each Unit as it responds to its particular context. Whilst this autonomy appears to be one of the favourable aspects that draws people to join a Unit it could create difficulties in terms of presenting a cohesive, unanimous message to others.

Theoretically a Unit could form having little or nothing that is recognisable as CoI within it. If this were the case it would actually have no connection to Nhat Hanh's teachings and, in practice, where this has manifested these Units tend not to continue for long; 'if the practice is strong people are drawn to that and the *Sangha* will prosper' (SI, Person 17 2011). Thus they appear to self-regulate without much influence from the national organisation. Furthermore, if the CoI is practising openness and non-judgement as denoted in the MTs there has to be acceptance that each Unit is developing autonomously without judging its practice or the content of its programme.

There is, however, recognition that one belongs to the CoI UK as part of a family and national retreats and gatherings are offered to bring Units together. The description of geese flying in formation (Appendix 7) is an accurate analogy of the requirements needed for *Sangha*-building demonstrating Nhat Hanh's elucidation that 'when we are part of a spiritual community, we have a lot of joy and we can better resist the temptation to be overwhelmed by despair' (Nhat Hanh 2009c: 90). Sixteen of the thirty-six interviewees concur with Nhat Hanh's position that it is easier to practise as part of a Unit and receive support from being connected to it. As an example, the established Cambridge Unit is able to offer many and varied activities within which to practise Mindfulness, such as informal morning mindful walks as well as a more usual evening session. In reciprocity, it is the Unit rather than Plum Village that becomes the focus of the practice for many people.

As discussed in section 7:3:2 Nhat Hanh repeatedly expresses the greater power and momentum of a collective as opposed to an individual (2003a: 176-177; 2003e: 7; 2007d: 70-71; 2009b: viii; 2009c: 90) and thereby gives encouragement to people joining or creating a Unit to support their practices at home (2009d: 69-71). He proposes one has to work together to create a viable Unit;
> I think that my contribution to the building of community life is to say, Do not judge each other too easily, too quickly, in terms of ideology, of point of view, strategies, things like that. Try to see the real person, the one with whom you live. You might discover aspects that will enrich you. It's like a tree that can shelter you (Nhat Hanh & Berrigan 2001: 138).

A non-judgemental atmosphere is crucial in creating a harmonious Unit and trusting in a mutual understanding of confidentiality, which is an implicit requirement in *Sangha*-building. This is demonstrated by the sense of being at 'home' within a Unit, it is a place of belonging. Members of a Unit work together to resist the habit energies running in society, especially rampant individualism, with an awareness of sharing a load rather than one person carrying the burden. This works better within some Units than others. It may depend on whether the Unit has been initiated by one person or several. This does not mean that the aim is to produce clones where everyone thinks and acts the same. Diversity is an important aspect of a Unit and I suggest steps are being taken in a positive direction to offer people an encouraging and mutually respectful atmosphere in which to practice and grow. This is a positive viewpoint with which to take forward Nhat Hanh's teachings once he is no longer able to offer it personally.

Two interviewees expressed 'I felt I had found my spiritual home' (Person 2 2010; Person 27 2010) in describing their Unit. In the present moment there are no doubts that one is in the right place and one is calm and peaceful. These emotions can be tangible during a Unit meeting. This could also explain why many people are attracted to attending retreats and joining Units rather than just reading Nhat Hanh's books, or listening to a *Dharma* talk on CD. One distinctive quality that cannot be found in books is an enhanced aspect of the community experienced in a Unit. 'You receive a kind of energy from being with the Sangha, or find a place of rest ... and that carries you through the rest of the week' (SI, Person 6 2010). The inclusive nature of a Unit allows for 'personal enrichment' as well as support in the practice (IC, York Sangha 2010). It also gives a chance to evaluate how one has been practising, not in terms of a quantitative measurement but in terms of appreciating any new understanding or shift in understanding. A key practice of the Unit is the ability to let go of one's personal ideas and limitations and open up to the democratic voice of the larger body. For example, in inaugurating York *Sangha* the Cambridge Unit was proposed as an ideal to copy, meeting in people's houses with no expense involved in hiring a room. However, this was not possible in York as those who lived centrally had smaller houses and those with larger rooms were too geographically widespread. The idea had to be dropped that the Unit *should* meet in houses, that what works in one place *should* be replicated in another in order to discover what was actually possible. Indeed, the rented room in York is in a beautiful ecumenical centre that is welcoming and accessible. It is not useful or necessary to have an ideal picture of what a Unit should be like, it is only necessary to be present with it each step of the way as it evolves and grows, and being aware of the changing form (Knott 1986: 12). What it becomes is up to those involved and whether or not they are practising, whether it is something that grows and nurtures others or remains stuck in an idea of what a Unit should be. At each point along the way there is the capacity for liberation or bondage. The choice depends on whether one is mindful or not.

7:6:2 Challenges of the Community of Interbeing units

As noted above a further difficulty can be created when the balance of democracy and personal input is too uneven. On the Facilitators' Retreat concern was expressed that if one person inaugurated and facilitated a Unit they could be seen as the facilitator for all time and other people may be reluctant to take on the task, thereby devolving ownership to one person instead of the entire Unit. This can be a problem for some Units and creative ways have to be found to overcome this, such as dividing the tasks on the evening so that the facilitator and the bell master (inviting the bell) are two separate roles. In this way people can be eased into organising roles for the Unit without taking on more than they are comfortable with. For a Unit to progress it needs the input of many people not just one or two, people who are prepared to breathe out as well as breathe in for the healthy growth of a Unit. In this respect *breathing in* is receiving the teachings and *breathing out* is offering them to others, whether this is within the Unit in terms of fulfilling the various administrative roles or speaking about one's personal experience, or outside the Unit in how one relates to others. Yet there also has to be acceptance for someone not to contribute verbally in an evening. Although one may hope that people are at ease to speak freely I propose it is also important for people to know they need not speak, their presence is enough. There are different roles within a Unit and some people are comfortable facilitating a group whereas for others this poses difficulties. From my field research I propose the desire of the majority of the CoI is to use Nhat Hanh's teachings to make a difference to their lives and not to be a sedentary receptor. 'It's not what the *Sangha* can do for you but what you can do for the *Sangha*' (SI, Person 6 2010) emphasises Nhat Hanh's words that one has to be there for the Unit physically and mentally. It is a reciprocal relationship and an expression of interbeing which will ensure the survival and growth of the Unit.

The way Units are currently forming within the UK, as discussed by Henry in section 7:1, is that '... the C of I are ethnically white (94%),

Western converts (69%), middle aged, well educated and largely middle class' (2008: 233). Whilst not deliberately excluding people from other ethnic groups Person 17 indicates, 'my experience of Buddhism in the UK is that it's very much a middle class preoccupation' (SI, 2011) which I would concur with. If this is a national situation as Person 17 suggests there may be little that an individual Unit can do to change this except ensure its doors are open to everyone. Whilst there is little financial consideration within the UK Units, if one is attending a retreat at Plum Village this requires the financial means necessary to pay the £300 plus for a week. This is addressed by a bursary scheme within the national CoI but it may not be reaching those people who would most benefit from a retreat if they are unaware of it. However, all one can do is make sure the Units are open and available to those who are looking for what they have to offer and I suspect a substantial drive in advertising may assist here.

Currently most groups increase by word-of-mouth rather than a concerted advertising campaign. Units do not generally advertise themselves except in localised circumstances, perhaps in free newspapers. There have been discussions within the national *Sangha* how best to advertise local Units yet it appears a decision was taken nationally not to spend funds on advertising. The CoI website provides a means of finding local Units but people have to know of its existence in order to access it. In recent studies on Buddhism in the UK (Bell 1991, Kay 2004, Bluck 2006, Kennedy 2006, Henry 2008) the CoI only features in Henry's thesis. Bell and Kay separately concentrated on two Buddhist groups in the UK and Kennedy did not choose to use the CoI in his research. Bluck intimates although the CoI is too small a group to be included initially further research on his part would include this group (2011). Whilst this has not stopped Units manifesting I suggest it could prevent people from joining simply because they are unaware of the existence of a local Unit within their vicinity. Having said that, other Units have large numbers and in the case of the York Unit this has grown in two years to achieve fifteen to twenty regular attendees from word-of-mouth and the CoI website alone. However, Units of this size do seem to be in the minority.

7:6:3 Moving the Plum Village model forward

I now consider how the CoI are embracing Nhat Hanh's teachings in a way that indicates a mature understanding of 'when you yourselves know' (*Kalama sutta*). I suggest the growth of a Unit signifies the transition when the teachings move from being Nhat Hanh's teachings to being *my practice*. This is an important step for the individual and the Unit to take to appreciate that the teachings do not belong to Nhat Hanh and in many respects are not related to him. He is the mouthpiece through which they are being relayed at this moment in time yet part of the retransplantation process involves how the teachings, traditions and practices evolve through second and future generations. I propose this is when the teachings are accepted as *mine*, i.e. they are 'guiding means to help me look deeply and to develop my understanding and compassion' (1st training).

This development from theory to praxis is expounded in James Fowler's *Stages of Faith* (1981). It begins at the level of 'imitative' acceptance (1981: 133) and hopefully moves to an 'adult' appreciation or judgement for oneself rather than having to be told what to do, and how to behave. This movement does not necessarily take place, one can stay at the level of acquiescence, yet the nature of Nhat Hanh's teachings encourage people to test things out for themselves rather than blindly accepting what they are being offered. This is an aspect Nhat Hanh strongly emphasises especially with regard to the way people can view him as a wise person or a guru. 'He's not teaching a practice that depends on him' (SI, Person 4 2010) is one perception denoting the teachings do not emanate from him. It continues through him, being passed on continuously for over forty generations. Likewise, 'he isn't the path, the practice is important' (SI, Person 19 2010). This can be hard to comprehend especially when he is such a charismatic figure (see Chapter 5), but it is a necessary development to ensure the continuation of the teachings once Nhat Hanh has passed on.

The emphasis is on finding out for oneself rather than being instructed, 'knowing that answers discovered are more valuable than answers given, we trust the Sangha's wisdom' (Cushing 2002: 118). Part of a Unit evening usually consists of a sharing session similar to a retreat (see Chapter 5). One can bring problems and difficulties to the Unit without expecting to be told what to do or given an answer, but more importantly emotional support and wisdom are offered (SI, Person 10 2010) through deep listening, which provides the space to find the answer for oneself. All the members of the community contribute in their own way by offering their 'own understanding and willingness to practise and transform, and be the practice' (SI, Person 21 2010). As well as offering a place of refuge and safety, protection and support the Unit is the place where Mindfulness can be tested before going *out into the world*. A further question concerning the retransplantation issue relates to whether the monasteries are sustainable and where future monastics will come from.

7:6:4 Are the growing numbers of monasteries sustainable?

In adapting the Plum Village Model through retransplantation one pertinent question is whether there is a saturation point for the monasteries worldwide. If the satellite monasteries are being run by monastics who train firstly at Plum Village will there be a point at which they become unsustainable? EIAB was in need of more monastics to complete the building project in which they intended to live. Not only did it require funds it also needed manpower to undertake the work, much of which the monastics aimed to do themselves. Likewise at Blue Cliff, Monk A highlighted an issue in that the small numbers of monastics made it difficult to cope with the growing number of lay 'friends' who wished to visit (SI, 2010). It is a fine balance in that the monastery is growing and wishes to encourage laypeople to visit and attend DoMs and retreats, yet it also needs a considerable number of monastics to support and care for these visits 'to maintain [the] energy, to make it available for people' (SI, Monk A 2010).

One benefit for both EIAB and Blue Cliff, which comes out of the misfortune of *Bat Nha* (see Appendix 4) is that monastics who were able to get to Thailand and have been continuing their practice there, are now moving on to these monasteries or Plum Village. However, they are mostly young people in their twenties and will require a lot of support and training themselves and may not be immediately ready to offer the provision EIAB and Blue Cliff are requiring. When I interviewed Monk A in 2010 he had recently requested more monastics from Plum Village and, whilst this is happening, they come in small numbers only, one or two at a time, as there is a similar need for them at Plum Village. There is a fine logistical balance taking place between the monasteries which whilst ensuring continuity in the teachings could present problems in there being a finite number of monastics available. Is this why there is currently so much emphasis on attracting young people for a 5-year monastic programme?[71]

As can be seen by EIAB and the 5-year monastic programme Nhat Hanh has big plans but can they be fulfilled? Are there sufficient monastics to physically undertake them? Nhat Hanh appears to have many schemes that he wishes to put into action, but it is left up to the monastics to implement them and this could cause difficulties. However, as was demonstrated in America in 2009 the monastics had to step up and replace him (2010d). There is, nonetheless, clearly a tension between proliferating the teachings through new monasteries throughout the world and ensuring there are sufficient numbers of monastics to implement them. Therefore, adopting a slow-growth policy as discussed in section 7:1 ensures they are not taking on more than is manageable. This relates back to the

---

[71] At the 2010 Nottingham retreat Nhat Hanh announced the instigation of a new 5-year programme intended to attract young people to the monastic life without them having to commit the rest of their lives to it. This new venture is also offered as an alternative to university, where the monastics are concerned about the overuse of drugs and alcohol and wish to submit a viable alternative. Those who complete the 5-year programme will return to the lay community as *Dharmacharyas*.

discussion on balancing being and doing in subsection 4:5:1 in that burnout can be the result unless one balances the input from meditation practice with the output of compassionate work. There is understandable caution in opening new monasteries. First it has to be ascertained whether there is enough support from the lay community before undertaking a considerable new project. This is demonstrated through ongoing conversations in the UK.

7:6:5 Is a satellite monastery possible for the UK?

For several years there have been discussions amongst the CoI UK as to whether it is feasible to have a monastery in the UK (SI; Person 17 2010) but it largely depends on whether the lay Community can maintain it. After the Nottingham retreat in 2010 Nhat Hanh expressed an idea that the next monastery to open would be in the UK (SI, Person 22 2011) and it certainly seems that it requires his support although not necessarily his consent (SI, Person 17 2011).

Since 2008 the CoI has owned the Being Peace Cottage in Dorset, which is open for all Units to use and is available for small residential retreats or meetings. Although the cottage sleeps only six an adjacent field centre can house a further forty people and is ideal for small CoI retreats but not a retreat led by Nhat Hanh, such as the Nottingham retreats which accommodated over eight hundred people. The proposal is for the cottage to become, at least, a base for monastics from Plum Village if not a permanent monastery from which they can then support the Units. Contact with and teaching from the monastics trained at Plum Village plays an essential part in the growth and sustenance of the CoI UK and therefore, having a residence which can offer accommodation to visiting monastics will enable this to happen more frequently. Henry suggests the development of the CoI 'largely depends on the outcome of the Being Peace centre' (2008: 233), which was still being purchased when he conducted his interviews. Whilst I recognise the truth of what he says I would propose the continuation of the CoI depends wholly on the efforts and practice of its members and others who attend the Unit meetings and support for this can come from Plum

Village, as it currently does, as easily as monastics within the UK. Plum Village is not so remote as to make it inaccessible for the majority of the CoI. Although having a permanent monastery in the UK would be a great asset I would not argue the continuation of the CoI UK is dependent on this and it should not be vital to the growth of the lay community in the UK.

However, a permanent community within the UK, either monastic or lay, would be a step forward for the CoI. Whether the Being Peace cottage will become a local retreat centre for large numbers, replacing the need to travel to Plum Village, is currently unclear but there may be hopes to move in that direction. Its location does make it a long travelling distance for those in the north of England or Scotland who may still find it easier to go to Plum Village. The Being Peace Cottage in Dorset could be the base for a small number of monastics although there is not enough accommodation for both monks and nuns; it would have to be one or the other. A strong and supportive local Unit would need to be in place, as well as the backing of the community nationally, committed to providing financial as well as physical support. This is not going to happen overnight, but it seems the enthusiasm and support of many people in the lay community are factors that will move it in this direction if it is considered appropriate. As of 2014 it is not certain that this will be the way forward for the UK and instead the influx of monastics to lead retreats, as regularly happens, is a viable compromise.

In this section I have discussed aspects that relate to the possible progression or regression of the CoI as a retransplantation of Nhat Hanh's teachings. The forms of lay practice that are currently being followed indicate the Plum Village Model is being adapted to suit a smaller timeframe, signifying the autonomy of the Units in finding ways of adapting Nhat Hanh's teachings to suit their own context. I have discussed some of the challenges being met in adapting what has become a monastic practice into a lay setting. Although there are questions about the narrow ethnicity of and size of many Units the national membership is increasing, particularly after each time Nhat Hanh leads a retreat in the UK. Therefore, there is an indication of positive growth in the lay community. I have concluded with a challenge for the monasteries in providing a sustainable means of proliferating the teachings, traditions and practice into the lay community. There are several matters for the satellite and lay communities to address in working with the retransplantation process.

7:7 Conclusion

In discussing the individual points of Knott's theory I have argued that the Plum Village Model confirms this theory. Through using Knott's theory as a framework for this chapter I have examined the ways in which the Plum Village community has adapted the practices that Nhat Hanh originated in Vietnam and have been able to implement his ideas of adaptation in a way that was not possible in Vietnam.

I suggest one of the biggest '... consequent religious changes' (Knott 1986: 10) from the Plum Village Model is the expansive growth of the lay community, by which means Nhat Hanh's teachings, traditions and practices are permeating out into the world in a way that is accessible and approachable. Nhat Hanh has developed a teaching that does not deny the history or traditions on either side (Eastern or Western), but seeks to blend these together.

As well as considering how the Plum Village Model is rippling out into society from the hub to the satellites, I have also reflected on the impact of this within the CoI UK which whilst small at the moment, is growing. In using Knott's theory I have identified the aspects of home traditions, identity of the individual and the group, leadership and the impact of Western religious ideas as key components affecting the Plum Village Model. Furthermore I have merged the two aspects of host traditions and response to consider how effective Nhat Hanh has been in transplanting a Vietnamese tradition into a mainly Christian country. Most relevant to Nhat Hanh's approach are the facets of home traditions and engagement with a Western culture.

The Plum Village Model, working towards harmonious relationships, has demonstrated this, whether this is with the diverse cultures and ethnicities on a retreat or an Eastern tradition locating in a Western culture. By continuing to emphasise the home traditions Nhat Hanh has been able to maintain charitable aid into Vietnam as well as implement his ideas of Engaged Buddhism that began in Vietnam. He is fortunate to be able to do this in a Western setting as it was not possible in Vietnam.

I have identified areas in which the transplantation process has adapted the practices that originated from Vietnam. Of particular relevance to this discussion are a fourfold community, addressing the psychological suffering of the West as opposed to the physical suffering of the East, and working with Western religious ideas, in particular demonstrating how the Institutes (EIAB) are presenting Mindfulness in a more secular way.

The fourfold community is addressed through Nhat Hanh's emphasis on *Sangha*, something that is being implemented in the monasteries and in the lay community. This is further accentuated by his understanding that *Maitreya*, the next *Buddha* to come, will be a *Sangha* rather than an individual. It highlights another question of leadership versus the autonomy of each satellite. The key teaching is to practise Mindfulness in any situation and this does not depend on the promotion of Nhat Hanh as a charismatic figure. Although he is currently the focus of retreats there are many other monastic *Dharmacharyas* who are able to competently and skilfully deliver a *Dharma* talk, as discovered in America in 2009 when Nhat Hanh fell ill. The fourfold community is also examined through the reciprocal way in which the monasteries and lay community support one another. Plum Village and the satellite monasteries have been able to work alongside their respective local communities rather than imposing what could be an alien teaching on them. This is particularly demonstrated by projects where monastics are bringing Mindfulness to prison inmates and schools. These aspects have come about through working with retreatants and co-operating with work they are already undertaking. Furthermore, each monastery demonstrates being detached from society so as not to feel its influences yet engaging with it enough, through the lay community, to be able to help retreatants with their problems.

The meeting of Eastern and Western worldviews is addressed with the issue of secularisation. Nhat Hanh embraces the issue of secularisation, which can be a problem for some religious organisations, in the move towards Institutes of Applied Buddhism. I propose Nhat Hanh has successfully balanced the tension between tradition and interpretation by retaining faithfulness to the early Buddhist teachings as discussed in Chapter 2. I have demonstrated that what appears to be Nhat Hanh's pedagogy is deeply rooted in the *Buddha*'s teachings.

As far as the CoI UK is concerned, I have shown it operates in much the same autonomous way as the satellites. I have expressed my reservations about the lack of nationwide advertising which leaves some individual Units with only a handful of members. The regular Unit meetings are not carbon copies of what takes place at Plum Village but are living entities changing and morphing as each Unit finds out what suits it best. The practices as demonstrated by the Cambridge Unit, 'based on Plum Village forms, are simplified to suit our needs' (Corke 2002: 231). They take components of the Plum Village Model approach to Mindfulness, but Nhat Hanh does not want people to merely replicate what happens in Plum Village, that is not Mindfulness, neither is it a true indication of transplantation. In his non-dogmatic approach he encourages retreatants to discover for themselves how to apply Mindfulness into their daily lives in a particular way relevant to their own circumstances. Therefore, I have indicated an area of adaptation for the Units in that they are not upholding the home traditions in the energetic way Plum Village and the satellite monasteries do. Being mindful is being aware of the needs of a particular group of people and responding to those needs. The Units retain the same aim of the Plum Village Model in seeking to transform suffering into happiness as Nhat Hanh has taught and demonstrated throughout his life.

One question in the retransplantation process is whether the monasteries are sustainable given the finite number of monastics throughout the world. It is hoped there will be new monastics entering the tradition and it will be interesting to see, when the time comes, what effect Nhat Hanh's death will have on these numbers and whether there be a flood of people wishing to join the tradition. Yet they do seem to be adhering to a slow-growth approach as denoted by the caution with which the installation of a monastery in the UK proceeds.

8. Conclusion

I have arrived, I am home ... "I have arrived" is a practice, not a statement or declaration. I have arrived in the here and now, and I can touch life deeply with all of its wonders ... I have arrived in the present moment, because only the present moment contains life ... and by doing so I stop running ... We have been running all our life. We believe that peace, happiness, and success are present in some other place and time. We don't know that everything – peace, happiness and stability – should be looked for in the here and now (Nhat Hanh 2009d: 30-31).

The phrase Thich Nhat Hanh uses to articulate Mindfulness, 'I have arrived, I am home', expresses the present moment as the only place to be alive, to be fearless and to have insight into what is actually taking place. The present moment is the only place to experience freedom and true happiness which is not related to or limited by material possessions, people, particular conditions or outcomes and it is this to which Nhat Hanh's teachings point.

The above statement further expresses the acknowledgement and appreciation of interbeing, which can be particularly tangible on a retreat and in a Unit. Interbeing is a foundational aspect of Nhat Hanh's teachings, by which one recognises oneself as one cell of a greater body, thus inferring one's actions have an effect both on the other cells and the whole body. Nhat Hanh strongly recommends interbeing as a counterbalance to rampant individualism, because of his belief that humanity needs to recognise its innate oneness for the planet and humanity to survive. In recognising the interdependence of all beings the desire is for all to be free from suffering by transforming suffering into happiness, which is the foundation of Nhat Hanh's pedagogy.

This book began with an examination of the *Satipatthana Sutta*, a key text of the *Buddha*'s teaching on Mindfulness in the four areas of body, feelings, mind and objects of mind which encompass every action one undertakes in daily life. I have demonstrated how Nhat Hanh has adopted this *sutra* in particular, along with the *Anapanasati Sutta* on breathing as the foundations of his own pedagogy and has particularly emphasised the experiential aspects of this teaching as well as its practical application. His understanding and embracing of the *Satipatthana Sutta* has been a firm foundation from which the rest of his teachings have emanated. This *sutta* represents the roots from which Plum Village, the satellite monasteries and the lay communities have grown.

The development of Nhat Hanh's pedagogy of Engaged Buddhism and Mindfulness has been addressed through an examination of his inspirations and aspirations that helped to formulate *meditation in action* whilst he was in Vietnam. This originates from his recognition that Buddhism in Vietnam in the 1940s, when he became a novice monk, was not offering the country the practical means of coping with war. For Nhat Hanh, Buddhism is essentially an applied practice not a theoretical teaching or a purely intellectual pursuit. Buddhism should engage with society rather than withdraw from it and this fervent belief led to his formulation of Engaged Buddhism supported by Mindfulness. I established that Nhat Hanh's teachings were grounded in practices of Buddhism that had previously been implemented in Vietnam in earlier centuries, providing a holistic economic and social support. This reassured Nhat Hanh it could work in the conflict situation he grew up in. Furthermore, seeing the effect of the teachings of Gandhi, King and Merton convinced Nhat Hanh that a nonviolent and compassionate approach was not only possible but necessary to balance the prevailing atmosphere of conflict at that time.

In the Tradition of Thich Nhat Hanh

The mindful communities that Nhat Hanh established in Vietnam did not have the conditions to survive for long yet they provided the basis for Plum Village and confirmed for Nhat Hanh that a nonviolent way of living may be possible. Whilst this is adequately demonstrated within the Plum Village monasteries I also suggest it is a reality for retreatants who practise Mindfulness on a retreat in order to benefit their lives and those around them back at home. The key message here is that being rather than doing is the prerequisite, one works on one's own practices before effecting change for others. Although Nhat Hanh was considered to be a vocal peace protestor in Vietnam this book has established he concentrated on the aspect of peace rather than protestation by demonstrating that one has to *be* peace before one can *do* peace.

With regard to being peace, I proposed the most relevant question is one of visibility and whether Engaged Buddhism is only visible, social activist work. Nhat Hanh has demonstrated this is not the case as the practice he propounds is based on the individual working on oneself before aiming to effect change for others. Perhaps further pertinent questions are, how long one works on oneself before being ready to help others? Or do these aspects work concurrently? These questions could be one reason the CoI is apparently unclear in its focus, as addressed by Henry (2008: 229-230). Nhat Hanh himself had seven years of preparation to become a monk and learning the art of Mindfulness before he moved to Saigon to practise Engaged Buddhism. Furthermore, *Tiep Hien* observed seventeen years of experimentation before accepting their seventh member. However, they were still involved in engaged practices during this time, therefore I would suggest *being* and *doing* work concurrently. It is not a case of practising sitting meditation for a set period before one is ready to engage with the world. They feed each other. Or, as Nhat Hanh indicates,

> How can we practice at the airport and in the market? That is engaged Buddhism. Engaged Buddhism does not only mean to use Buddhism to solve social and political problems, protesting against the bombs, and protesting against social

injustice. First of all we have to bring Buddhism into our daily lives (2007a: 53).

The key aspect of Engaged Buddhism is not only relevant to a warlike situation; the pedagogy Nhat Hanh developed is equally applicable to any local or familial circumstance where conflict may or may not arise. Thus, the relationship between Engaged Buddhism and Mindfulness is expressed as closely interlinked, bringing together the 'hard' end of social activism and the 'soft' end of individual practice in daily life that Jones demarcates (2003: 175).

Nhat Hanh has a long-term view of peace and has not been diverted by being unsuccessful in Vietnam in terms of not bringing the Vietnam/American War to a peaceful conclusion sooner; this is not a criterion by which to approach Engaged Buddhism and Mindfulness. His particular method is to aim for peace and reconciliation through understanding and compassion; these are the guiding principles on which he has based his life, his practice and his teachings. Nhat Hanh was influenced by Gandhi's method of *Satyagraha* and he has employed this himself despite it not apparently working in the particular situation of Vietnam. Nhat Hanh's *battle* of Vietnam may have been lost, but not the war, to use an inappropriate analogy! Time means nothing in the practice of Mindfulness. In this line of work one forgoes the idea of tangible results and proceeds on a step-by-step basis. It is only in the present moment that one has the opportunity to appropriate change or make a difference. Nhat Hanh's approach is to let things grow and develop naturally rather than try and rush or force things along. His practice at Plum Village has only been established for thirty-two years and is still developing. He indicates the practices themselves as well as the practitioners have '... matured like the cedars' (Nhat Hanh 2003c: 20). This maturation takes time and I suggest one should not be in too much of a hurry to decide how this role of Mindfulness in daily life is being played out. As the emphasis is on the practice of Mindfulness - being peace - this will take time to establish itself as the practice deepens for each individual. Yet this slow-growth approach aims to ensure a firm foundation is being developed from which many aspects of Mindfulness can grow and spread.

The evolution of Nhat Hanh's teaching of Mindfulness as demonstrated in Plum Village reveals the substantial qualities of gentleness, kindness, patience, perseverance and happiness that pervade Plum Village, in contrast to the extreme poverty, depravation and imminent threat of death palpable in Vietnam. Yet this is not to suggest Plum Village is a naïve, unrealistic utopia. There are necessary processes for conflict resolution in place, particularly Beginning Anew, which demonstrate an aim of nonviolence. Plum Village is a community that is consciously implementing Mindfulness in all activities that comprise the daily programme, thus teaching through osmosis by being full-time practitioners. The areas I have suggested to address here, such as clarifying the practice of sitting meditation and offering retreatants more immediate access to a *Dharmacharya* for the course of their stay do not negate the appeasement of suffering that is available, due to the awakening to the present moment. Plum Village offers an approach that is accessible to anyone interested in developing Mindfulness rather than following a specifically Buddhist path. This is consistent with Nhat Hanh's message that Buddhism is about awakening to the present moment rather than following rigid rules or dogma and is further reflected in the MTs.

Although the MTs are offered as an ethical path for anyone wishing to live a more compassionate and nonviolent lifestyle they are deliberately termed trainings rather than precepts to indicate the fluidity and flexibility with which they can be applied. They are the principal teachings from which all else has evolved. Nhat Hanh's particular version was developed in 1966 in Vietnam and they are regularly updated to ensure their continued relevance to current society. The MTs address the human condition of suffering by proposing it is possible to transform this into happiness thereby presenting a more compassionate way of living both for the individual and wider society. They can be examined and executed afresh in each situation, they are not a one-fits-all answer.

Mindfulness is the consistent thread that provides cohesion to Nhat Hanh's teachings; it was the foundation underpinning Engaged Buddhism and continues to be the substance of his teachings at Plum Village and beyond.

In order to assist with the practice of the MTs Nhat Hanh maintains that operating within a *Sangha* is essential. Through evaluating how and why Nhat Hanh's teachings have proliferated worldwide to other monasteries, institutes and lay Units I propose *Sangha*, a palpable aspect of Plum Village, is the key facet that underpins Mindfulness. The emphasis in the satellite monasteries, as established in Vietnam with the inauguration of *Tiep Hien*, is the necessity of practising alongside like-minded people. Nhat Hanh's particular interpretation of *Sangha* as a fourfold community rather than just monastic contributes to the originality of his teachings. The growing presence of the satellite monasteries demonstrates a worldwide need for Mindfulness, which they are beginning to meet. Likewise the Institutes (in Germany and Hong Kong) are fulfilling the need that Nhat Hanh recognised many years earlier in Vietnam of offering Buddhist teachings in a practical rather than theoretical way, which allows the teachings to reach a wider audience.

The implementation of *Sangha* continues through the practices of the lay community and specifically the CoI UK. Whilst this setting is very much removed from 1940s Vietnam onwards and the extremes of war, the practices of Mindfulness developed there are equally applicable here. Nhat Hanh recognises a tension between the rise of individualism and the natural human need to be part of a community and offers Mindfulness as a means of developing one's personal compassionate, ethical outlook in order to then respond within a community in a peaceful, nonviolent way. The Units examined here are a viable means for people to practise and maintain Mindfulness beyond a retreat situation.

The transplantation process has allowed Nhat Hanh to implement and practice the teachings of Mindfulness he wished to bring to the peace process in Vietnam. I suggest this has been successful because he accepted that Buddhism in the West would take on a different form to the East and he is prepared to work with different cultures and worldviews to find a way forward expressing harmony and reconciliation. Through living his teachings of Mindfulness and interbeing he demonstrates how it is possible for others to do the same. In reflecting on Nhat Hanh's transplantation process I have found Knott's theoretical framework invaluable, from which I have discussed the various aspects pertaining to Nhat Hanh's situation. Using this theory I have established the home traditions, relating back to Vietnam, are still a high priority for Nhat Hanh himself and he has appealed to the fourfold Sangha to continue this work on his behalf. He has been able to achieve more in this direction from the West than was possible in Vietnam. Furthermore, his emphasis on a fourfold Sangha demonstrates an adaptation of the transplantation process that has manifested in the West for the Plum Village community.

I have investigated Nhat Hanh's work and teachings in a more in-depth approach than has been used before to critique his work and due to this I conclude Mindfulness has always been at the heart of any actions he has undertaken. The terms of his practice may have changed from Engaged Buddhism to Applied Buddhism and more recently to Applied Ethics but the essence of his teachings remains consistent, founded in the *Satipatthana Sutta*. I have expressed my concern at the recent change of the term to Applied Ethics as this suggests hiding the Buddhist roots from which the teachings emanate. However, this again is an ongoing practice and if the term Applied Ethics is found not to be useful it will be re-adapted.

One question directing this book was whether Nhat Hanh's pedagogy has changed from one of collective social action (i.e. Engaged Buddhism) to practices of Mindfulness that focus on the individual. I have argued this is not the case because Nhat Hanh has responded to the immediate need in each context he has lived and practised in, meeting each circumstance from a perspective of Mindfulness and applying relevant action to the context. The different worldviews he has connected with have provided diverse settings for his pedagogy of Mindfulness, yet the teachings themselves are consistent. Now he focuses on an individual practice of Mindfulness that is suitable to the West, and accentuates the need for a *Sangha* within which the individual practises, learns and operates. His message of Mindfulness in all features of daily life, 'washing the dishes to wash the dishes' (Nhat Hanh 2008e: 3), has not changed in the seventy years he has been practising Mindfulness. However, I am not arguing that Nhat Hanh has dropped the teachings of Engaged Buddhism in favour of Mindfulness, but advocating that in the transplantation process, which was forced upon Nhat Hanh due to his exile from Vietnam, Mindfulness has come to the fore, especially in the European countries where the extremes of war that existed in Vietnam are not present. I suggest it is only a matter of emphasis, as in accentuating Mindfulness he has not abandoned Engaged Buddhism. It depends on what one's understanding of Engaged Buddhism is, and for Nhat Hanh it includes the minutiae of cleaning one's teeth or caring for one's child as much as overt practices of social activism. In Chapter 4 I established a Summation of Engaged Buddhism, incorporating the balance of being and doing, interbeing and, participation in the world. I proposed these aspects are indicative of any practice of Engaged Buddhism and are particularly relevant to Nhat Hanh's teachings, combining the main aspects of his pedagogy. Furthermore, I have ascertained that the Engaged Buddhism he practised in Vietnam was established in Mindfulness and not a separate characteristic.

In examining the evolution of Nhat Hanh's teachings I denoted that his pedagogy has developed by meeting the need of the circumstances in which he found himself rather than having a long-term plan to which to adhere. Having said that, the only aspiration guiding Nhat Hanh's life was renewing the practices of Buddhism in Vietnam in order for them to be of better service at grassroots for the Vietnamese people. This aspiration continues to be paramount for Nhat Hanh even though he can no longer return to the country and he has expressly stated his wish for the fourfold *Sangha* to take on this aspiration.

What does it mean to be 'in the tradition of Thich Nhat Hanh'? It means living a practice of full awareness that can be imparted to any activity one undertakes based in early Buddhist teachings. Nhat Hanh has interpreted these as the 5 and 14MTs, guidelines requiring the practitioner to look deeply into a situation in order to take the most mindful path. Furthermore, it is an awareness of body and mind so that one cognises from moment to moment what is taking place internally, what perceptions are being formed and what they are based on. Although Plum Village in many respects represents the culmination of Nhat Hanh's work that began in Vietnam it is by no means the end of the journey simply a new beginning. There are new ways to implement Mindfulness that Nhat Hanh is still addressing. Currently his focus is on education and ecology issues, which the Dalai Lama also deemed needing urgent attention on his 2012 tour of the UK. Although I have only briefly mentioned ecology as a concern of Nhat Hanh's throughout this book it is something he is deeply interested in and could be the focus of further research. There are many strands to the application of Mindfulness that will continue once Nhat Hanh has passed on as it appears he has been creating a community, as an embodiment of *Maitreya,* which will ensure the teachings are carried forward into the future.

Nhat Hanh's name, given to him at ordination, means *one action* and I have been considering what the one action is, towards which his life is focussed. I now propose his life's purpose is to make people aware of Mindfulness as a means of becoming peaceful human beings. In this sense Mindfulness becomes a path that aids peaceful thinking, speaking and acting, both for oneself and towards others. Nhat Hanh describes Mindfulness as 'the practice of peace' (1993: 70).

In conclusion, I propose Nhat Hanh's understanding and pedagogy of Mindfulness is something that could benefit many people, especially those living a demanding and stressful life, and that by taking even a few moments out of one's day to 'learn the art of stopping – stopping our thinking, our habit energies, our forgetfulness, the strong emotions that rule us' (Nhat Hanh 1999d: 24) would affect not only oneself but one's wider community.

Postscript 2016

Since writing my thesis, which was concluded in 2014, there have been significant changes at Plum Village. In November 2014 Thich Nhat Hanh suffered a brain tumour that resulted in a major stroke. At the time it was not clear, given his age of 88, whether he would survive. After many months in hospital in Bordeaux he returned to Plum Village unable to speak and with very limited movement down his right side. However, it is clear he is still practising Mindfulness and there were reports from the hospital of him exceeding doctors' expectations of recovery because of his long-term practice of mindful breathing. There were also anecdotal reports that in the hospital nurses would come into his room at the end of their shifts to sit and relax because this was the most peaceful place in the building. It was as if he was leading a retreat from his hospital bed despite being unable to speak. Whilst being supported in the hospital by a group of monastics who stayed with him the Plum Village community had to go about its everyday business. The 3-month winter retreat that usually takes place from mid-November to mid-February went ahead as normal with senior monastic *Dharma* teachers taking on the role of teacher that Nhat Hanh had thus far held. The everyday practices of Mindfulness (as examined in Chapter 5) continued and in many respects life proceeded as it does in the satellite monasteries. The senior *Dharma* teachers began to find their own voice and offer the teachings from their own perspective, rather than attempting to parrot Nhat Hanh's words. Here was the chance to demonstrate their own understanding of the teachings and to learn from any mistakes in the presentation.

In this time Nhat Hanh went to San Francisco for some months to work with experienced therapists before returning to Plum Village in

January 2016. Whilst in America he was able to speak a few words and these were offered to the worldwide community as a guided meditation; 'in, out, happy, thank you'. It is my personal understanding that his return to Plum Village indicates he will not recover or that his speech or walking will not improve any further. Nhat Hanh now uses a wheelchair to move around and if he wishes to walk he needs someone to literally move his right leg forward as it no longer functions by itself.

Whilst these occurrences could be viewed as devastating by the community it is fortunate that they are practising Mindfulness and therefore have an approach to this current situation that means the emotions are not highly involved. As discussed in Chapter 7, the community has to consider what will happen once Nhat Hanh passes away and is no longer present in his physical form. It seems to me that with these circumstances the community is gradually being introduced to this idea in a gentle way that is entirely reminiscent of Nhat Hanh himself. Now back at Plum Village he joins in with the community when he can and is reported as often being in the *Dharma* hall for morning meditation before the other monastics (IC, Monk E 2016). He has also begun practising calligraphy with his left hand by drawing the Zen circle '... about a hundred times each day' (IC, Monk E 2016) demonstrating his stamina and determination to not only recover as much as possible but to continue with as many aspects of life as he previously enjoyed.

Although he no longer has the ability to speak and therefore cannot deliver *Dharma* talks, his presence is still a profound teaching in itself. My first encounter with Thich Nhat Hanh in person was him walking into the Meditation hall to give a *Dharma* talk. He did not speak, he just walked mindfully and his deep practice of Mindfulness was tangible. I suggest this presence is still available to the community through him just being there. It is a great learning for all concerned to accept this new situation in mindfulness and see it for what it is. These circumstances have allowed many other *Dharma* teachers to step into Nhat Hanh's shoes, as it were, and the community as a whole to take on board the teaching that the next

Buddha, Maitreya, will be a Sangha and not an individual. It is my view that this is how the Plum Village community is moving forward and this will be the flowering of all that Thich Nhat Hanh has offered in particular to the West.

Bibliography

Alden, Ann (2006), *Religion in Dialogue with Late Modern Society: a Constructive Contribution to a Christian Spirituality informed by Buddhist-Christian Encounters.* Frankfurt, Peter Lang.

Amore, Roy & Ching, Julia (2002), 'The Buddhist Tradition'. In, Willard Oxtoby ed. *World Religions: Eastern Traditions*, 2nd ed. Ontario, Oxford University Press, pp. 199-315.

Analayo (2006), *Satipatthana : The Direct Path to Realization.* (3rd ed.) Birmingham, Windhorse Publications.

Anderson, Pamela Sue (2005), 'Postmodernism and Religion', in Stuart Sim ed. *Postmodernism: Its History and Cultural Context.* Abingdon 2nd ed. Oxon, Routledge, pp.45-50.

Armstrong, Karen (2000), *Buddha.* London, Orion Publishing Group.

Baer, Ruth (2011), 'Measuring Mindfulness'. In *Contemporary Buddhism,* vol. 12 no 1, May, pp. 241-261.

Batchelor, Martine (2011), 'Meditation and Mindfulness'. In *Contemporary Buddhism,* vol. 12 no 1, May, pp. 157-164.

Batchelor, Stephen (1994), *The Awakening of the West.* London, HarperCollins.

Bauman, Zygmunt (2003), *The Individualized Society.* Oxford, Blackwell Publishing Ltd.

Behm, Allan (1971), 'The Eschatology of the Jatakas'. In *Numen,* vol. 18 fasc. 1, April, pp. 30-44.

Bell, Sandra (2000), 'A Survey of Engaged Buddhism in Britain'. In Christopher Queen & Sallie King eds. *Engaged Buddhism in the West.* Boston, Wisdom Publications, pp. 397-422.

Berrigan, Daniel (1993), 'Foreword'. In, Thich Nhat Hanh *Love In action: Writings on Nonviolent Social Change.* Berkeley, Parallax Press, pp. 3-8.

Bluck, Robert (2006), *British Buddhism: Teachings, Practice and Development.* Abingdon Oxon, Routledge.

Bodhi, Bhikkhu ed. (2005), *In the Buddha's Words: an Anthology of Discourses from the Pali Canon.* Somerville MÃ, Wisdom Publications.

---- (2011), 'What Does Mindfulness Really Mean? A Canonical Perspective'. In *Contemporary Buddhism,* vol. 12 no 1, May, pp. 19-39.

Bond, George D. (1996), 'A.T. Ariyaratne and the Sarvodaya Shramadana Movement'. In Christopher Queen & Sallie King eds. *Engaged Buddhism: Buddhist Liberation Movements in Asia.* Albany, State University of New York Press, pp. 121-146.

Bonner, Ann & Tolhurst, Gerda (2002), 'Insider-outsider Perspectives of Participant Observation'. In *Nurse Researcher,* vol. 9, no. 4, Feb, pp. 7-19.

Boyatzis, Richard & McKee, Annie (2005), *Resonant Leadership: Renewing Yourself and Connecting with Others Through Mindfulness, Hope and Compassion.* Boston, Harvard Business School Press.

Brazier, David (2001), *The New Buddhism: A Rough Guide to a New Way of Life.* London, Constable Publishers.

Brazier, Caroline (2003), *Buddhist Psychology: Liberate Your Mind, Embrace Life.* London, Constable & Robinson Ltd.

Brown, Sid (2008) 'For the Record'. In: *Tricycle,* vol. xvii, no.3, spring, p9.

Bryman, Alan (2008), *Social Research Methods* 3rd ed. Oxford, Oxford University Press.

Buswell, Robert ed. in chief (2004), *Encyclopedia of Buddhism, Vol. 2.* New York, Macmillan Reference.

Cantwell, Cathy & Kawanami, Hiroko (2002), 'Buddhism'. In Linda Woodhead et al, *Religions in the Modern World.* London, Routledge, pp. 41-69.

Chan Khong, Sr (2007), *Learning True Love.* Berkeley, Parallax Press.

Chapman, John (2007), 'The 2005 Pilgrimage and Return to Vietnam of Exiled Zen Master Thich Nhat Hanh'. In Philip Taylor *Modernity and Re-enchantment in Post-revolutionary Vietnam.* Singapore, Institute of Southeast Asian Studies, pp. 297-341.

Chappell, David (1999b), 'Engaged Buddhists In A Global Society: Who Is Being Liberated?'. In Sulak Sivaraksa hon. ed. *Socially Engaged Buddhism For The New Millennium.* Bangkok, The Sathirakoses-Nagapradipa Foundation, pp. 70-78.

Chhaya, Mayank (2007), *Dalai Lama, Man, Monk, Mystic.* New York, Doubleday.

Clark, Herbert (2005), *Using Language*. Cambridge, Cambridge University Press.
Clough, Bradley (2005), 'Altruism in Contemporary Buddhism: Thich Nhat Hanh's Socially Engaged Buddhism'. In Jacob Neusner & Bruce Chilton eds. *Altruism in World Religions*. Washington D.C., Georgetown University Press, pp. 115-138.
Cohen, Louis, Manion, Lawrence & Morrison, Keith (2011), *Research Methods in Education* 7th ed. Abingdon, Oxon, Routledge.
Coleman, J.W. (2001), *The New Buddhism: The Western Transformation of an Ancient Tradition*. New, York, Oxford University Press.
Conze, Edward (2001), *Buddhism its Essence and Development*. Birmingham, Windhorse.
Corke, Murray (2002), 'The Cambridge Sangha'. In Thich Nhat Hanh & Jack Lawlor, *Friends on the Path*. Berkeley, Parallax Press, pp. 231-232.
Corfield, Justin (2008), *The History of Vietnam*. Westport, Conn., Greenwood Press.
Cushing, Caleb (2002), 'Some Experiences With Local Sangha Organising'. In Thich Nhat Hanh & Jack Lawlor, *Friends on the Path*. Berkeley, Parallax Press, pp. 115-121.
Deitrick, James (2003), 'Engaged Buddhist Ethics: Mistaking the Boat for the Shore'. In Christopher Queen, Charles Prebish & Damien Keown eds. *Action Dharma: New Studies in Engaged Buddhism*. London, RoutledgeCurzon, pp. 252-265.
Denscombe, Martyn (2003), *The Good Research Guide for Small-scale Social Research Projects* 2nd ed. Maidenhead, Open University Press.
Do, Thien (1999), 'Buddhism in Contemporary Vietnam'. In Ian Harris ed. *Buddhism and Politics in Twentieth-century Asia*. London, Continuum, pp. 254-284.
Dreyfus, George (2011, 'Is Mindfulness Present-centred and Non-judgemental? A Discussion of the Cognitive Dimensions of Mindfulness'. In *Contemporary Buddhism*, vol. 12 no 1, May, pp. 41-54.
Duiker, William (1998), *Historical Dictionary of Vietnam* 2nd ed. Maryland, Scarecrow Press Inc.
Dunne, John (2011), 'Towards an Understanding of Non-dual Mindfulness'. In *Contemporary Buddhism*, vol. 12 no 1, May, pp. 71-88.
Eppsteiner, Fred ed. (1988), *The Path of Compassion: Writings on Socially Engaged Buddhism*. Berkeley, Parallax Press.

---- (2000), 'Editor's Introduction'. In Thich Nhat Hanh, *Interbeing: Fourteen Guidelines for Engaged Buddhism.* New Delhi, Full Circle, pp. vii-x.
Fasching, Darrell & Dechant, Dell (2001), *Comparative Religious Ethics.* Oxford, Blackwell Publishers.
Feldman, Christina & Kuyken, Willem (2011), 'Compassion in the Landscape of Suffering'. In *Contemporary Buddhism,* vol. 12 no 1, May, pp. 143-155.
Fernando, Jude Lal (2007), *A Paradigm for a Peace Movement: Thich Nhat Hanh and Martine Luther King Jr.* Dublin, The Columba Press.
Fielding, Nigel & Thomas, Hilary (2005), 'Qualitative Interviewing'. In Nigel Gilbert ed. *Researching Social Life* 2nd ed. London, Sage Publications, pp. 123-144.
Forest, James (2008), 'Nhat Hanh: Seeing With the Eyes of Compassion'. In Thich Nhat Hanh, *The Miracle of Mindfulness.* London, Rider, pp. 101-108.
Foster, Nelson (1988), 'To Enter the Marketplace'. In Fred Eppsteiner ed. *The Path of Compassion: Writings on Socially Engaged Buddhism.* Berkeley, Parallax Press, pp. 47-64.
Fowler, James (1981), *Stages of Faith: the Psychology of Human Development and the Quest for Meaning.* San Francisco, Harper & Row.
Fronsdal, Gil (2002), 'Virtues Without Rules: Ethics in the Insight Meditation Movement'. In Charles Prebish & Martin Baumann (eds.), *Westward Dharma: Buddhism Beyond Asia.* Berkeley, University of California Press, pp. 285-308.
Gandhi, M. K. (2001), *An Autobiography.* London, Penguin.
Garfinkel, Perry (2007), 'Politics of a Still Mind'. In *Shambhala Sun,* Sep, pp. 62-65.
Gethin, Rupert (1998), *The Foundations of Buddhism.* Oxford, Oxford University Press.
---- (2001), *The Buddhist Path to Awakening.* Oxford, Oneworld.
---- (trans.) (2008), *Sayings of the Buddha : a Selection of Suttas from the Pali Nikayas.* Oxford, Oxford University Press.
Ghosananda, Maha (1992), *Step by Step.* Berkeley, Parallax Press.
Gombrich, Richard F. (1998), *Buddhist Precept and Practice: Traditional Buddhism in the Rural Highlands of Ceylon.* Delhi, Motilal Banarsidass Publishers.
Gowans, Christopher (2003), *Philosophy of the Buddha.* London, Routledge.

Grossman, Paul & Van Dam Nicholas T. (2011), 'Mindfulness By Any Other Name ...: Trials and Tribulations of Sati in Western Psychology and Science'. In *Contemporary Buddhism*, vol. 12 no 1, May, pp. 219-239.

Gunaratana, Henepola (2002), *Mindfulness in Plain English*. Somerville MA, Wisdom Publications.

Habito, Ruben L. F. (2007), 'Environment or Earth Sangha: Buddhist Perspectives on our Global Ecological Well-being'. In *Contemporary Buddhism*, vol. 8, no 2, November, pp. 131-147.

Hammersley, Martin & Atkinson, Paul (2007), *Ethnography: Principles in Practice* 3rd ed. Abingdon, Oxon, Routledge.

Harris, Elizabeth J. (2001), *What Buddhists Believe*. Oxford, Oneworld Publications.

---- (2006), *Theravada Buddhism and the British Encounter*. Abingdon, Oxon, Routledge.

---- (2010), *Buddhism for a Violent World*. London, Epworth Press.

Harris, Ian ed. (1999), *Buddhism and Politics in Twentieth-century Asia*. London, Continuum.

Helmbrecht, Johannes (2002), 'Grammar and function of *we*'. In Anna Duszak ed. *Us and Others*. Amsterdam, John Benjamins Publishing Co., pp. 31-50.

Hobsbawm, Eric (2002), *Age of Extremes: The Short Twentieth Century 1914-1991*. London, Abacus.

Hope, Marjorie & Young, James (1977), *The Struggle for Humanity: Agents of Nonviolent Change in a Violent World*. New York, Orbis Books.

Huang, C. Julia (2003), 'The Buddhist Tzu-chi Foundation of Taiwan'. In, Christopher Queen, Charles Prebish & Damien Keown eds. *Action Dharma: New Studies in Engaged Buddhism*. London, RoutledgeCurzon, pp. 136-153.

Hunt-Perry, Patricia & Fine, Lyn (2000), 'All Buddhism is Engaged: Thich Nhat Hanh and the Order of Interbeing'. In Christopher Queen ed. *Engaged Buddhism in The West*. Boston, Wisdom Publications, pp. 35–66.

Irons, Edward A. (2008), *Encyclopedia of Buddhism*. New York, Checkmark Books.

Johnson, Phil & Duberley, Joanne (2000), *Understanding Management Research: An Introduction to Epistemology*. London, Sage Publications.

Jones, Ken (2003), *The New Social Face of Buddhism: a Call to Action*. Somerville MA, Wisdom Publications.

Kabat-Zinn, Jon (1996), *Full Catastrophe Living*. London, Piatkus.
---- (1997), 'Mindfulness as Medicine'. In Daniel Goleman ed. *Healing Emotions: Conversations with the Dalai Lama on Mindfulness, Emotions and Health*. Boston, Shambhala Publications Inc., pp. 107-144.
---- (2005), *Coming To Our Senses*. London, Piatkus.
---- (2009), *Wherever You Go, There You Are*. London, Piatkus Books.
---- (2010), 'Toward a Mindful Society'. *Shambhala Sun*, March, p62.
---- (2011), 'Some Reflections on the Origins of MBSR, Skillful Means, and the Trouble With Maps'. In *Contemporary Buddhism*, vol. 12 no 1, May, pp. 281-306.
Karnow, Stanley (1997), *Vietnam, A History* rev ed. New York, Penguin.
Kay, David (2004), *Tibetan and Zen Buddhism in Britain: Transplantation, Development and Adaptation*. London, RoutledgeCurzon.
Keown, Damien (2003), *Dictionary of Buddhism*. Oxford, Oxford University Press.
King, Robert (2001), *Thomas Merton and Thich Nhat Hanh: Engaged Spirituality in an Age of Globalization*. New York, Continuum.
King, Sallie (1996), 'Thich Nhat Hanh and the Unified Buddhist Church of Vietnam: Nondualism in Action'. In Christopher Queen & Sallie King eds. *Engaged Buddhism: Buddhist Liberation Movements in Asia*. Albany, State University of New York Press, pp. 321-364.
---- (2005), *Being Benevolence: The Social Ethics of Engaged Buddhism*. Honolulu, University of Hawaii Press.
---- (2009), *Socially Engaged Buddhism*. Honolulu, University of Hawaii Press.
Kipling, Rudyard (1996), 'If'. In BBC (compiler) *The Nation's Favourite Poems*. London, BBC Books.
Kloppenborg, Ria (trans.) (1973), *The Sutra on the Foundation of the Buddhist Order: Catusparisatsutra*. Leiden, The Netherlands, E.J. Brill.
Knott, Kim (1986), *Religion and Identity, and the Study of Ethnic Minority Religions in Britain*. Community Religions Project Monograph: Leeds, University of Leeds.
---- (1991), 'Bound to Change? The Religions of South Asians in Britain'. In Steven Vertovec ed. *Aspects of South Asian Diaspora*. Delhi, Oxford University Press, pp. 86-111.
---- (2005a), 'Insider/Outsider Perspectives and the Study of Religion'. In Hinnells, J.H. (ed.) *The Routledge Companion to the Study of Religion*. London and

New York; Routledge: pp. 243-258
---- (2005b) *The Location of Religion: A Spatial Analysis*. London, Equinox Publishing.
Kollontai, Pauline (2007), 'Transplanting Religion: Defining Community and Expressing Identity'. In Sebastian Kim & Pauline Kollontai eds. *Community Identity: Dynamics of Religion in Context*. London, T&T Clark, pp. 57-68.
Kornfield, Jack (1996), *Living Dharma: Teachings of Twelve Buddhist Masters*. Boston, Shambhala Publications Inc..
Kraft, Kenneth (1988), 'Engaged Buddhism: an Introduction'. In Fred Eppsteiner ed. *The Path of Compassion: Writings on Socially Engaged Buddhism*. Berkeley, Parallax Press, pp. xi-xviii.
---- (1992), *Inner Peace, World Peace: Essays on Buddhism and Nonviolence*. Albany, State University of New York Press.
---- (1995), 'Practicing Peace: Social Engagement in Western Buddhism'. In *Journal of Buddhist Ethics*, vol. 2, pp. 152-172.
---- (1999), *The Wheel of Engaged Buddhism*. New York, Weatherhill.
---- (2004), 'Wellsprings of Engaged Buddhism'. In Susan Moon, *Not Turning Away: The Practice of Engaged Buddhism*. Boston, Shambhala Publications Inc., pp. 154-161.
Krus, David & Blackman, Harold (1980), 'Contributions to Psychohistory: V. East-West Dimensions of Ideology Measured by Transtemporal Cognitive Matching'. In *Psychological Reports*, vol. 47, pp. 947-955.
Kuan, Tse-fu (2008), *Mindfulness in Early Buddhism: new Approaches through Psychology and Textual Analysis of Pali, Chinese and Sanskrit Sources*. Abingdon, Oxon, Routledge.
Laity, Sr Annabel (1991), 'The History of Buddhism in Vietnam'. In *The Mindfulness Bell* 5 (autumn), pp. 31-32. A synopsis translated from Thich Nhat Hanh's 'The History of Buddhism in Vietnam' in 3 volumes.
---- (2003), 'The Pure Land is Now or Never'. In Thich Nhat Hanh, *Finding Our True Home: Living in the Pure Land Here and Now*. Berkeley, Parallax Press, pp. 7-11.
Laumakis, Stephen (2008), *An Introduction To Buddhist Philosophy*. Cambridge, Cambridge University Press.
Lockhart, Bruce M & Duiker, William J (2006), *Historical Dictionary of Vietnam* 3rd ed. Lanham, Maryland, Scarecrow Press Inc.
Macy, Joanna (1988), 'In Indra's Net: Sarvodaya & Our Mutual Efforts for Peace'. In Fred Eppsteiner ed. *The Path of Compassion: Writings*

on *Socially Engaged Buddhism*. Berkeley, Parallax Press, pp. 170-181.

Maex, Edel (2011), 'The Buddhist Roots of Mindfulness Training: A Practitioners View'. In *Contemporary Buddhism*, vol. 12, no 1 May, pp. 165-175.

McCutcheon, Russell T. (ed.) (1999), *The Insider/Outsider Problem in the Study of Religion*. London, Cassell.

McLeod, Melvin (2009), 'Editor's Preface'. In Thich Nhat Hanh, *You Are Here*. Boston, Shambhala Publications Inc., pp. vii-xiii.

Mitchell, Donald W. (2002), *Buddhism: Introducing the Buddhist Experience*. New York, Oxford University Press.

Monier-Williams, Monier (1990), *A Sanskrit-English Dictionary*. Oxford, Oxford University Press.

Nguyen, Cuong Tu & Barber, A. T. (1998), 'Vietnamese Buddhism in North America: Tradition and Acculturation'. In Charles Prebish and Kenneth Tanaka eds. *The Faces of Buddhism in America*. Berkeley, University of California Press, pp. 129-146.

Nguyen, Tai Thu (ed.) (2008), *The History of Buddhism in Vietnam*. Washington D.C., The Council for Research in Values and Philosophy.

Nhat Hanh, Thich (1967), *Vietnam, Lotus In a Sea of Fire*. London, SCM Press.

---- (1988), *The Heart of Understanding*. Berkeley, Parallax Press.

---- (1990), *Our Appointment with Life*. Berkeley, Parallax Press.

---- (1992a), *Breathe! You are Alive*. London, Rider.

---- (1992b), *The Diamond that Cuts Through Illusion*. Berkeley, Parallax Press.

---- (1992c), *Old Path, White Clouds: The Life Story of the Buddha*. London, Rider.

---- (1992d), *The Sun My Heart*. London, Rider.

---- (1992e), *Touching Peace: Practicing the Art of Mindful Living*. Berkeley, Parallax Press.

---- (1993a), *Love In Action*. Berkeley, Parallax Press.

---- (1993b), *Thundering Silence*. Berkeley, Parallax Press.

---- (1995) *Peace is Every Step*. London, Rider.

---- (1996), *The Long Road Turns to Joy*. Berkeley, Parallax Press.

---- (1997), *Stepping into Freedom*. Berkeley, Parallax Press.

---- (1999a), *Call Me By My True Names*. Berkeley, Parallax Press.

---- (1999b), *Fragrant Palm Leaves*. New York, Riverhead Books.

In the Tradition of Thich Nhat Hanh

---- (1999c), *Going Home: Jesus and Buddha as Brothers.* New York, Riverhead Books.
---- (1999d), *The Heart of the Buddha's Teaching: Transforming Suffering into Peace, Joy and Liberation.* London, Rider.
---- (2000a), *Interbeing: Fourteen Guidelines for Engaged Buddhism.* New Delhi, Full Circle.
---- (2000b), 'The Sun My Heart', in: Stephanie Kaza & Kenneth Kraft, *Dharma Rain: Sources of Buddhist Environmentalism.* Boston, Shambhala Publications Inc., pp. 83–90.
---- (2001), *Anger: Buddhist Wisdom for Cooling the Flames.* London, Rider.
---- (2002a), *Be Free Where You Are.* Berkeley, Parallax Press.
---- (2002b), *My Master's Robes.* Berkeley, Parallax Press.
---- (2003a), *Creating True Peace.* London, Rider.
---- (2003b), *Finding our True Home: Living in the Pure Land Here and Now.* Berkeley, Parallax Press.
---- (2003c), *I Have Arrived, I Am Home.* Berkeley, Parallax Press.
---- (2003d), 'Interview with Thich Nhat Hanh'. In, Catherine Ingram, *In the Footsteps of Gandhi: Conversations with Spiritual Social Activists.* Berkeley, Parallax Press, pp. 81-95.
---- (2003e), *Joyfully Together.* Berkeley, Parallax Press.
---- (2004a), *Peace Begins Here.* Berkeley, Parallax Press.
---- (2004b), *True Love: A Practice for Awakening the Heart.* Boston MA, Shambhala Publications Inc.
---- (2006a), 'A Century of Spirituality', in Melvin McLeod (ed.), *The Best Buddhist Writing 2006.* Boston, Shambhala Publications Inc., pp. 291-300.
---- (2006b), *Present Moment, Wonderful Moment.* Berkeley, Parallax Press.
---- (2006c), *Transformation and Healing.* Berkeley, Parallax Press.
---- (2007a), *Being Peace.* New Delhi, Full Circle Publishing.
---- (2007b), *Chanting From the Heart: Buddhist Ceremonies and Daily Practices.* Berkeley, Parallax Press.
---- (2007c), *For A Future to be Possible: Buddhist Ethics for Everyday Life.* Berkeley, Parallax Press.
---- (2007d), 'Love Without Limit: an Interview with Thich Nhat Hanh' in Melvin McLeod (ed.), *The Best Buddhist Writing 2007.* Boston, Shambhala Publications Inc., pp67-81.
---- (2007e), *Nothing To Do, Nowhere To Go.* Berkeley, Parallax Press.
---- (2007f), *Teachings on Love.* Berkeley, Parallax Press.
---- (2008a), *Buddha Mind, Buddha Body.* Mumbai, Jaico Publishing House.

---- (2008b), *Cultivating the Mind of Love.* Berkeley, Parallax Press.
---- (2008c), 'History of Engaged Buddhism', in *The Mindfulness Bell,* Autumn (49) pp. 4-9.
---- (2008d), *Mindful Movements: Ten Exercises for Well-being.* Berkeley, Parallax Press.
---- (2008e), *The Miracle of Mindfulness,* translated by Mobi Ho. London, Rider.
---- (2008f), *The Path of Emancipation.* New Delhi, Full Circle Publishing.
---- (2008g), *Peaceful Action, Open Heart.* Berkeley, Parallax Press.
---- (2008h), *Understanding Our Mind.* Uttar Pradesh, India, HarperCollins.
---- (2009a), *Answers From The Heart.* Berkeley, Parallax Press.
---- (2009b), *The Blooming of a Lotus.* Boston, Mass., Beacon Press.
---- (2009c), *Calming the Fearful Mind.* New Delhi, Amber Books.
---- (2009d), *Happiness.* Berkeley, Parallax Press.
---- (2010a), *A Key to Peace: Bat Nha.* Florence, Bagno a Ripoli.
---- (2010b), *Beyond the Self.* Berkeley, Parallax Press.
---- (2010c), 'The Long Arm of the Fourfold Sangha'. In *The Mindfulness Bell,* Autumn (55), pp. 4-9.
---- (2010d), *One Buddha is Not Enough.* Berkeley, Parallax Press.
---- (2010e), *Reconciliation.* Berkeley, Parallax Press.
---- (2010f), *Together We are One: Honoring our Diversity, Celebrating our Connection.* Berkeley, Parallax Press.
---- (2011), *Your True Home: the Everyday Wisdom of Thich Nhat Hanh.* Boston, Shambhala Publications Inc.
---- (2012a), *Awakening of the Heart: Essential Buddhist Sutras and Commentaries.* Berkeley, Parallax Press
---- (2012b), *Fear: Essential Wisdom for Getting Through The Storm.* London, Rider.
---- (2013), *Work.* Berkeley, Parallax Press.
---- (2014), *The Mindfulness Survival Kit: Five Essential Practices.* Berkeley, Parallax Press.
Nhat Hanh, Thich & Berrigan, Daniel (2001), *The Raft is Not the Shore.* New York, Orbis Books.
Nhat Hanh, Thich & Cheung, Lilian (2010), *Savor.* New York, HarperOne.
Nhat Hanh, Thich & Lawlor, Jack (2002), *Friends on the Path.* Berkeley, Parallax Press.
Nyanaponika, Thera (1996), *The Heart of Buddhist Meditation.* (3rd ed.) London, Rider.
Paramananda (1999), *Change Your Mind: A Practical Guide to Buddhist Meditation.* Birmingham, Windhorse Publications.

Payutto, P.A. (2002), 'Buddhist Perspectives on Economic Concepts'. In Allan Hunt Badiner ed. *Mindfulness in the Marketplace*. Berkeley, Parallax Press, pp. 77-92.
Payne Geoff & Payne Judy (2006), *Key Concepts in Social Research*. London, Sage Publications.
Pike, Kenneth L. (1999), 'Etic and Emic Standpoints for the Description of Behaviour'. In, Russell T. McCutcheon (ed.) *The Insider/Outsider Problem in the Study of Religion*. London, Cassell, pp. 28-36.
Powers, John (2000), *A Concise Encyclopedia of Buddhism*. Oxford, Oneworld Publications.
Puri, Bharati (2006), *Engaged Buddhism: The Dalai Lama's Worldview*. New Delhi, Oxford University Press.
Pye, E.M. (1969), 'The Transplantation of Religions'. In *Numen: International review for the History of Religions*, vol. 16, fasc. 3, December, pp. 234-239.
Queen, Christopher (1996), 'Introduction'. In Christopher Queen & Sallie King eds. *Engaged Buddhism: Buddhist Liberation Movements in Asia*. Albany, State University of New York Press, pp. 1-44.
---- ed. (2000), *Engaged Buddhism in the West*. Boston, Wisdom Publications.
---- (2003), 'From Altruism to Activism'. In Christopher Queen, Charles Prebish, & Damien Keown eds. *Action Dharma: New studies in Engaged Buddhism*. London, RoutledgeCurzon, pp. 1-36.
Queen, Christopher & King Sallie eds. (1996), *Engaged Buddhism: Buddhist Liberation Movements in Asia*. Albany, State University of New York Press.
Rahula, Walpola (2000), *What the Buddha Taught*. New York, Atlantic Books.
Reat, Noble Ross (1983), 'Insiders and Outsiders in the Study of Religious Traditions'. In *Journal of American Academy of Religion*, 51 no. 3 S pp. 459-476.
Rothberg, Donald & Senauke, Alan (2008), 'Active Visions: Four Sources of Socially Engaged Buddhism'. In *Turning Wheel*, summer/fall, pp. 21-25.
Saddhatissa, Hammalawa (1987), *Buddhist Ethics: the Path to Nirvana*. London, Wisdom Publications.
Saliba, John (2003), *Understanding New Religious Movements*. Walnut Creek, CA, AltaMira Press.
Salzberg, Sharon (2011), 'Mindfulness and Loving-Kindness', in *Contemporary Buddhism*, vol. 12 no 1, May, pp.177-182.

Sangharakshita (2003), *Living with Awareness*. Birmingham, Windhorse.
SarDesai, D R (2005), *Vietnam Past and Present.* Boulder, Colorado, Westview Press.
Sawatsky, Jarem (2009), *The Ethic of Traditional Communities and the Spirit of Healing Justice: studies from Hollow Water, the Iona Community and Plum Village.* London, Jessica Kingsley Publishers.
Schmied, Karl (2002), 'What the geese know'. In Thich Nhat Hanh & Jack Lawlor, *Friends on the Path.* Berkeley, Parallax Press, pp. 259-260.
Shakespeare, William (1985), *The Complete Works of Shakespeare: The Alexander Text.* London, Collins. (First published 1951).
Shaw, Sarah (2009), *Introduction to Buddhist Meditation.* Abingdon, Routledge.
Singh, Rajinder (2003), *Inner and Outer Peace Through Meditation.* London, Element.
Sivaraksa, Sulak (1988), 'Buddhism in a World of Change: Politics Must be Related to Religion'. In Fred Eppsteiner ed. *The Path of Compassion: Writings on Socially Engaged Buddhism.* Berkeley, Parallax Press, pp. 9-18.
---- (1992), *Seeds of Peace.* Berkeley, Parallax Press.
Smart, Ninian (1987), *Religion and the Western Mind.* Basingstoke, Macmillan.
Soma, Thera (1975), *The Way of Mindfulness.* 4th ed. Kandy, Buddhist Publication Society.
Sponberg, Alan ed. (1988), *Maitreya, The Future Buddha.* Cambridge, Cambridge University Press.
Styles, Joseph (1979), 'Outsider/insider: researching gay baths', in *Urban Life*, 8,2: 135-152.
Swearer, Donald (1996), 'Sulak Sivaraksa's Buddhist Vision'. In Christopher Queen & Sallie King eds. *Engaged Buddhism: Buddhist Liberation Movements in Asia.* Albany, State University of New York Press, pp. 195–235.
Teasdale, John D (2004), 'Mindfulness-based Cognitive Therapy'. In Jenny Yiend ed., *Cognition, Emotion and Psychopathology.* Cambridge, Cambridge University Press, pp. 270-289.
Teasdale, John D. & Chaskalson, Michael (2011), 'How Does Mindfulness Transform Suffering? II: The Transformation of *Dukkha*'. In *Contemporary Buddhism*, vol. 12 no 1, May, pp. 103-124.

Thomas, Claude (2006), *At Hell's Gate: A Soldier's Journey From War to Peace*. Boston, Shambhala Publications Inc.
Tomalin, Emma (2006), 'Religion and a Rights-based Approach to Development'. In, *Progress in Development Studies*, 6, 2, pp. 93-108.
---- (2009), 'Buddhist Feminist Transnational Networks, Female Ordination and Women's Empowerment'. In *Oxford Development Studies*, vol. 37, no.2, pp. 81-100.
Toms, Michael (1998), *Buddhism in The West: Spiritual Wisdom for the 21st Century*. Carlsbad, Hay House Inc.
Topmiller, Robert (2002), *The Lotus Unleashed*. Kentucky, The University Press of Kentucky.
Trai Nghiem, Sr (2011), 'The True Musician'. In *The Mindfulness Bell*, Autumn (58) pp. 24-28.
Tricycle (no author acknowledged) (1995), 'Interbeing; an Interview with Thich Nhat Hanh'. *Tricycle* 4 no 4 Summer, pp. 30–38.
Trungpa, Chogyam (1991), *Meditation in Action*. Boston, Shambhala Publications Inc.
Truong, Thanh-dam (2006), 'Reflections on Human Security: A Buddhist Contribution'. In Gerrie Ter Haar and James Busuttil eds. *Bridge or Barrier : Religion, Violence, and Visions for Peace*. Leiden, The Netherlands, Brill, pp. 275-295.
Tucker, Spencer (1999), *Vietnam*. Kentucky, The University Press of Kentucky.
Van der Veer, Peter (2002), 'Transnational Religion: Hindu and Muslim Movements'. In *Global Networks* 2,2, pp. 95-109.
Ward, Keith (2000), *Religion and Community*. Oxford, Clarendon Press.
Weber, Max (1966), *The Sociology of Religion*. Translated from German by E. Fischoff. London, Methuen & Co.
Weiner, Matthew (2003), 'Maha Ghosananda as a Contemplative Social Activist'. In Christopher Queen, Charles Prebish & Damien Keown eds. *Action Dharma: New Studies in Engaged Buddhism*. London RoutledgeCurzon, pp. 110-127.
Williams, Mark & Kabat-Zinn, Jon (2011), 'Mindfulness: Diverse Perspectives on its Meaning, Origins and Multiple Applications at the Intersection of Science and Dharma'. In *Contemporary Buddhism,* vol. 12 no 1, May, pp1-18.
Winzeler, Robert (2008), *Anthropology and Religion: What we Know, Think and Question*. Plymouth, AltaMira Press.

Woods, Shelton (2002), *Vietnam, An Illustrated History*. New York, Hippocrene Books.
Yamaguchi, Susumu (1956), 'Development of Mahayana Buddhist Beliefs'. In Kenneth Morgan ed. *The Path of the Buddha*. New York, The Ronald Press Company, pp. 153-181.
Yarnall, Thomas (2003), 'Engaged Buddhism: New and Improved(?) Made in the U. S. A. of Asian Materials'. In Christopher Queen, Charles Prebish & Damien Keown eds. *Action Dharma: New studies in Engaged Buddhism*. London, RoutledgeCurzon, pp. 289-303.

Website addresses

Bluck, Robert (2008), *Mapping The Buddhist Landscape*. Available from: http://video.google.com/videoplay?docid=3746040976351058704# [Accessed 19 Mar 2011].
---- (2011), *Dr Robert Bluck Research Affiliate*. Available from: http://www.open.ac.uk/Arts/religious-studies/bluck.shtml [Accessed 21 May 2011].
Bodhi, Bhikkhu (2010), *Arahants, Bodhisattvas, and Buddhas*. Available from: http://www.accesstoinsight.org/lib/authors/bodhi/arahantsbodhisattvas.html [Accessed 25 Mar 2014].
Britannica. Available from: http://www.britannica.com/EBchecked/topic/536626/seventeenth-parallel [Accessed 26 June 2014].
China Buddhism Encyclopedia. Available from: http://www.chinabuddhismencyclopedia.com/en/index.php?title=Dharmaguptaka [Accessed 2 July 2014].
EIAB/events. Available from: http://eiab.eu/events [Accessed 2 December 2011].
EIAB/health retreat. Available from: http://eiab.eu/events/health-retreat [Accessed 15 March 2011].
Hartford (1996). Available from: http://www.hartford-hwp.com/archives/45a/025.html [Accessed 22 October 2008].
INEB. Available from: http://www.inebnetwork.org/web/index.php?option=com_content&task=view&id=46&Itemid=48 [Accessed 8 May 2009].
Interbeing/groups. Available from: http://interbeing.org.uk/groups/ [Accessed 12 November 2010].

Loy, David (2004), 'What's Buddhist about Socially Engaged Buddhism?'. Available from: http://www.zen-occidental.net/articles1/loy12-english.html [Accessed 18 July 2011].
Macy, Joanna (2009a). Available from: http://www.joannamacy.net/dependent-co-arising.html [Accessed 16 Nov 2011].
Macy, Joanna (2009b). Available from: http://www.joannamacy.net/3rd-turning-of-the-wheel.html [Accessed 16 Nov 2011].
Mindfulness Bell/international. Available from: http://www.mindfulnessbell.org/international.php [Accessed 16 Sep 2010].
Minh Chau, Dr Thich (1994), *A Brief History of Vietnamese Buddhism*. Available from: http://daophatngaynay.com/english/vietnam/country/003-buddhism%20in%20VN.htm [Accessed 17 Jun 2010].
NBCUniversal (2011). Available from: http://www.nbcnewyork.com/video/#!/news/local/Monks-Help-Teens-in-Brooklyn-Detention-Center/134431233 [Accessed 30 November 2011].
Nhat Hanh, Thich (2000MB), 'Dharma Talk: Transforming Negative Habit Energies'. In *The Mindfulness Bell* 26 (summer. Available from: http://www.mindfulnessbell.org/wp/2013/08/transforming-negative-habit-energies/ [Accessed 10 September 2014].
Nhat Hanh, Thich (2012c), *Body and Mind Are One: an Online training in Mindfulness with Thich Nhat Hanh*. Available from: http://www.soundstrue.com/onlinecourses/bodymindone/home;jsessionid=CXGLA6coHIgUTYTSWWFF.app02 [Accessed 23 April 2012].
Nhat Hanh Vimeo (2012), *One Cell in the Buddha Body*. Available from: http://vimeo.com/44054397 [Accessed 7 July 2014].
Nobelprize. Available from: http://nobelprize.org/nobel_prizes/peace/laureates/ [Accessed 26 June 2010].
Oxfordmindfulness. Available from: http://oxfordmindfulness.org/all-party-parliamentary-launch/ [Accessed 22 September 2014].
Plum Village Online Monastery. Available from: https://www.facebook.com/home.php#!/plumvillage [Accessed 1 December 2011].

Plum Village1. Available from: http://www.plumvillage.org/dharma-talks/video/144-history-of-engaged-buddhism-.html [Accessed 29 September 2009].
Plum Village2. Available from: http://www.plumvillage.org/lettersfromThich Nhat Hanh/152-a-young-monastics-dream.html [Accessed 29 September 2009].
Plum Village3. Available from: http://www.plumvillage.org/members-currently-in-pv/becoming-a-monastic.html [Accessed 29 September 2009].
Plum Village4. Available from: http://www.plumvillage.org/sangha.html, [Accessed 9 October 2010].
Plum Village5. Available from: http://www.plumvillage.org/mindfulness-trainings/3-the-five-mindfulness-trainings.html [Accessed 20 August 2009].
Plum Village6. Available from: http://www.plumvillage.org/mindfulness-trainings.html [Accessed 4 April 2012].
Plum Village7. Available from http://plumvillage.org/mindfulness-practice/mindfulness-software/ [Accessed 12 May 2014].
Thinkexist. Available from http://thinkexist.com/quotation/the_only_thing_necessary_for_the_triumph_of_evil/158330.html [Accessed 22 July 2014].
Triratna. Available from https://thebuddhistcentre.com/text/ethics [Accessed 24 June 2014].
UNESCO. Available from: http://www.unesco.org/bpi/eng/unescopress/99-38e.htm [Accessed 26 June 2012].
Wallace, Alan (2008), *A Mindful Balance: What did the Buddha Really Mean by Mindfulness?* Available from: http://buddhanet.net/budsas/ebud/ebdha344.htm [accessed 26 November 2013].

Semi-structured Interviews (SI)

Person 1, Plum Village, 12 July 2009.
Person 2, Cambridge, 24 May 2010.
Person 3, Skype, 7 April 2011.
Person 4, Cambridge, 22 May 2010.
Person 5, Plum Village, 13 July 2009.
Person 6, Cambridge, 26 May 2010.
Person 7, Cambridge, 25 May 2010.

Person 8, York, 13 October 2009.
Person 9, Sheffield, 13 October 2009.
Person 10, Cambridge, 27 May 2010.
Person 11, Plum Village, 13 July 2009.
Person 12, Sheffield, 13 October 2009.
Person 13, Cambridge, 20 May 2010.
Person 14, Cambridge, 24 May 2010.
Person 15, Plum Village, 11 July 2009.
Person 16, Cambridge, 19 May 2010.
Monk A, Blue Cliff Monastery NY, 5 August 2010.
Monk B, Blue Cliff Monastery NY, 7 August 2010.
Person 17, Cambridge, 20 May 2010.
Person 17, Phone, 25 March 2011.
Person 18, Cambridge, 18 May 2010.
Person 19, York, 13 October 2009.
Person 20, Cambridge, 20 May 2010.
Person 21, Cambridge, 26 May 2010.
Person A, Plum Village, 12 July 2009.
Person B, Cambridge, 25 May 2010.
Person C, Cambridge, 25 May 2010.
Person D, Skype, 27 March 2011.
Person 22, Skype, 26 February 2011.
Person 23, email 3 April 2011.
Person 24, London, 11 November 2010.
Person 25, Plum Village, 12 July 2009.
Sr Chan Khong, Plum Village, 10 July 2009.
Sr Chan Khong, Plum Village, 26 July 2011.
Person 26, Plum Village, 11 July 2009.
Person 27, Cambridge, 21 May 2010.
Person 28, email, 1 April 2011.
Person 29, Plum Village, 11 July 2009.

Informal Conversations (IC)

Facilitators' Retreat, Harwich, 19 September 2010.
Monk A, Blue Cliff Monastery NY, 5 August 2010.
Monk C, Leeds, 9 March 2011.
Monk D, Leeds, 10 March 2011.
Monk E, Stourbridge, 2 June 2016.
Nun A, Plum Village, 11 July 2009.
Nun B, Nottingham, 17 August 2010.
Person E, Plum Village, 7 July 2009.
Person F, Plum Village, 23 January 2011.
Person G, Plum Village, 24 July 2011.
Person H, Leeds, 5 May 2012.
Person 29, Sheffield, 2 November 2010.
York Sangha, 4 October 2010.

Public Talks

Kabat-Zinn, Jon, Public talk, Oxford, 10 Nov 2010.
Monk E, *Dharma* Talk, Nottingham, 8 April 2012.
Nhat Hanh, Thich, *Dharma* Talk, Plum Village, 8 July 2009.
Nhat Hanh, Thich, *Dharma* Talk, Nottingham, 14 August 2010.
Nhat Hanh, Thich, *Dharma* Talk, Nottingham, 9 April 2012.
Nhat Hanh, Thich, Q&A, Nottingham, 18 Aug 2010.
Nhat Hanh, Thich, Q&A, Nottingham, 9 Apr 2012.
Nhat Hanh, Thich, Q&A, Plum Village, 12 Jul 2009.
Sr Chan Khong, comment after *Dharma* talk, Nottingham, 14 August 2010.
Unnamed Monk, *Dharma* Talk, Nottingham, 14 Aug 2010.

DVD

Nhat Hanh, *Peace is Every Step* (1997), Directed by Gaetano Kazuo Maida, Festival Media release [DVD].

Unpublished Theses

Bell, Sandra (1991), *Buddhism in Britain: Development and Adaptation.* Ph.D. thesis, University of Durham.

Goss, Janet (2012), *Honouring Individuality, Creating Community: Mindfulness-Based Emotional Development and Wellbeing.* Ph.D. thesis, Lancaster University.

Henry, Philip (2008), *Socially Engaged Buddhism in the UK: Adaptation and Development Within Western Buddhism.* Ph.D. thesis, University of Liverpool.

Kennedy, Andrew (2006), *The Dilemma of Mind in Contemporary Buddhism: Some British Testimony.* Ph.D. thesis, University of Leeds.

Minh Pham, Van (2001), *Socio-political Philosophy of Vietnamese Buddhism: A Case Study of the Buddhist Movement of 1963 and 1966.* Ph.D. thesis, University of Western Sydney. Available from: http://handle.usw.edu.au:1801/1959.7/382 [Accessed 23 March 2009].

List of Abbreviations

5MTs 5 Mindfulness Trainings
14MTs 14 Mindfulness Trainings
AIAB – Asian Institute of Applied Buddhism
CoI – Community of Interbeing
DoM – Day of Mindfulness
EIAB – European Institute of Applied Buddhism
GVN – South Vietnamese Government (during Vietnam/American War)
IC – Informal Conversations
MBCT – Mindfulness Based Cognitive Therapy
MBSR – Mindfulness Based Stress Reduction
NRMs – New Religious Movements
OI   Order of Interbeing
P   Pali
Q&A – Question and answer session
SEB – Socially Engaged Buddhism
SI – Semi-structured Interviews
Skt   Sanskrit
Sr – Sister (ordained nun)
UBC – United Buddhist Church

Texts from the Pali Canon
A   Anguttara Nikaya
DN   Digha Nikaya
MN   Majjhima Nikaya
Vin   Vinaya Pitaka

Appendices

Appendix 1: Field research

The field research has been conducted over the following dates,
Plum Village Summer Retreat, one week, July 2009;
Blue Cliff Monastery, USA, five days, August 2010;
Nottingham Retreat, UK, five days, August 2010;
CoI Facilitators' Retreat, Harwich, UK, three days, September 2010;
Plum Village, one week, January 2011;
EIAB, Germany, one week, February 2011;
Leeds University, 2 day introduction to Mindfulness by monastics from Plum Village, March 2011;
Plum Village Summer Retreat, one week, July 2011;
Nottingham Retreat, UK, five days, April 2012.

Appendix 2: Interview questions

Original questions asked to those attending the Summer retreat, Plum Village 2009

1. Have you visited Plum Village before?
2. How long are you staying?
3. Can you say something of your experience of Plum Village?
4. What would you say was the most fulfilling part of your visit so far?
5. Are there any aspects you would like to change?
6. What do you understand Engaged Buddhism to be?
7. What do you think about Thich Nhat Hanh as a teacher?
8. Do you think Plum Village will continue when Thich Nhat Hanh's no longer living?
9. Do you feel Plum Village is only for Buddhists?
10. How did you become involved in Buddhism?
11. Do you think what you've got from this week will enrich your practices at home?

After this first set of interviews I added two further questions

1) What is your view on the bell?
2) What is your view on Noble Silence?

I deemed these to be important aspects of the practice that I was not aware of before my first visit.

The above questions were adapted slightly to CoI members back in the UK as we were not on a retreat at the time of interviews.

1) Can you say something of your experience of retreats; at Plum Village (or other monasteries) and in the UK?
2) When was your last visit? / How long was your stay?
3) Can you say something of your experience at Plum Village?
4) What would you say was the most fulfilling part of your visit? (What does Plum Village offer to you?)
5) Are there any aspects you would like to change?
6) What would you say are the key aspects of Plum Village?
7) What is your view on the bell?
8) What is your view on Noble Silence?
9) What do you understand Engaged Buddhism to be?

In the Tradition of Thich Nhat Hanh

10) How do you feel about Thich Nhat Hanh as a teacher?
11) Do you think Plum Village will continue when Thich Nhat Hanh is no longer living?
12) How did you become involved in Buddhism? / What made you decide to visit Plum Village?
13) Do you think what you got from Plum Village will enrich your practices at home?

Whilst writing the latter part of the thesis I decided further questions about the practice of the laypeople in their Sangha was relevant and so I arranged as many second interviews as possible or added these questions to the interview.

1) What is your understanding of Sangha?
2) What does your local Sangha provide for you?
3) What do you offer to the Sangha?
4) Do you feel Thich Nhat Hanh's teachings are adequately understood by the lay community?
5) What do you think creates a good Sangha?
6) Are there aspects of the Sangha you don't agree with, or would like to change?
7) How do you decide which aspects of Plum Village practices to use and which not to use?
8) Is there anything else you would like to say related to these questions? (anything you feel has not been asked?)

Appendix 3: The 14 Mindfulness trainings (14MTs)
Original version written in 1964

1. Do not be idolatrous about or bound to any doctrine, theory, or ideology, even Buddhist ones. Buddhist systems of thought are guiding means; they are not absolute truth.
2. Do not think the knowledge you presently possess is changeless, absolute truth. Avoid being narrow-minded and bound to present views. Learn and practice nonattachment from views in order to be open to receive others' viewpoints. Truth is found in life and not merely in conceptual knowledge. Be ready to learn throughout your entire life and to observe reality in yourself and in the world at all times.
3. Do not force others, including children, by any means whatsoever, to adopt your views, whether by authority, threat, money, propaganda, or even education. However, through compassionate dialogue, help others renounce fanaticism and narrowness.
4. Do not avoid contact with suffering or close your eyes before suffering. Do not lose awareness of the existence of suffering in the life of the world. Find ways to be with those who are suffering, including personal contact, images, and sound. By such means, awaken yourself and others to the reality of suffering in the world.
5. Do not accumulate wealth while millions are hungry. Do not take as the aim of your life fame, profit, wealth, or sensual pleasure. Live simply and share time, energy, and material resources with those who are in need.
6. Do not maintain anger or hatred. Learn to penetrate and transform them when they are still seeds in your consciousness. As soon as they arise, turn your attention to your breath in order to see and understand the nature of your anger and hatred and the nature of the persons who have caused your anger and hatred.
7. Do not lose yourself in dispersion and in your surroundings. Practice mindful breathing to come back to what is happening in the present moment. Be in touch with what is wondrous, refreshing, and healing both inside and around you. Plant seeds of joy, peace, and understanding in yourself in order to facilitate the work of transformation in the depths of your consciousness.
8. Do not utter words that can create discord and cause the community to break. Make every effort to reconcile and resolve all conflicts, however small.
9. Do not say untruthful things for the sake of Personal interest or to impress people. Do not utter words that cause division and hatred. Do not

spread news that you do not know to be certain. Do not criticize or condemn things of which you are not sure. Always speak truthfully and constructively. Have the courage to speak out about situations of injustice, even when doing so may threaten your own safety.

10. Do not use the Buddhist community for personal gain or profit, or transform your community into a political party. A religious community, however, should take a clear stand against oppression and injustice and should strive to change the situation without engaging in partisan conflicts.

11. Do not live with a vocation that is harmful to humans and nature. Do not invest in companies that deprive others of their chance to live. Select a vocation that helps realize your ideal of compassion.

12. Do not kill. Do not let others kill. Find whatever means possible to protect life and prevent war.

13. Possess nothing that should belong to others. Respect the property of others, but prevent others from profiting from human suffering or the suffering of other species on Earth.

14. Do not mistreat your body. Learn to handle it with respect, preserve vital energies (sexual, breath, spirit) for the realization of the Way. Be fully aware of the responsibility of bringing new lives into the world. Meditate on the world into which you are bringing new beings (Nhat Hanh 2000a).

Updated version, April 2012

The Fourteen Mindfulness Trainings are the very essence of the Order of Interbeing. They are the torch lighting our path, the boat carrying us, the teacher guiding us. They allow us to touch the nature of interbeing in everything that is, and to see that our happiness is not separate from the happiness of others. Interbeing is not a theory; it is a reality that can be directly experienced by each of us at any moment in our daily lives. The Fourteen Mindfulness Trainings help us cultivate concentration and insight which free us from fear and the illusion of a separate self.

The First Mindfulness Training: Openness

Aware of the suffering created by fanaticism and intolerance, we are determined not to be idolatrous about or bound to any doctrine, theory, or ideology, even Buddhist ones. We are committed to seeing the Buddhist teachings as guiding means that help us develop our understanding and compassion. They are not doctrines to fight, kill, or die for. We understand that fanaticism in its many forms is the result of perceiving things in a dualistic and discriminative manner. We will train ourselves to look at everything with openness and the insight of interbeing in order to transform dogmatism and violence in ourselves and in the world.

The Second Mindfulness Training: Non-attachment to Views

Aware of the suffering created by attachment to views and wrong perceptions, we are determined to avoid being narrow-minded and bound to present views. We are committed to learning and practicing non-attachment to views and being open to others' experiences and insights in order to benefit from the collective wisdom. We are aware that the knowledge we presently possess is not changeless, absolute truth. Insight is revealed through the practice of compassionate listening, deep looking, and letting go of notions rather than through the accumulation of intellectual knowledge. Truth is found in life, and we will observe life within and around us in every moment, ready to learn throughout our lives.

The Third Mindfulness Training: Freedom of Thought

Aware of the suffering brought about when we impose our views on others, we are determined not to force others, even our children, by any means whatsoever – such as authority, threat, money, propaganda, or indoctrination – to adopt our views. We are committed to respecting the right of others to be different, to choose what to believe and how to decide. We will, however, learn to help others let go of and transform fanaticism and narrowness through loving speech and compassionate dialogue.

The Fourth Mindfulness Training: Awareness of Suffering

Aware that looking deeply at the nature of suffering can help us develop understanding and compassion, we are determined to come home to ourselves, to recognize, accept, embrace and listen to suffering with the energy of mindfulness. We will do our best not to run away from our suffering or cover it up through consumption, but practice conscious breathing and walking to look deeply into the roots of our suffering. We know we can realize the path leading to the transformation of suffering only when we understand deeply the roots of suffering. Once we have understood our own suffering, we will be able to understand the suffering of others. We are committed to finding ways, including personal contact and using telephone, electronic, audio-visual, and other means, to be with those who suffer, so we can help them transform their suffering into compassion, peace, and joy.

In the Tradition of Thich Nhat Hanh

The Fifth Mindfulness Training: Compassionate, Healthy Living
Aware that true happiness is rooted in peace, solidity, freedom, and compassion, we are determined not to accumulate wealth while millions are hungry and dying nor to take as the aim of our life fame, power, wealth, or sensual pleasure, which can bring much suffering and despair. We will practice looking deeply into how we nourish our body and mind with edible foods, sense impressions, volition, and consciousness. We are committed not to gamble or to use alcohol, drugs or any other products which bring toxins into our own and the collective body and consciousness such as certain websites, electronic games, music, TV programs, films, magazines, books and conversations. We will consume in a way that preserves compassion, wellbeing, and joy in our bodies and consciousness and in the collective body and consciousness of our families, our society, and the earth.

The Sixth Mindfulness Training: Taking Care of Anger
Aware that anger blocks communication and creates suffering, we are committed to taking care of the energy of anger when it arises, and to recognizing and transforming the seeds of anger that lie deep in our consciousness. When anger manifests, we are determined not to do or say anything, but to practice mindful breathing or mindful walking to acknowledge, embrace, and look deeply into our anger. We know that the roots of anger are not outside of ourselves but can be found in our wrong perceptions and lack of understanding of the suffering in ourselves and others. By contemplating impermanence, we will be able to look with the eyes of compassion at ourselves and at those we think are the cause of our anger, and to recognize the preciousness of our relationships. We will practice Right Diligence in order to nourish our capacity of understanding, love, joy and inclusiveness, gradually transforming our anger, violence and fear, and helping others do the same.

The Seventh Mindfulness Training: Dwelling Happily in the Present Moment
Aware that life is available only in the present moment, we are committed to training ourselves to live deeply each moment of daily life. We will try not to lose ourselves in dispersion or be carried away by regrets about the past, worries about the future, or craving, anger, or jealousy in the present. We will practice mindful breathing to be aware of what is happening in the here and the now. We are determined to learn the art of mindful living by touching the wondrous, refreshing, and healing elements that are inside and

around us, in all situations. In this way, we will be able to cultivate seeds of joy, peace, love, and understanding in ourselves, thus facilitating the work of transformation and healing in our consciousness. We are aware that real happiness depends primarily on our mental attitude and not on external conditions, and that we can live happily in the present moment simply by remembering that we already have more than enough conditions to be happy.

The Eighth Mindfulness Training: True Community and Communication

Aware that lack of communication always brings separation and suffering, we are committed to training ourselves in the practice of compassionate listening and loving speech. Knowing that true community is rooted in inclusiveness and in the concrete practice of the harmony of views, thinking and speech, we will practice to share our understanding and experiences with members in our community in order to arrive at a collective insight. We are determined to learn to listen deeply without judging or reacting and refrain from uttering words that can create discord or cause the community to break. Whenever difficulties arise, we will remain in our Sangha and practice looking deeply into ourselves and others to recognize all the causes and conditions, including our own habit energies, that have brought about the difficulties. We will take responsibility for the ways we may have contributed to the conflict and keep communication open. We will not behave as a victim but be active in finding ways to reconcile and resolve all conflicts however small.

The Ninth Mindfulness Training: Truthful and Loving Speech

Aware that words can create happiness or suffering, we are committed to learning to speak truthfully, lovingly and constructively. We will use only words that inspire joy, confidence and hope as well as promote reconciliation and peace in ourselves and among other people. We will speak and listen in a way that can help ourselves and others to transform suffering and see the way out of difficult situations. We are determined not to say untruthful things for the sake of personal interest or to impress people, nor to utter words that might cause division or hatred. We will protect the happiness and harmony of our Sangha by refraining from speaking about the faults of other persons in their absence and always ask ourselves whether our perceptions are correct. We will speak only with the intention to understand and help transform the situation. We will not spread rumours nor criticize or condemn things of which we are not sure. We will do our best to speak out about situations of injustice, even when doing so may make difficulties for us or threaten our safety.

The Tenth Mindfulness Training: Protecting and Nourishing the Sangha

Aware that the essence and aim of a Sangha is the realization of understanding and compassion, we are determined not to use the Buddhist community for personal power or profit, or transform our community into a political instrument. As members of a spiritual community, we should nonetheless take a clear stand against oppression and injustice. We should strive to change the situation, without taking sides in a conflict. We are committed to learning to look with the eyes of interbeing and to see ourselves and others as cells in one Sangha body. As a true cell in the Sangha body, generating mindfulness, concentration and insight to nourish ourselves and the whole community, each of us is at the same time a cell in the Buddha body. We will actively build brotherhood and sisterhood, flow as a river, and practice to develop the three real powers – understanding, love and cutting through afflictions – to realize collective awakening.

The Eleventh Mindfulness Training: Right Livelihood

Aware that great violence and injustice have been done to our environment and society, we are committed not to live with a vocation that is harmful to humans and nature. We will do our best to select a livelihood that contributes to the wellbeing of all species on earth and helps realize our ideal of understanding and compassion. Aware of economic, political, and social realities around the world, as well as our interrelationship with the ecosystem, we are determined to behave responsibly as consumers and as citizens. We will not invest in or purchase from companies that contribute to the depletion of natural resources, harm the earth, or deprive others of their chance to live.

The Twelfth Mindfulness Training: Reverence for Life

Aware that much suffering is caused by war and conflict, we are determined to cultivate nonviolence, compassion, and the insight of interbeing in our daily lives and promote peace education, mindful mediation, and reconciliation within families, communities, ethnic and religious groups, nations, and in the world. We are committed not to kill and not to let others kill. We will not support any act of killing in the world, in our thinking, or in our way of life. We will diligently practice deep looking with our Sangha to discover better ways to protect life, prevent war, and build peace.

The Thirteenth Mindfulness Training: Generosity

Aware of the suffering caused by exploitation, social injustice, stealing, and oppression, we are committed to cultivating generosity in our way of thinking, speaking, and acting. We will practice loving kindness by working for the happiness of people, animals, plants, and minerals, and sharing our time, energy, and material resources with those who are in need. We are determined not to steal and not to possess anything that should belong to others. We will respect the property of others, but will try to prevent others from profiting from human suffering or the suffering of other beings.

The Fourteenth Mindfulness Training: True Love

[For lay members]: Aware that sexual desire is not love and that sexual relations motivated by craving cannot dissipate the feeling of loneliness but will create more suffering, frustration, and isolation, we are determined not to engage in sexual relations without mutual understanding, love, and a deep long-term commitment made known to our family and friends. Seeing that body and mind are one, we are committed to learning appropriate ways to take care of our sexual energy and to cultivating loving kindness, compassion, joy and inclusiveness for our own happiness and the happiness of others. We must be aware of future suffering that may be caused by sexual relations. We know that to preserve the happiness of ourselves and others, we must respect the rights and commitments of ourselves and others. We will do everything in our power to protect children from sexual abuse and to protect couples and families from being broken by sexual misconduct. We will treat our bodies with compassion and respect. We are determined to look deeply into the Four Nutriments and learn ways to preserve and channel our vital energies (sexual, breath, spirit) for the realization of our bodhisattva ideal. We will be fully aware of the responsibility of bringing new lives into the world, and will regularly meditate upon their future environment.

[For monastic members]: Aware that the deep aspiration of a monk or a nun can only be realized when he or she wholly leaves behind the bonds of sensual love, we are committed to practicing chastity and to helping others protect themselves. We are aware that loneliness and suffering cannot be alleviated through a sexual relationship, but through practicing loving kindness, compassion, joy and inclusiveness. We know that a sexual relationship will destroy our monastic life, will prevent us from realizing our ideal of serving living beings, and will harm others. We will learn appropriate ways to take care of our sexual energy. We are determined not

In the Tradition of Thich Nhat Hanh

to suppress or mistreat our body, or look upon our body as only an instrument, but will learn to handle our body with compassion and respect. We will look deeply into the Four Nutriments in order to preserve and channel our vital energies (sexual, breath, spirit) for the realization of our bodhisattva ideal (Plum Village6).

Appendix 4: Plum Village satellite monasteries

Blue Cliff Monastery, NY State
Blue Cliff, established in 2007, reflects the early days of Plum Village with small numbers of monastics. There were thirty monastics when I visited (in 2010) and 350 people on retreat including children and teens, all American apart from me. It is therefore less international than Plum Village. Blue Cliff is a spacious open site divided down the middle by a public road which provides a convenient boundary between the monks' and nuns' living quarters. They operate as two entirely separate monasteries coming together for DoMs and public retreats. On the monks' side is the large meditation hall used by everyone on retreats. Otherwise the nuns have their own, smaller hall which they use outside of retreat events. It also reflects Plum Village in that it is housed in an existing farmhouse which already had buildings for weekend visitors, with the meditation hall as a separate addition. This stands majestically apart from other buildings indicating the prominence meditation plays in the daily life of any monastery. The monastery is surrounded by forests that provide ideal spaces for walking meditation.

European Institute of Applied Buddhism (EIAB), Germany
EIAB has a more urban setting than Blue Cliff as it is in a town close to a hospital. However, there are forests for walking meditation within easy reach. EIAB's setting is an ex-Nazi[72] building that required a huge fundraising project and several years to complete. When I visited in 2011 most of the activities and living quarters took place in the building next door. The institute is significantly different to Plum Village in that everything happens in one building including lay men and women sleeping in the same building although on different floors. The monks currently reside in the unfinished building and it must be the intention for lay men to also live there once it is closer completion. In order to assist sexual restraint (14th MT) monks and nuns or lay men and women do not normally share living accommodation unless they are married.

---

[72] The main building at EIAB was built as a military building for the Nazis, and once housed a mental asylum hospital, whose inmates were rounded up by the Nazis.

***Bat Nha*, Vietnam, 2005-2009**
In 2005 Thich Nhat Hanh returned to Vietnam to undertake a teaching tour which was strictly regulated by the government (SI, Person 10 2010). Vietnam relaxed its imposed exile as it desired to join the World Trade Organisation and therefore had to demonstrate it had policies on religious freedom (IC, Monk A 2010; Chapman 2007: 312). The tour only went ahead after rigorous limitations imposed by the Vietnamese government restricting Nhat Hanh's talks to temples in order to contain numbers. Many people who have been reading his books for years and perhaps knew him previously did not know he was there (IC, Monk A 2010) as the tour was advertised mainly by word of mouth. Despite these restrictions many young people attended talks and wished to join the Plum Village tradition. Six monasteries throughout Vietnam agreed to accept them (Chapman 2007: 317) including *Bat Nha* and Nhat Hanh's own root temple in Hue. An abbot at *Bat Nha*, the Venerable Duc Nghi, publicly offered his monastery to Nhat Hanh with the new novices following Nhat Hanh's tradition (Nhat Hanh 2010a: 12). Many of Nhat Hanh's students in the international community contributed towards a building programme to house the extra monastics. In 2007 he returned to Vietnam to care for the young monastics and this further swelled numbers. By 2009, 500 young people had been ordained in the Plum Village tradition at *Bat Nha* alone (Nhat Hanh 2010a: 12).

However, these large numbers of young people caused suspicion amongst the government scared by the idealism Nhat Hanh was offering (SI, Person 10 2010). The Vietnamese government believed he worked for the CIA and that his true intention was to overthrow the government in a coup (IC, Monk A 2010) and to them here was further proof. They believed he was amassing forces to oust the government. It is also understood that pressure was brought to bear upon Vietnam by China after Nhat Hanh publicly spoke out in support of the Tibetans, encouraging them to believe that like Vietnam their country could be free from the Chinese again (IC, Monk A 2010). Therefore the Vietnamese Government secretly brought pressure to bear firstly on the Venerable Duc Nghi to rescind his offer and secondly on the monastics themselves to disrobe and return home. Details of the brutal methods employed to achieve this can be found in Nhat Hanh's book *A Key to Peace* (2010a). Many young people disrobed and some went into hiding after *Bat Nha* was destroyed. More than one hundred got into Thailand and have been supported in setting up Thai Plum Village. Initially this was a temporary measure before the monastics could transfer to other Plum Village monasteries (IC, Monk A 2010). However, in May 2011 Nhat Hanh

In the Tradition of Thich Nhat Hanh

and a delegation from Plum Village returned to Thailand not only to support the monastics but also the countrywide *Sangha*. Due to the unparalleled situation of the influx of monastics from Vietnam, Thailand (practising in the *Theravada* tradition) now finds itself with a growing *Sangha* following Nhat Hanh's pedagogy.

Although *Bat Nha* was in many ways an exceptional situation that cannot be compared with the satellite monasteries in the West, its demise is indicative of Vietnam's continued suspicion of Nhat Hanh's motives and their lack of acceptance towards his teachings. Despite the grassroots support for Nhat Hanh the Vietnamese government remain resolutely opposed to Nhat Hanh and it now seems certain that 2008 was the last time he would return.

Appendix 5: A unit meeting

A Unit evening (or in some cases, a Saturday morning) will usually include a sit-walk-sit meditation practice; that is a sitting meditation, a slow walking meditation called *Kinh Hanh*, followed by a second period of sitting meditation with each period taking about 20 minutes. One of the sittings could be a guided meditation. A refreshment break will feature at some point in the evening, either half way through or at the end. The second half of the evening will usually include a reading from one of Thich Nhat Hanh's books, or CD or DVD of a *Dharma* talk he has given. This will be followed by a *Dharma* discussion, which is actually a sharing rather than a conversation, and offers people the opportunity to share something with the rest of the group, if they so choose. The key aspects of an evening are a communal practice of meditation, some connection to Thich Nhat Hanh's teachings, Mindfulness and a chance to speak either about one's personal practice from the previous week, or something that arises in response on the evening.

It cannot be emphasised too strongly that each Unit decides on its own format, so all of the above are suggestions only, and not requirements. Other activities may include the Mindful Movements (a sequence of movements based on Qigong), singing, recitation of 5 and/or 14 MTs, practices from Plum Village such as Beginning Anew or Touching the Earth and other experiments or meditations that the facilitator deems appropriate. The Cambridge Unit has a monthly programme, which begins with the sit-walk-sit and continues with; week 1, a discussion on the practice from the last month; week 2, reading from a book and discussion (the book is eventually read all the way through); week 3, a reading but no discussion, more time for tea and informal chat; week 4, facilitator's choice; week 5 (if there is one), as week 3. Other Units may be more fluid in deciding what takes place from week to week.

The roles within the Unit will differ from group to group. One Unit is led by one facilitator (often the person who inaugurated the group), whereas another will have a rotation of facilitators from within the group. Another task is the bell-master, the person who invites the bell throughout the evening at various intervals, and this could be the facilitator, or another individual. Matters such as these are up to the individual Unit to decide upon.

In the Tradition of Thich Nhat Hanh

The Day of Mindfulness is an extension of the evening, with 6 or 7 hours in which to practice together. A possible structure for the day, beginning between 10 and 11am, is;
Tea and Catch up
Sit walk sit (20 minutes each)
Reciting the 5 MTs
Shared lunch
Outside walk/movement
Dharma discussion/share, usually based on a reading or talk from a *Dharmacharya*
Tea and informal chat to finish.
Again, there are a variety of other possibilities to be included, which will depend upon the nature of the group.

Appendix 6: Details of the 4 units researched

Cambridge is a well-established Unit that has been operating for about 20 years. It began with a core of six people (who met through another Buddhist group before experiencing Thich Nhat Hanh's teachings on retreat) most of who are still central to the group. Two of these are *Dharmacharyas*, ordained by Thich Nhat Hanh, and both have a large input into COI UK activities and events, including UK retreats with Thich Nhat Hanh. The Cambridge Unit is a stable Unit, and I would suggest is a paradigm that other Units may aspire to. As well as weekly meetings and regular monthly DoMs, they have in the past organised other activities, such as a choir, writing a Vietnamese cookbook, a Unit walk once a month, a study group on particular books of Thich Nhat Hanh's, a Unit library, sailing holidays, and an annual Christmas retreat. They meet in people's houses, organised on a rotation. Facilitation is also organised on a monthly rotation, with 2 facilitators being responsible for a whole month, and deciding between themselves who takes which evening. The person who is hosting the evening at their house is not the facilitator as well. They have monthly facilitation meetings where only matters relating to facilitation are decided, all other matters are brought to the whole Unit. As with other groups they will have a large email or contact list, with a smaller number attending the evenings on a regular basis; the two evenings I attended had about 16 people to each.

The Sheffield Unit was inaugurated in 1987, originally run by a *Dharmacharya* who no longer lives in Sheffield, so although it has been running for several years the people involved have changed significantly. It meets mainly in one house and has a monthly meeting in the central Quaker Meeting house. Between 4 and 14 people attend the evenings. Facilitation is led by the two Order members whose house is used for most of the meetings. DoMs are held monthly, with an attendance of about 6 people. As with Cambridge, the 2 Order members are involved in CoI activities throughout the UK.

Although Leeds has been running for 4 years it has not really established itself with a strong core group of people – in contrast to Cambridge. This could be due to the limited input of the person running it due to illness, but it hasn't been taken up by other people. There are 3 core people who are joined by others intermittently. The evening meetings are held monthly, the second Friday of the month at the home of the inaugurator. A new recent venture has been to organise DoMs. These are successful in terms of attracting 10-20 people, but these people generally do not live close to Leeds, and therefore attendance to the evening meetings is not possible. The originator now wishes to step aside and it will be interesting to see whether the baton is taken up by others in the months to come.

The York Unit is a nascent group started in September 2010 immediately after Thich Nhat Hanh's Nottingham retreat. It meets in a hired venue, on a weekly basis and has a strong core group of people, who share facilitation week by week, on a voluntary basis. Between 15 to 20 people attend the evening each week. It holds DoMs approximately four times a year. Although it is new, it has quickly developed due to the commitment of many involved and incorporates people travelling some distance to attend the evening meetings, from Guisborough, Malton, Pickering, Beverley, Hull and Wetherby as well as those more local to York. It would appear the strength and size of this group is unusual compared to others within the UK, where the standard of a core group of 3 people is more normal.

Appendix 7: What the geese know

The following five lessons of the geese make clear the foundations for building a Sangha.

By flapping its wings, each goose creates an upwind for the ones following it. Flying in a V-formation allows the flock to fly seventy-one percent further than would be possible for an individual goose.
Lesson 1: People who share a common direction and a sense of community reach their goal more quickly and easily, because they benefit from the energy of others.
Whenever a goose swerves out of formation, it immediately becomes aware of the resistance present when one bird flies alone and quickly reenters the formation, in order to be able to use the lift caused by the preceding geese.
Lesson 2: If we are as sensible as a goose is, we will stay in formation with those wanting to go the same place as we do, and we accept their support in the same way in which we are willing to support others.
When the lead goose becomes tired, it falls back and another goose takes the lead position.
Lesson 3: It pays to relieve one another working and to take turns in the leadership position.
The geese flying in the rear rally the ones in flying up front with their calls.
Lesson 4: We should be sure of the encouragement resulting from our rallying calls.
When a goose is sick or wounded and is no longer able to fly, then two other geese leave the formation and accompany it in its way down in order to help and protect it. They stay with the goose until it can either fly again or until it dies. Then they join another formation and try to catch up to their own flock again.
Lesson 5: Sangha members should feel secure that they are not abandoned by their spiritual family. When faced with a serious illness, physical or mental problems, they can rely on the support of experienced and sympathetic Sangha friends (Schmied 2002: 259-260).

About the author

This book is the result of six years of Ph.D. research and many years' practice of mindfulness! Lauri's Ph.D. came on the back of a degree in Theology & Religious Studies, as a diversion from her original intention to undertake a PGCE and train to be a Primary school teacher. Her practice of mindfulness developed within the Community of Interbeing alongside her research and has continued to deepen, as Lauri became an Order member in 2014. She practices on a weekly basis with the York Sangha http://www.coiuk.org/sangha-pages/york-sangha/. As an outcome of the research she now teaches mindfulness with York MBSR http://www.yorkmbsr.co.uk/ and the Community of Interbeing http://www.coiuk.org/. Lauri also discovered that writing poetry is an outlet for her mindful practice and regularly posts her poems on the *Mindful Living* blog http://lauribower.blogspot.co.uk/
She is particularly interested in the relationship between mindfulness and creativity and is open to exploring this in many ways, particularly poetry and bookbinding. This is an appropriate means for Lauri as the words and the books fit together neatly!
She lives in Yorkshire with her husband and son, and has a daughter in Australia.

Printed in Great Britain
by Amazon